Pupils, Potholes & Poor Relief

The Great Seal of Queen Elizabeth I attached to the charter of
The Town Lands of Wantage

Pupils, Potholes & Poor Relief

The Town Lands of Wantage
from
Elizabeth I to Elizabeth II

Hazel Brown

Garden Shed
Publications

ISBN 978-0-9554979-3-3

©Hazel Brown2012

Published by
Garden Shed Publications
Bridge House, Main St, East Challow,
Wantage, Oxfordshire
OX12 9SS

Acknowledgments

I would like to offer my sincere thanks to everyone who has helped in the writing of this book. Firstly to the staff at the Berkshire Record Office, where many of the documents are now kept, especially Peter Durrant, County Archivist, and Sabina Sutherland who have been unfailingly helpful; to the Governors, who have given access to documents still in their possession, particularly David Castle, who has been a great support, Anne Shone and Moya Lee, who made helpful comments on an early draft of the book, and Carol Clubb, the present clerk to the Governors; to the staff at the Vale and Downland Museum; and to Bill Jestico, the clerk of the Trustees of the Almshouse of Robert Stiles. Some of the early history on Robert Stiles had been given to the Trustees by Mr E.J. Hughes, a descendant of the Stiles family.

I am also grateful to my sister, Hilary Austin, who proof read the book; to Tim Weekes, then the tenant at the King Alfred's Head; to Barbara Allison, Joan Dils and David Clark for their advice; and to all those who lent photographs or maps, separately acknowledged on page 197.

My heartfelt thanks go to my husband for his hours of work on the maps, photographs and the design of this book, and for all his support. Last, but most certainly not least, I and the Governors of the Wantage Town Lands are most grateful to Anne Shone, a Governor for thirty one years until 2010, who has facilitated a gift from the Dolphin Trust towards the cost of this book.

Notes

1) When the Act of Parliament, which set up the Wantage Town Lands on a proper legal footing, was signed in February 1597, this was at a time when the new year started on 25th March. So by modern dating, with the beginning of the year on January 1st, this date should now be referred to as February 1598. As all references to the beginning of the Wantage Town Lands give the year as 1597, I have kept to that date in this book.

2) From the early days of the Wantage Town Lands until February 1971, money was recorded in pounds, shillings and pence. There were twenty shillings in a pound and twelve pennies in a shilling.

> One pound (as now) was shown as £1
>
> One shilling could be shown as 1s or 1/-
>
> One penny was shown as 1d
>
> I have shown one pound, two shillings and three pence, for example, as £1 2s 3d

3) Writing any history book relies on having access to documents, of which the Wantage Town Lands have a plentiful archive. It also depends to a certain extent on guesswork and detective investigation. Three words used frequently throughout this book — "possibly", "probably" and "perhaps" — tell their own story. I have tried to be as close to the truth as possible, but I could be wrong in some of my suggestions, so you have every right to disagree with any assumptions made in the following pages.

October 2012

Contents

Illustrations

Maps & Plans

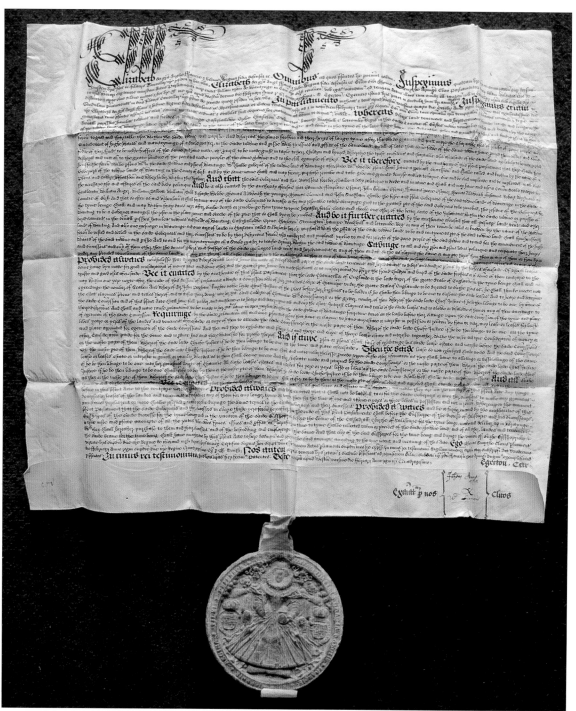

The original Act of Parliament setting up the Wantage Town Lands Trust in 1597

1

In the beginning ...

The setting up of the Charity

There is no way of knowing just how and when the Wantage Town Lands charity originally came into existence. The first documented reference was towards the end of Queen Elizabeth I's reign, when an Act of Parliament was passed, setting up the trust under which the Governors of the Wantage Town Lands still operate. This came about because it was reported that certain men, particularly William Wordnam and Francis Cator, who were administering the Town Lands at the time, were benefiting themselves and their families and friends, rather than using the proceeds for the intended charitable uses. A petition on behalf of the Wantage inhabitants was drawn up at the time, which described William Wordnam as "a man of evill name and fame .... and a man of notorious sedicious troblesome disposicion well known in the whole country." The Act of Parliament set out that in future there should be twelve Governors to run the affairs of the Town Lands and it named the men originally chosen for this office. When a Governor either died or for other reasons resigned, the other Governors were to elect someone to replace him from "the better sort of the inhabitants of Wantinge". The Act was passed in the

The Great seal of Elizabeth 1
top obverse, bottom reverse
BRO D/QW1

39th year of the "raigne of our Soveraigne Lady Queen Elizabeth" and was signed in February 1597, but as at that time in history the year ended on 24th March, we would now consider the year to be 1598.

When the Act was passed, it was obvious that no-one really knew how long the charity had been in existence, as it stated that the lands had been given by "sundry persons", some in the time of Henry VI (1422-1461) and some in the time of Henry VII (1485-1509): in other words, by persons unknown and before anyone living could remember. Many charities for helping the poor and for providing education dated back to medieval times, when people would leave money for these purposes when they died, as well as endowing chantry chapels and paying chantry priests to sing masses for their souls, in order to make sure that they got to heaven. Schools would often be held in the chantry chapels at the church. Towards the end of his reign, Henry VIII banned chantry chapels and the praying for souls. When his young son, Edward VI, became king, chantry lands given to finance chapels and masses for souls were confiscated for the Crown. However, many towns with religious chantries turned them and their lands into lay organisations with charitable purposes, to avoid them passing to the crown. This was possibly what happened in Wantage. The lands originally given to support a chantry chapel could have become the Town Lands around 1547. A clue as to the possible original donors of the land comes from the Governors' seal which has two devices on it which were used by the Bouchier family — the Bouchier knot and two water bougets. Thomasina, the niece of the last male Fitzwarin, an important medieval Wantage family, married Sir William Bouchier about 1442 and it is likely that this couple gave land which later became part of the Town Lands. Although of course, nothing is certain. There is a hint that some of the Town Lands could originally have been given to finance a chantry in the town when, in 1640, the charity commissioners held an investigation in Wantage regarding the Trust and the Governors gave them hospitality: the accounts have an entry showing that 14d was spent "for a quort of sack" (a dry white wine from Spain) "that was given to the Commissioners about the Channtrye Land".

Originally, the income from the Town Lands was supposed to have been used to relieve the poor, to maintain the Grammar School and to keep the highways in good repair: in future the Governors were to make sure that the profits of the

Armorial devices used by the Bouchier family. A stylised bouget or water carrying device, and what appears to be a granny knot

Governors' seal with Bouchier devices.
The outer circle reads:
THE SEALE OF THE TOWNE LANDES OF WANTING
and the inner circle refers to the county: BARK
BRO D/QW49

Town Lands were used for these purposes only. The cost of getting the Act passed, £88 12s 6d, was met by loans from most of the men who were the new Governors and they were repaid these loans out of the income of the Town Lands over the next few years. This absorbed most of the available money and resulted in very little being left to help the needy for several years, although the schoolmaster was paid his wages and some repairs were done to the school. By 1604, money was being spent on the poor, the school and in mending the roads, so the charity was by then beginning to run smoothly, with the initial expenses of putting the charity on a sound legal footing having been paid off. The income also increased over the initial years of the new Trust, partly as a result of more property being acquired and partly because it appeared that rents were increased. In 1598, 21 people paid rent but by 1620 the Governors were collecting rent from 40 people. In 1598 Ellys Digweed's rent was 10s a year but by 1613 he was paying 50s. Over the same period, Thomas Aldworth saw his rent rise from 10s to 30s and William Wilmott's rent increased from 6s 8d to 15s; with most others experiencing the same trend.

The Act of Parliament listed where land was held at the time of the Act, referring to land and buildings in "Wantinge, East Challowe, Grove, Charleton, Stevington, Hanney, Woodhill and Letcombe Regis" including a house and land which had recently been bought with the profits of the Town Lands. The house was in Wantage and had the lovely name of Silverlocks; the land which went with it was two half acres in the fields of Charlton. Many of the houses had land which belonged to them but was situated in fields at a distance from the house, not next to it. In later years a house and its land were not necessarily rented by the same person. Although the Act mentions land in Letcombe Regis, later descriptions of the Town Lands make it fairly clear that this was in White Mead, the large area of meadow in what is now East Challow, that was shared by three other parishes, including Letcombe Regis, and was usually regarded by the Governors as being in East Challow. Woodhill is also a part of East Challow. The Act stipulated that every three years the accounts were to be shown to the Bishop of Salisbury, as the Wantage area was at that time in the Diocese of Salisbury; no doubt to prevent any misappropriation of the funds in the future.

Later donations

The early, unknown, benefactors had given lands and properties with the intention that the profits from the rents could be put to "good charitable uses" in Wantage. From the end of the sixteenth century, after the passing of the Act of Parliament, records exist setting out the various transactions carried out by the Governors on behalf of the charity, and from these it appears that donations of property continued to take place: over the years various donors left land and houses or money to the Governors, to become part of the Town Lands and to be used to benefit the Charity. Most benefactors had been inhabitants of Wantage or had family connections with the town: some left the Governors to use their gift for the general benefit of the charity but others stipulated how they wished the income from their gift to be used. Thomas Aldworth, one of the first Governors, specifically asked that

The site of part of Robert Payne's bequest, Newbury St.

money he left should be used to provide income for the almshouse. His gift was put with the bequests left between 1584 and 1608 by Ann Latton of Chilton and Alexander Carter of Charlton, along with an additional £60 from the Town Lands profits, to buy land in East Challow in 1617, which comprised a close of two acres of pasture and meadow ground, behind a house called 'Goddes' (or 'Geddes') and nine and a half acres of arable land in the common fields, along with grazing for one horse and one cow in Cowleaze.

Also in 1617, Robert Payne of Abingdon, who had been born in Wantage, left property in Newbury Street opposite the old almshouse, some arable land in a common field in Wantage, near what is now Manor Road, and pasture land at Grove which was enough for four rotherbeasts (horned cattle). These properties were to be let and £5 of the annual income was to be used to provide bread for the "poor, aged and impotent" of Wantage and for two sermons to be preached each year on Christmas Day & Easter Day. The bread, in the form of twenty penny wheaten loaves, was to be shared out to twenty of the poorest inhabitants of Wantage at the church every Sunday. In the accounts for 1617, there were entries "to the poor in bred - 12d"; "to Mr Wills for a sermon - 6s 8d" and "to Mr Floyd for a sermon 6s 8d", so this would have been the first time that Payne's gift was used. Later the full £5 was spent each year as Payne had wished. There

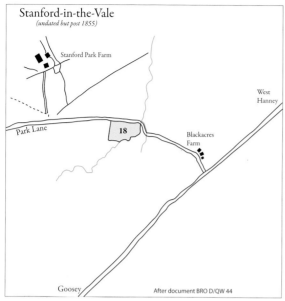

Stanford-in-the-Vale
(undated but post 1855)

Stanford Park Farm

West Hanney

Park Lane

18

Blackacres Farm

Goosey

After document BRO D/QW 44

Meadow at Stanford-in-the-Vale called Gentlemans Mead belonging to the Wantage Town Lands

could have been an earlier benefactor who left money for sermons from before 1597, as in the early 1600s ten shillings was paid each year for two sermons, although if this was a bequest it was not recorded as such. The ten shilling payments seemed to stop once sermons were being paid for from Payne's bequest.

William Masemore, a Governor who died in 1709, left £100 to the Town Lands: it was decided to add a further sum from the Trust's money and to buy estate with the joint amount. Five Governors were given the responsibility of deciding what to buy, but the only purchase recorded at that time was the land called Gentlemans Mead in Stanford in the Vale, which cost £18 18s 6d for the seven acres of meadow ground; the remainder of Mr Masemore's legacy and money from the Trust did not appear to be used to buy land.

Like Robert Payne, Thomas Willis who gave land in East Challow, in 1713, also asked that the income obtained by letting this land be used to provide bread and sermons. The bread was to be distributed to the poor every Sunday after the service at church; also twenty shillings each year from this income was to be given to the vicar for preaching two afternoon sermons, one on the Sunday before Ascension Day and the other

on the Sunday before All Saints Day (the last Sunday in October). Wantage bakers were paid regularly for baking the bread supplied to the poor under Willis's and Payne's bequests. In October 1720, the accounts show that Mr Hibberd the baker was paid £5 4s 0d to provide Willis's Bread; John Belcher was paid £4 6s 8d for Mr Payne's Bread; and Mr Birch the vicar was paid for four sermons, two at 10s each and two at 6s 8d each. All the items in both Willis's and Payne's gifts were being honoured. The four sermons continued to be paid for until the late 1970s but after 1851, the giving of bread was gradually phased out. Named charities like these gradually became part of the general funds.

This happened with other bequests too. One that survived for many years under the name of the benefactor was Brooke's Charity: Thomas Brooke in his will of 1677 left land called Black Croft in Wantage, with the instructions that £10 a year out of the rent was to be distributed to the town poor each year at the time of the severest winter weather. Poor people would be given sums ranging from sixpence to two shillings, depending on their need. The present day road named Black Croft, on Belmont Park estate off Denchworth Road, is the approximate site of the original field mentioned in Thomas Brooke's will. Black Croft did not belong to the Governors; their only connection with this land was to distribute the £10 each year. In 1691, a special book was bought to keep account of this, listing who was paid and the amount, and at the same time the clerk was paid an extra two shillings for entering these names in the book. So no recipients' names were ever given in the end of year accounts, just comments such as "Brooke's money - £10", or "Distributed Brooke's money among a great many paupers". During the 1760s, the town crier was paid sixpence for advertising to the townspeople that Mr Brooke's money was to be given away and "for crying the bread" or letting people know that they could apply for either Willis's or Payne's bread. Brooke's charity was shared out amongst the poor until the middle of the nineteenth century; when the Governors decided in

1851 that it would no longer be specifically distributed as money to the poor but would become part of the general fund, the same as Payne's charity: it had existed for nearly two hundred years in the form Thomas Brooke had originally laid down in his will.

Mrs Sarah Whitfield gave two sums of £100 in May and September 1831 to Robert Pumfrey and on her death in 1832 she left a further £100. All this money was given for the use of the old almshouses in Newbury Street and was to be used there as Mr Pumfrey thought best. He invested the money and used the income from it, which he shared between the inmates of the almshouses, giving each person there half a crown (2s 6d) a month with the balance used to provided them with a Christmas dinner. In 1854, the Governors decided that they were not too happy that the inmates of the Newbury Street almshouses were getting this extra 2s 6d a month; the Governors' payment to the almspeople was 3s 6d a week, at the time. They felt that they could not make changes for the almspeople already being paid this extra, but decided that when anyone died in those almshouses, any new tenant would be paid 2s 6d less a month by the Governors, which would once more make their income the same as the people living in the Mill Street almshouses. When Robert Pumfrey died in 1861, the invested money was transferred to the Governors of Wantage Town Lands, who wished to put it towards the building of the new almshouses in Eagles Close. This request was initially refused by the Charity Commissioners, but later the investment became part of the general income of the Trust.

Another charitable donation to the Town Lands, where the donor originally specified how the dividends should be spent, was the £400 given by William Cless, a coachmaker of Wantage who died in 1845. His gift was actually £392 in Consolidated Bank Annuities (or Consols), as when he died his assets were insufficient to realise the full £400. In his will he asked that £5 be distributed to the poor on the Sunday before Easter each year, and also £5 worth of coal was to be given to the poor on the 12th of January, that being the date of his wedding day. Anything left over each year from the dividends was to be shared equally between the parish clerk and the sexton of Wantage. The old almshouses in Newbury Street were still in existence at that time and the Governors agreed to share Cless's money between the eight houses in Mill Street and the seven in Newbury Street, as well as distributing coal to the fifteen houses in the winter. The remaining money, to be shared between the parish clerk and the sexton, was usually between one pound and one pound fifteen shillings, which did not sound very much but the smaller sum gave each of them the equivalent of a local farm worker's weekly wage. Shortly after 1900, however, the annual income from Cless's funds fell to just below £10 and after that time there was never any surplus to share between the two men.

In 1861, Mrs Mary Burd bought the land where the old almshouses had stood in Newbury Street, for £100. By the time she died in 1871, Eagles Close almshouses were in existence, and she left £2,000 in her will to be invested and for the dividends to be distributed by the Governors every half year in clothing and bedding amongst the inmates of Eagles Close, Mill Street and Stiles Almshouses; Stiles normally being the responsibility of the churchwardens. At the time, the Governors were contemplating additional building at the Grammar School and they asked the Charity Commissioners if they might borrow a thousand pounds of the Burd bequest to use for this purpose, paying it back over thirty years. The almspeople did receive the benefit of Mrs Burd's gift, although it appeared that the Governors decided to use it with Cless's and Whitfield's charities to increase the weekly sums given to the almshouse inmates, rather than distributing it as clothing and bedding.

As we have seen, people donating sums of money during their lifetime or leaving money in their wills usually set down how they wished the money to be spent, some wishing the church to benefit by sermons or by donations to clerk and sexton as well as contributing

Passageway at the top of Grove Street to Falcon Cottages, which had previously been the Cowheel Inn

to the charitable work of the Town Lands. One gift, which was given during the person's lifetime, totally involved church people as beneficiaries; the Governors were only intermediaries. In 1864, Mr Richard Belcher donated £3 a year from the rent of his property in Grove Street which was by then two cottages but had previously been the Cowheel Inn. This inn was behind what was then the Town Hall but is now HSBC Bank. The two cottages were still there in 1908 but by 1972 they had been pulled down and the plot was called Falcon Court and belonged to Woolworths. This firm paid £60 to the Governors in 1972 as a final redemption of the rent charge, which meant that the firm no longer had to pay the £3 a year over to the Governors. Mr Belcher's original document of 1864 stated that the Governors were to hand over the money each year to the vicar and churchwardens of Wantage church, who were to distribute the £3 on St Matthias Day (May 14th); 15s was for a sermon, 3s was for the parish clerk, 2s for the sexton, 3s for the organist and 6s to be shared between the parish singers with a maximum amount of one shilling each. The recipients were to be in church to receive these handouts but if any of them failed to attend, the money was to be spent on bread which was to be given to the poor who were members of the church instead. As all the beneficiaries were involved

in some way with the parish church, it is not clear why the Governors were left the responsibility of handing over the money each year, and why Richard Belcher did not donate the £3 directly to the churchwardens to distribute. After 1972, when the £3 from the rent was no longer handed over to the Governors, they were still to pay this amount each year to the vicar and churchwardens, out of the £60 from Woolworths which had been invested, but as with Willis and Payne's sermon money, the payments ended in the late 1970s.

A bequest to be used exclusively for the educational side of the Governors' responsibilities was left by Mary Harbert, or Herbert, in 1763. She asked for the £100 she left to be used for the free school in Wantage (i.e. the Grammar School) but the Governors decided to use it to educate poor girls, as discussed in the chapter on education. When Mrs Harbert's donation was received, the Governors suggested that an inscription should be put up in the church to record her gift. This had not been done when the Governors met the following year, but the year after that they made the decision to have a list of all the donations to the Trust inscribed, framed in canvas, and put up in the church at the expense of the Trust. There was no record of anything being spent on this project and if it was carried out, the framed list has long since disappeared. Mary Harbert's name was not mentioned again after the first few years, so the dividends from her donation must have been treated as general income.

Another donor who gave strict instructions as to how the Town Lands should use his gift was Thomas Fewson Eagles, who made a donation of land in 1832. This was a small meadow in Wantage, which came to be known as Eagles Close, and it was given on condition that the Governors were to build almshouses on part of it for the use of people of the town: the details of this will be dealt with in the chapters about the Town Lands' almshouses and other properties.

In more modern times, three donations were made specifically for medical help and treatment for the poor of Wantage. Two of the charities were related in that they were made by a brother and sister, although neither were originally anything to do with the Town Lands and it was only later that one of these charities involved the Governors. In 1885, Mrs Harriet Firth left £2,000 in her will towards a dispensary for the "poor and deserving inhabitants" of Wantage and its neighbourhood, particularly Letcombe Bassett. The term deserving poor usually meant those people of limited means who were managing to support themselves, not the paupers in the workhouse or on union benefits. This seems to be the case here as the will stipulated that the people to be helped were to be people who were not able to pay medical bills but were not receiving parish relief. A house was rented in Newbury Street to be used by the dispensary, known as the Firth Provident Medical Dispensary, where a book-keeper received any applications for relief and passed them on to the medical officers, or doctors, in the town. Anyone wanting to take advantage of the dispensary made a nominal weekly payment, so it was like a friendly society, giving medical insurance. Working people and servants were eligible, as were their wives and children. Anyone too ill to attend in person was visited in their homes. Harriet Firth's brother, Percy Smith of Letcombe Bassett, had died two years before Harriet, in 1883, leaving £5,000 to rent a suitable building and maintain it as a cottage hospital for the poor and sick in Wantage, the town at that date having no hospital for the poor except the infirmary at the workhouse. He wanted the hospital to serve some of the surrounding villages as well as Wantage town, and he particularly mentioned East Hanney and Letcombe Bassett. Funds raised by public subscription were used to buy a house at Belmont which was considered suitable for use as

Wantage Cottage Hospital at Belmont

a hospital. The building was furnished by Mrs Silver of Letcombe Manor at Letcombe Regis, her husband being one of the Town Lands' Governors at the time, and it was opened in February 1886. The hospital was run by trustees and had no connection with the Wantage Town Lands.

Originally the trustees of the Firth Provident Medical Dispensary were individuals such as members of the Jotcham and Ormond families and Albert Castle's wife Maria, and the charity at that time had no connection with the Town Lands. After the National Health Service was set up in 1946, the previous work of Harriet Firth's dispensary became redundant. Discussions took place between the Charity Commissioners and other medical charities in Wantage which supported the district nurses or provided amenities for patients and staff at Wantage Hospital and the Downs Hospital (the old workhouse). It gradually became clear that amalgamation of Harriet Firth's charity with these other Wantage charities was not going to be possible, as their charitable aims were different. The trustees of the other medical charities were reluctant to take on the extra duties of running Harriet Firth's trust, and finally the Governors of the Wantage Town Lands agreed to do so. From 1953, this charity became known as the Harriet Firth Charity and would now be for the benefit of the sick poor in ways not provided for by the National Health Service, such as giving money for convalescence, or supplying extra bedding or fuel, or domestic help for the sick or infirm. One year £25 was used for the district nurses to distribute Bovril; on another occasion taxi fares were paid to enable an elderly person from an outlying village to get to Wantage Hospital; and on

EXTRACTS FROM THE RULES OF THE
FIRTH PROVIDENT MEDICAL DISPENSARY.
WANTAGE.

1.—Every Provident Member above 14 years of age shall pay 1d. per week, but 3d. per week will be considered sufficient for a man, his wife, and all his children under 14 years of age. Servants who may be judged eligible by the Committee shall pay 4/- a year in quarterly payments. Wives of members of Sick Benefit Clubs, or widows with children under 14 years of age, shall pay 2d. per week.

2.—The payments of Provident Members shall be made in advance. No one in arrear will be entitled to the benefits of the Institution, and each family or member shall pay a fine of 1d. for the arrears of every week. If any member be more than two months in arrear, his or her name shall be erased from the books.

3.—No one actually labouring under sickness shall be admitted a Provident Member unless he pay an entrance fee of 5/-, in addition to the usual weekly subscription, and all his family enter at the same time. If treatment be required within a fortnight after joining, the sick entrance fee shall, as a general rule, be exacted.

4.—If any person, whose name has been erased from the books, shall desire to be re-admitted, there being at the time no sickness in the family, he shall pay the monthly subscription, and 1d. for the card, and also a re-admission fee of 2/- for a family, and 1/- for a single person. After one re-admission, the re-admission fee to be doubled. If any person or member of a family desiring re-admission be sick, then a fine of 5/-, in addition to the ordinary sick fee of 5/-, must be deposited with the ordinary monthly subscription and the payment for the card, at the time of application. The sums deposited in accordance with this Rule shall be dealt with at the discretion of the Committee.

5.—Every Provident Member shall have the choice of whichever Medical Officer he may prefer, but he shall not make any change during the current year without the sanction of the Committee.

6.—Those patients who are able must attend at the Surgery of the Medical Officer chosen by them, between the hours of 9.30 and 10.30 in the morning, bringing their admission tickets. Those who are too ill to attend at the Surgery must send their tickets before 9 o'clock in the morning to their Medical Officer, and he will visit them at their own homes. In case of accident or sudden illness, members can have the attendance of any of the Medical Officers on sending their admission ticket to his residence. Patients can only be attended at their own homes when within a distance of five miles from Wantage. Members requiring the attendance of a Medical Officer at their own homes after 6 o'clock p.m., must pay a fee of 2/6 to the Medical Officer, to be returned if, in the opinion of the Medical Officer, the case be an urgent one.

DIRECTIONS FOR MEMBERS.

1.—The card must accompany *every* application for the Medical Officer, at other times it *must* be kept *at home* for his inspection.

2.—Read carefully the Extract of Rules above.

3.—Send for the Doctor *before* 10 a.m.

4.—The Rules as to *fines* will be *strictly enforced*.

5.—All patients must bring their own bottles and gallipots clean to the Surgery of their Medical Officer.

6.—On Sundays, the Surgery is *only* open for *urgent cases* at 9.30 a.m.

7.—The Medical Officer will *not* prescribe for any Member in arrear of payment.

8.—The Pay Office of the Dispensary, in Newbury Street, Wantage, is open *every morning* from 10 o'clock to 12.30, and on *Tuesday and Friday Evenings*, from 5.30 to 6.30.

several occasions chiropody treatment was paid for. Fifty pounds was given to the appeal for providing a lift at Wantage Hospital; and other donations were made to the Red Cross, the Wantage Silver Threads Club and the Berkshire Mental Hospital Welfare Fund. The main payments from the charity were made to supply coal in winter to the almspeople, and later to give them all a small donation at Christmas.

The third modern bequest was made by Walter Joseph Regis Kirby; born in New Zealand in 1874 he became known as "the Auckland boy soprano" and after training in Australia he went on to become a fine tenor who sang in Europe as well as Australia and New Zealand. He died in London in 1934, having written a will leaving money to various religious bodies, colleges and hospitals in Australia and New Zealand, including money to set up two singing scholarships to be named after him. Quite why is not clear, but the residue of his estate was to be shared by charities in Wantage, to be chosen by Lady Jane Lindsey of Abingdon who selected Wantage Cottage Hospital and the Wantage Town Lands as the joint beneficiaries. Each received around £6,000. This all seemed fine, with Wantage people benefiting as Walter Kirby had wished, except that there was an addition to the story revealed in a series of letters to the Governors from Walter's relatives in Australia. It transpired that Walter had later added a codicil to his will, leaving part of his estate to be shared between his three nieces and two nephews. He had had the codicil witnessed but had not signed it himself, so it was not legally binding. Having sent it to his solicitor, he wrote to one of the nieces, "... I am afraid I will never be strong again, but don't worry I am leaving you and your sisters and JG in Sydney all I have left, during your lifetime and to go to charities at death." It was signed, "Your affectionate Uncle Walter". His solicitor noticed that Walter had not signed the codicil but put it away for safe keeping and did not inform Walter that it was unsigned, so that this did not come to light until after his death. The relatives, including Walter's only brother wrote to the Governors, begging that the Governors would see their way to at least making some small financial contribution to the family, who had expected some of the money to be left to them rather than the Wantage Town Lands and Wantage hospital. Walter's brother explained that he and Walter had been on affectionate terms, sending one of Walter's letters to prove it: this letter ended, "With my everlasting love, Jack dear, your affectionate brother Walter", and he had written across the corner, "Give my warmest love to my nieces and nephews without fail". The brother told the Governors, "My financial position is almost desperate. If your Institutions who have been bequeathed by my brother such a vast amount of money could see your way to make me some allowance, I should be for ever grateful. I have a wife as poor as myself". The Governors were moved by these letters to consider helping the family in Australia in some way and Mr Jotcham, the clerk to the Governors, wrote to the solicitors in Australia that it was "the definite desire on the part of the Governors to make some provision for the relatives of the deceased". However, the Charity Commissioners were impelled to carry out the letter of the law as far as the will and the unsigned codicil were concerned, and even an approach to the Attorney General had no success; the reply to that appeal was that "Charity Trustees cannot, without committing a breach of trust, surrender any property to which they are entitled ... however much sympathy they may properly feel with those who make an appeal ... as in this case". So although Walter Kirby had decided to leave some of his fortune to his family, who were "all persons of small means" with one niece being a war-widow, and although the Governors were sympathetic, the law had to be strictly upheld. The missing signature on the codicil meant those later wishes expressed by Walter could not be acted upon and the bequest to the Wantage Town Lands in the main will had to be honoured.

Shortly after this bequest was finalised and the Governors had invested the Town Lands' share of the money, they asked permission of the Charity Commissioners to pay some of the income to the churchwardens to be used to benefit the inmates of Stiles almshouses. This request was granted as it did not break the rules of the Town Lands charity, set out in the original Elizabethan Act of Parliament, to give relief to the poor of Wantage. As well as the Stiles almspersons who were to collect 10s from the clerk's office on the first day of every month, each of the six In-town Governors nominated "one poor and deserving person resident in Wantage", who would receive 30s a month. It was suggested that the Governors would give preference to people on the waiting list for the almshouses in Mill Street or Eagles Close. These monthly payments out of the income generated by the Kirby bequest were to be known as Kirby Pensions. Later, in 1971, as income was increasing, two extra pensioners were appointed.

A further very small gift was made to the Governors in 1939, when George Pearce, an elderly gentleman, sent a cheque for £25. His mother had lived in an Eagles Close almshouse for some years and his aunt had been an almsperson in Mill Street. He originally hoped that the interest on this gift would enable the Governors to build another house and name it Leah Pearce's Home of Rest in memory of his mother. When it was pointed out to him that it would probably take many years to achieve this, from his £25, it was agreed that after ten years of building up the interest, annual payments would be made just before Christmas to the Eagles Close almspeople and this would be known as Leah Pearce's Gift. A small interesting paragraph in one of George Pearce's letters explained that one of his sisters had been nursemaid to Mr and Mrs Jotcham's children, so as a boy he had known the Jotchams, as well as Mr and Mrs de Vitre and Mrs Ormond, adding "but all at the proper distance of course, as we respected our betters in the 1870s". (Messrs Jotcham, de Vitre and Ormond were Governors at the end of the nineteenth century, all being gentlemen of standing in the area).

2

The Running of the Trust

Governors

The Act of Parliament which set up the Trust as the Wantage Town Lands, appointed twelve Wantage men "of the better sort" to be Governors. The original men chosen and named in the Act of Parliament were: Edmonde Fettyplace Esquire, John Dolman Esquire, Franncis Moore Esquire, Thomas Aldworth merchant, Robert Wirdnam gentleman, William Anger, William Talbotte, William Tubbe, Richard Webb, Thomas Aldworth the younger, Thomas Clement and John Snodham. However, some of the men lived in the area surrounding Wantage rather than in the town itself. Edmund Fettiplace and John Dolman appear to have lived in Childrey, Francis Moore was an inhabitant of Fawley, Robert Wirdnam of Charlton, and Thomas Aldworth was a merchant of the City of Bristol, although he must have had some connection with Wantage, possibly having been born there. Thomas Aldworth the younger was a relative of his, but not a son, and may have been a tanner in the town.

The reason Thomas Aldworth, the merchant of Bristol, was chosen as a Governor is perhaps explained in his will, when he died in 1598. In this will, he left money to the churchwardens and overseers of Wantage. It appeared that he had already lent them a large sum, which they could now keep, and the two amounts totalled £40, approximately equal to the annual income of the Town Lands in the early years. He wanted this money to be spent on buying wool so that the poor could be set to work spinning, for the following four years. The younger Thomas Aldworth, who lived in Wantage, was to oversee the spending of this money. If it was not used for giving work to the poor, then the older Thomas wanted it to be used to buy land or houses to be used towards the upkeep of the almshouse in Wantage. His generosity before his death must have decided the good men of Wantage to

include him as one of the twelve original Governors, although in the end he was only in office for a few months before he died. As was shown in Chapter 1, his bequest was combined with other donations and used to buy land in East Challow, which was then administered by the Governors for the benefit of the Town Lands.

Some families provided members as Governors over several generations, as in the case of the Collins family of Betterton where five of the family were Governors over a 200 year span. John Collins became a Governor in 1667 and was followed by his son Charles in 1686: Ferdinando Collins became a Governor in 1790, the Rev. John Collins was elected in 1812 and the Rev. John Ferdinando Collins took up the position in 1843. The last three men did not follow directly after the family member before them, but it is quite likely, from the Lockinge parish registers that sons followed fathers in all cases. Several members of the Butler family also became Governors over the years, starting in 1688 with Thomas Butler who was the father of Joseph Butler, Bishop of Durham. When Thomas died his son Robert was elected in his place and he was followed by his son, another Robert. This Robert's brother, John, became a Governor on Robert's death, with a George Butler being elected in 1822, who may also have been a relative. Other families, although not providing as many Governors as the Collins or Butler families, still had sons being elected to replace their fathers in many instances. This still continued into modern times. Amongst others, the Jotcham and Ormond families had sons following fathers, and current Governors David Castle, Robert Sharp and Thomas Loyd, were preceded by members of their families.

Over the years the Governors continued to be a mix of men from Wantage town and from the surrounding area, and it appeared that usually a town person would replace a Wantage inhabitant while a man from further afield would replace a similar person, when the situation arose where a new Governor was appointed. In 1856, the Governors were actually referred to as out-town and in-town Governors, when John Bowler of Milton Hill was elected as an out-town Governor to replace the Reverend Nelson of Sparsholt; and George Stone, who lived at The Ham in Wantage, was asked to replace the in-town Governor, Reverend Hayward of Charlton House on Charlton Road in Wantage. George Stone did not wish to become a Governor, so another Wantage man took the position instead. He was John Plumbe, a coal merchant operating from the wharf at the bottom of Mill Street. At the beginning of the twentieth century, the Charity Commissioners commented that the Governors were divided into these two groups by long standing custom but that in view of the terms of the original Act of Parliament it was probably not a valid division. It did, however, continue. Some of the out-town Governors were chosen for their standing as men of importance in the county and were usually landowners and magistrates, such as Sir Henry Moore of Fawley, elected in 1665, Bartholomew Tipping of Woolley Park who was elected in 1756, and Colonel Sir Robert James Loyd-Lindsay of Lockinge, later Lord Wantage, who became a Governor in 1860.

Quite often, these important gentlemen agreed to become Governors but rarely attended meetings. It is difficult to be exact in the number of attendances they made, as minutes are missing, but the above Bartholomew Tipping served for forty three years until he died in 1799 and only appeared to attend two meetings, while Sir Henry William Martin, elected in 1826, never put in an appearance, dying seventeen years later in 1843. Thomas Goodlake, JP of Letcombe, did slightly better as he attended eight meetings in the forty nine years he was a Governor, from 1805 to 1854. In a document drawn up in 1936, giving the duties of the Governors, it appeared that the out-town Governors at that time were only expected to attend

the annual meeting, when the accounts were presented, or on special occasions when their advice was needed. The in-town Governors carried on the business of the Charity and met throughout the year as necessary.

After the Governors were classed as either 'in-town' or 'out-town' members, there were several occasions where a Wantage man moved away, was replaced by another town inhabitant, but shortly afterwards was re-elected as an out-town Governor. This happened in the case of the last of the Butler family mentioned earlier; George Butler, appointed in 1821, moved from Wantage in 1826 and was replaced by Carew Packer who was a glazier trading in the town. The following year, George Butler, now living in Woolstone, was re-appointed to replace Rev. John Collins, an out-town Governor from Betterton near Lockinge who had died, and he went on to serve the charity for a further forty five years.

Although it seemed to be accepted that some of the gentry were non-attending members for many years, there were occasions when it was felt necessary to deal with men who had been elected as Governors, had accepted the position, but then were hardly ever seen at meetings. We are told that in 1667, John Jennens of Charlton had "long absented himself and not joyned with the rest of the Governors in the acting of anything with them." The Governors sent the bailiff, Hugh Snodham, to have a word with him about his lack of attendance but Mr Jennens sent back a message that "he cannot nor will not attend that imployment but is willing that another shall be chosen in his room." At which point he was replaced by the John Collins of Betterton mentioned above. Also in 1667, the Governors agreed to remove William Talbott. He was a woollen draper of Wantage but had left the town and gone to London to serve as a soldier in the King's service (this was King Charles II). Jasper Scholes, a gentleman, was elected in his stead. Bartholomew Wroughton, of Woolley Park, was asked by the Governors in 1814 to replace Lord Craven of Ashdown Park, as the latter had "neglected to attend any meeting of the trust since he was appointed" in 1790. Sometimes, like William Talbott, Governors moved away from the area and either asked to be discharged or were requested to resign. In 1665, Sir John Fettiplace, asked for a suitable person to be chosen to replace him, "his distance and occasions not permitting him to be present at the meetings" and William Moore Esquire was living at a distance, in 1701, when he told the Governors he no longer wished to serve. The above Governors asked to be replaced, but when another Moore, Sir John Moore, failed to attend meetings, the Governors felt he should be removed and they told the clerk to write to Sir John requesting to know his intentions about resigning "as he has seldom attended since being elected." Two years later, in 1768, it appeared that he had moved away but that they were still waiting for a reply about his intentions, as they sent another letter asking "if he is agreeable to resigning as he has left this part of the kingdom." In 1802, it was minuted that several of the Governors had not attended to carry out the business of the Trust and they were to be asked to be more regular in their attendance in future or to resign so that other people could be elected who would attend more frequently. The only person asked to resign for reasons other than non-attendance was William Ansell, in 1820, who had been the owner of a large tannery in the town but was considered an improper person to be a Governor as he had been made bankrupt.

Not all the Governors were as remiss as some of the above gentlemen. There were other men through the years who were very conscientious in their duties and attended very regularly. Thomas Aldworth and William Masemore were two of several Governors in the 1600s who gave the Town Lands their time and effort unstintingly: Henry Knapp, Thomas Butler and Sir Thomas Goodlake served regularly for forty five years, forty two years and thirty two years respectively before dying in the 1700s. (This Thomas Goodlake was an ancestor of the Thomas Goodlake who only attended eight times.) At the end of the 1800s, there were six men who attended almost every meeting;

Edward Ormond and Llewellyn Jotcham the solicitors, Walter Barker a doctor of the town, the Reverend Archer-Houblon the vicar, Mr de Vitre Esquire of Charlton House in Charlton Road and Philip Gibbons of Brooklands in Newbury Street.

The Governors tried various methods to improve attendance. In 1662, they ordered that any of their members who, having been given notice of a forthcoming meeting, did not put in an appearance should be fined twelve pence each. In 1738, it was agreed that if a Governor was absent for three years without giving a good reason, he would be asked to resign. The Governors living out of town were to be sent a copy of this notice before the next meeting, but this did not seem to have much effect on the numbers attending meetings, with an average of between seven and eight of the twelve Governors signing the minutes both before and after this edict. The minutes only record one meeting a year at this time, in October or November, so the meetings we know about may have been the annual general meetings with other less well attended meetings during the year, which had caused the Governors to worry about lack of attendance.

It appeared that at the general meeting each year the members who attended ate dinner. The Governors carried out all their duties on a voluntary basis, without any payment. even this annual dinner was paid for out of their own pockets, although the schoolmaster and clerk, who also attended, had their meals provided from the funds. In 1732 it was decided that any Governor who did not attend this annual meeting and dinner, after being given three days notice, "shall forfit and pay to the Landlord of the house where such meeting shall be held the sum of four shillings for his ordinary and extraordinary" (in other words for his meal). The landlord would have been asked to prepare dinner for the number of men expected at the meeting and if people did not turn up he would not be pleased to have several uneaten meals on his hands. This decision cannot have met with the approval of some of the Governors, as a few years later in 1738 it was decided that ten days

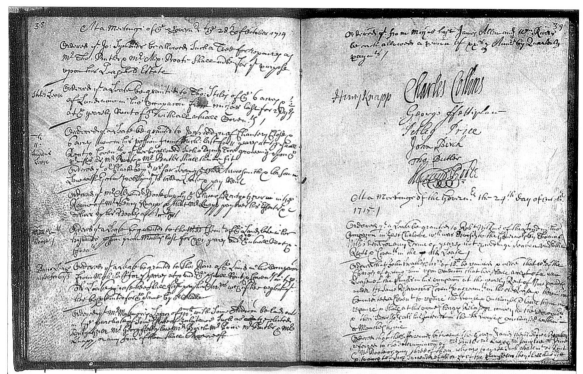

Governors' Minutes

The minutes of the annual meeting in 1714, signed by seven Governors, reads as follows:

At a Meeting of y^e [the] Governors the 28th of October 1714

Ordered y^t [that] Jo: Symonds be allowed Such a Tree for repaires as Mr Thos: Butler & Mr Alex: Boote shall make for ye purpose upon his Leasehold Estate

Stiles' Lease: Ordered y^t a Lease be granted to Tho: Stiles of ye 6 acres & 1/2 of land now in his occupacon [occupation] from Michas [Michaelmas] last for 21 yrs at ye yearly Rent of £3 with all usuall Covent^s [Covenants] [...][...] Hadden's Lease: Ordered y^t a Lease be granted to Jo: Hadden of Chantery Close & 6 acres now in his possion [possession] from Mich: [Michaelmas] last for 11 years at ye usuall Rent & Coven^ts & y^t he be allowed Such a Dying Tree groweing upon ye premises as Mr Boote & Mr Butler shall thinke fit

Ordered y^t or [officer?] Clarke be p^d (paid) 10s for Serving ye Widd (Widow) Arrowsmith & her son in Law with Ejectm^t (Ejectment) & obliging [...] to take a Lease & pay Rent

Ordered y^t Mr Alexander Boote Supply ye Place of Rentgatherer in the Room of [instead of] Mr Henry Knapp & that Mr Knapp pay over his Effects & deliver up his Bookes of Acc^ts [Accounts] [...]

Widd. Clemt's [Widow Clement's] Lease : Ordered y^t a Lease be granted to the Widd. Clem^t. of ye Land late in her husband's psson [possession] from Michas last for xxi [21] years under ye usuall Rent & Coven^ts

Barr's Lease made for 6 yrs: Ordered y^t a Lease be granted to Tho: Barr of ye Land in his occupacon [occupation] from Mich. [Michaelmas] last for 7 yeares at & under ye usuall Rent & Coven^ts [Covenants] in the old Lease in case hee shall first pay his Arrrs [Arrears] w^ch [which] if he neglect y^t hee be prosecuted for ye same by or (officer?) Clarke

Ordered that Mr Masemore's Legacy of £100 with Some Addicon [Addition] be laid out in the purchase of Some Estate of Zubitance [substance?] Such as the elected Rentgatherer Mr George Fettiplace Mr Birch Mr Price Mr Butler & Mr Knapp or any four of them shall Approve of

Ordered y^t from Michas. last James Allen & W^m. Rivers be each allowed a pencon [pension] of xxs [20s] per Annum by Quarterly paym^ts [payments]

Henry Knapp, Charles Collins, George Fettiplace, Petley Price, John Birch, Tho: Butler, Alexander Boote

notice would be given for a general meeting rather than three, following which absent members would have to forfeit the smaller sum of 2s 6d to the landlord where the meeting was held; while ten years later the amount was reduced to 2s. Each member was to have a copy of this latest order delivered to him, so there was to be no excuse for not complying.

As the in-town Governors were usually professional men or tradesmen, they were occasionally used by the governing body to carry out professional duties or to supply the charity in the way of their business. As a strict check was kept on the accounts by the Governors, there was no problem with one Governor benefiting his business in this way. He would not be claiming a larger sum than if a non-governor was used. Dr. Elias Clarke was a Governor in the seventeenth century and treated poor patients at the expense of the Town Lands. The Governors frequently needed the services of a solicitor, in dealing with the leases for their various properties and also, when land or cottages were let or sold by auction, this would involve the auctioneer and he would expect a payment. In 1803, William Wise, one of the local auctioneers and a Governor, was paid when several of the trust's estates were let by auction, while the solicitor William Beckett, also a Governor, was paid at the same time for drawing up the new leases. Over about twenty five years, Mr Beckett was paid regularly; the amount varying from about two pounds to about ten pounds, except for in 1818 when his bill came to the rather large amount of £24 7s 0d. Several leases had been granted or renewed that year, but this was not unusual. However, it had also been decided to take legal proceedings against George Roe to recover his unpaid rent, so this could have been the reason why Mr Beckett's charges had been unusually high that year. In 1825, another decision to sue a tenant in order to recover rent in arrears coincided with a higher than usual payment to Mr Beckett, this time for £13 5s 0d. When drawing up leases, Mr Beckett was paid half the cost. The leases would have two identical parts, one going to the person leasing the property

and the other staying in the Governors' hands, so the Governors would stand half the cost while one assumes the other half was met by the person taking out the lease. In 1830, we are told that Mr Beckett was paid £7 as half the cost of drawing up five pairs of leases and getting them signed. In a similar way Governors who were tradesmen in the town were allowed to provide goods and services to the Trust, although this only seemed to happen occasionally. Henry Knapp, a very conscientious Governor between 1684 and 1729, was paid for linen cloth for several years at the beginning of the 1700s, often quite large bills. Carew Packer, a plumber and glazier who was a Governor between 1826 and 1833, had been paid for glazing work before he became a Governor but was also paid in 1831 whilst a Governor. John Plumbe, a coal merchant at the wharf in Mill Street who was a Governor from 1856 to 1860 supplied coal each year to the almshouse inhabitants, which was paid for from the Town Lands accounts.

It appeared that a Governor could not be a tenant of the Town Lands at the same time that he was a Governor. John Price leased land in The Ham in Wantage, but when he became a Governor in 1758, his sister Mary Price took over the lease in trust for him, "he being elected a Governor". A similar situation had arisen a few years before this. John Bance of East Challow leased a close there known as Lambolls Close, for ten years before he was elected as a Governor. He became a Governor in 1730 but when the lease was renewed in 1737, it was minuted that it would be granted to "such person as Mr Bance shall appoint". He still continued to pay the rent each year, but when in 1745 the Governors viewed the land intending to discuss its value, it was recorded that "if Miss Bance shall refuse to accept a new lease" at the rent they set, then it would be offered to someone else. It appeared that John Bance's sister, Ann, had stood in for him as the person designated on the lease, in the same way that John Price's sister had become a trustee for Mr Price. It was perhaps not legally acceptable for a Governor to take a lease of Town Lands, although in the case of John Bance, it appeared that he continued to be financially responsible. Sometimes it is difficult to be certain whether a tenant and a Governor with the same name are one and the same person or not. Three of the original Governors were Thomas Aldworth, William Wilmott and William Anger: in the years immediately following the Act, three men of the same names were tenants of the Town Lands, but they may simply have been members of the same family, not the men who were the Governors. It appeared to be acceptable for members of Governors' families to be tenants.

The Governors played a part in the social life of Wantage, as can be seen by their involvement in the celebrations at the time of Queen Victoria's Golden Jubilee. Quoting from the minute book in June 1887: "This being the day of Jubilee appointed for celebrating the 50th anniversary of the Reign of Her Majesty The Queen, the Governors headed a procession consisting of the Town Commissioners, Odd Fellows, Foresters, and other Societies and the principal Inhabitants of the Town from the Town Hall to the Church where a special Thanksgiving service was held after which the Governors assisted in providing in the Market Place a public dinner to upwards of 900 persons and a Tea to upwards of 950 children. Various sports afterwards took place and at 10 o'clock in the evening many Beacon fires and fireworks were seen for several miles on the neighbouring hills." Other major events were marked: the almshouse inmates were given an extra week's allowance to celebrate the coronation of King George VI in 1937; and the Charity Commissioners agreed to the Governors making a donation of £25 towards a bungalow for the district nurse, which was to be the Wantage commemoration of this coronation. A teak seat at Eagles Close almshouses was also provided to mark the event. At the coronation of Queen Elizabeth II, the inmates of the almshouses and the other pensioners were each presented with a special gift from the Governors; £2 for the almspeople of Mill Street and Eagles Close and the Kirby pensioners; 10s each for the inmates of Stiles almshouses. Mrs

Cummins, who was the tenant of a shop at 24 Mill Street, one of the Governors' properties, also got £2. These gifts were given in a specially designed envelope and Mr Penney, one of the Governors, arranged for an attractive brochure to be distributed to the almspeople with the donations.

The two wars also had an impact on the Governors, not least the two deaths of members of the board killed on active service; Major Wroughton in 1917 and Captain Eyston in 1941. In WWII, investments were made to help the war effort, with several hundred pounds of funds being invested in Government bonds used to produce weapons: savings bonds for War Weapons Week in 1941, for Wantage and District Warships Week in 1942, for Wantage Wings for Victory Week in 1943 and Wantage Salute the Soldier Week in 1945. Towards the end of WWII, part of the land in Eagles Close was taken over by the Berkshire War Agricultural Committee as a depot.

Bailiffs, Rentgatherers and Clerks

The Governors employed a bailiff in the early years of the Trust. Gregory Webb, the first bailiff in the records, collected the rents from tenants and kept the accounts from 1598 until 1613, when one of the Governors, John Snodham (or Snadham), a draper in the town, took over these duties. The mid-1600s saw Hugh Snodham as the bailiff, so possibly a relative of John the Governor. Thomas Fewtrell was bailiff for many years from 1698, until in 1716 the Governors agreed that "in regard of his old age and disability he be discharged of the office of Bayliff." It is likely that Thomas was also the schoolmaster of the English school as a Thomas Fewtrell was appointed schoolmaster in 1699, the year after Thomas Fewtrell was appointed as bailiff. Whether Thomas had asked to be replaced as bailiff, when he gave up that office, or whether the Governors felt he was not fit for the job we are not told. He was given a pension of twenty shillings a year. Peter Martin, who replaced him as bailiff, was to be paid ten shillings a year while Thomas lived but this would be increased by twenty shillings a year when Thomas died. The accounts record Thomas being paid his pension until the end of 1719 and it appeared that when he died the following February, the Governors stood the cost of his funeral, as a man called Towsey was paid five shillings for burying Mr Fewtrell.

Peter Martin was paid "the usual salary of thirty shillings a year by quarterly payments" from Michaelmas 1720, so his salary had gone up as promised. He was also to be given a greatcoat; two of the Governors were to decide which coat was suitable for him. This annual payment to the bailiff was a small amount, which indicates that his duties were probably only part time, and which would fit in with Thomas Fewtrell also being the schoolmaster of the school teaching basics to the poor children. Peter Martin who followed him seemed to be a carpenter as payments were made to him for the type of jobs that a carpenter would do; for work done at the school with oak boards and nails, for mending a door and for making several coffins. Hugh Snodham, the earlier bailiff, also worked as a tailor as there were several entries in the accounts when he was paid to make clothes for the poor, such as when he was paid 1s 6d in 1680 for "makinge Edward Pinnock a Coate and Breeches". By 1760, the bailiff was paid forty shillings a year and he was now given a hat at that as well as a great coat. Richard Cox was the bailiff at that time, and his duties were to wait upon the Governors and assist them with his advice relating to timber repairs etc. He was also a carpenter as the Governors paid "Richard Cox, a carpenter, his bill for sundries" the previous year. By 1762 John Noke had taken over these duties and he also was to be paid forty shillings plus a great coat and laced hat, as was the bailiff William Savory in 1794, whose coat cost £2 6s 11d and his hat £1 7s 0d. The annual payment of forty shillings (£2) was less than the cost of the coat, which puts the amount the bailiff was paid into context.

In 1801, William Savory the bailiff, or Governors' Servant as he was called in the accounts, borrowed £6 from the Governors, which he promised to pay back at the rate of £1 four times a year. As he only earned £2 a year by his bailiff duties, he must certainly have had other employment as well. The money he borrowed would have been paid back by the middle of 1802 but the Governors then lent him a further £5 in 1806. This was paid back in ten instalments, so at the rate of 10s each time. At the time he paid back the last instalment on this, he borrowed a further £5. It seemed he was always living beyond his means. By now he was being paid £3 a year as the Governors' servant and in 1813, the Governors decided to raise this to £4 a year. Perhaps they had realised he was having difficulty making ends meet and felt his work for them deserved a higher salary. His salary rose to £8 a year in 1827 and remained at this figure until his death in 1838. Clothing was still part of the package given to the bailiff by the Governors; in 1815 they minuted that a great coat and hat was to be given to William Savory, and in 1825 a Mr Mattingly was paid £5 12s 6d for making a coat and hat for Savory. This might have meant he got a new one every ten years, although he could have been given others in the years between which have not been recorded. There were several Savorys in Wantage, a William and his son John were blacksmiths at the Shears in Mill Street but whether they were the same Savorys who were the Governors' servants it is not possible to tell. When William Savory, the bailiff, died in 1838 his son John was appointed in his place at a salary of £4 a year, half what his father had been getting. There is no mention of paying him or anyone else as bailiff after 1846.

As well as their annual salary, bailiffs were paid additional sums for extra work done for the Governors. In 1603 Gregory Webb went to London on behalf of the Governors and was given £1 "for his expences Riding to London and staying there." We are not told why he went but he might have been taking the accounts to the Bishop of Salisbury, who was in London on other occasions when the accounts were presented. In 1644, Hugh Snodham was paid 6s 8d for "waytinge and goeing upp and downe in the Governors business" and a further 3s for "goeing twise to Oxford"; and in 1706 Thomas Fewtrell earned 9s 6d "for his paines in summoning the Governors to elect a schoolmaster, and for horse hire." It sounded as though he rode round the countryside, taking a note or a verbal message to all the Governors, telling them of the special meeting which had been called to appoint a new schoolmaster.

After the first few years when the bailiff had collected the rents, the rent collecting became the responsibility of one of the Governors; sometimes the same person for several years. The man taking on this duty was known as the Rent Receiver or Rentgatherer until 1834 when he started being referred to as the Treasurer. The Governor who served longest as rent receiver was William Wise, a Wantage solicitor, who took on this responsibility for twenty five years, from 1798 to 1823, when on his death he was followed by his son John, also a Governor, who held this office for ten years. There were other men who served for long periods, including Robert Garrard who was rent receiver for fourteen years until his death in 1789, when his executors produced his accounts for the year. There were occasions when the rent receiver was replaced because of old age, after serving for several years. In 1658 Thomas Clement, a Wantage tanner, stopped collecting the rents as he was "growne in yeares and not able to undertake the office any longer"; and William Masemore was replaced in 1686 as it was reported that he was "growing ancient".

William Wise was perhaps becoming a little muddled towards the end of his twenty five years as rent receiver, as he did not carry out his duties quite as thoroughly as he should have done. When his son was elected a Governor in his place and also took over as rent receiver, he found that some of the payments, which his father should have been made, had not happened. Each year, the preaching of four sermons at the parish church was to be paid for but John found that his father had not paid the vicar for four out of the preceding five years; or possibly he had paid him but had not entered the amounts in the accounts, as

the money John paid was refunded a few years after he had given it to the vicar. Brooke's Charity which paid out £10 each year to the poor had also had been missed for several years, although the other Governors should have seen from the accounts that William had not carried this out. By the time it was noticed that Brooke's money was not being paid, six years had been missed, and so £30 was paid each year for the next three years, which brought the donations up to date.

The rentgatherer, or rent receiver, had the authority to make decisions, which included making small payments between meetings. In 1738, the Governors decided that from then on the rent receiver should not agree to spend money on repairs without first consulting three or more of the Governors and getting their consent, so perhaps he had been over generous with the amounts he had allowed tenants to spend. And then in 1754 the rent receiver was told not to pay out any sum of money greater than £1 1s 0d unless there was an order agreeing to the payment signed by six Governors; payments were being tightened up. Quite often a small group of Governors were appointed to carry out an agreed task. For instance in 1691 when it was decided at a meeting that the old almshouse should be made habitable once more for poor people, four of the Governors were named as the men responsible for carrying this out "as they think fit". And in 1727, John Symonds was to be allowed timber to repair the house he rented from the Town Lands in Grove Street, "as Mr Boote, Mr Pynner and Mr Pynnock or any two of them shall think fitt". Also it appeared from the accounts that between meetings, although small amounts were paid out by the rent receiver to the poor and needy, quite often it was recorded that this was done 'by consent' when other Governors had also given their approval. An example is in 1711, when William Patient and his wife were ill (he was possibly the landlord of the Camel, which was at the present Camel crossroads by the mini-roundabouts on the road to Challow). On several occasions he or his wife were given a shilling because of their illness, but when William was given five shillings, it was recorded as being given by consent; so other Governors besides the rentgatherer had agreed to that larger payment to the sick man.

After 1830, when the rent receiver began to be referred to as the treasurer, the in-town Governors took the duties of treasurer in turn, for a year at a time, being appointed at the annual general meeting. As well as being responsible for keeping the accounts, the treasurer for the year also arranged for necessary repairs to be carried out at his discretion, signed the cheques to pay for these and appointed new inhabitants for any almshouses that fell vacant. The treasurer would also be responsible for making sure rents were collected, so being the holder of this post was quite time consuming and a big responsibility. By the twentieth century, rents were paid at the clerk's office and he also kept the accounts, although one of the Governors was still treasurer, filling the position of chairman as well. The early to mid twentieth century also saw much of the property being sold and so the work of collecting rents gradually became less onerous.

For many years, the rentgatherer or later the treasurer seemed to be responsible for producing the annual account sheet, which was inspected and passed by the other Governors at the annual meeting. It was not until 1913 that the accounts were professionally audited: for several years after that the Wantage firm of Adkin, Belcher and Bowen were paid £3 3s 0d for carrying out the audit; the accounts are now audited each year by an accountant. The later accounts lack the wonderful detail given in the seventeenth and eighteenth centuries, which give a small picture of the poor people of the town and their lives.

The Governors employed a clerk who wrote the letters and dealt with the legal business, so he must have been someone trained in law. It was the clerk who took legal proceedings against tenants in arrears with their rent, sorted out the money left in a will for the benefit of the Town Lands, and on one occasion even dealt with the Court of Chancery in London on behalf of the Governors. The Boote family filled the position of clerk for around a hundred years from the late 1600s to the late 1700s, with at least four of the family following one another in succession. The clerk was originally paid 6s 8d a year for making up the accounts and keeping the register book, where the rents and payments were recorded, but in 1751 this increased to 16s 8d because the Governors thought that "the present fee of 6s 8d for ingrossing the annual accounts is not sufficient for the trouble in doing it."

In 1895, a decision was made to appoint a permanent clerk to take over the duties previously carried out by the treasurer, and William Clarke Jotcham, son of Llewellyn Jotcham one of the Governors, offered to become honorary clerk without remuneration because of the state of the Town Lands' finances at the time. William was appointed a Governor on the death of his father but continued as clerk until 1935, when he had to resign because of ill health. Mr Ormiston, another Wantage solicitor, took over as clerk with an annual honorarium of £10. The clerks throughout the twentieth century were all Wantage solicitors, although the present clerk (in 2012) is not. As the clerks gradually took on more administrative work, they began to be paid more for doing so. From 1940, Mr Ormiston was paid a salary plus commission for collecting the cottage rents, distributing the almspeople's allowances and paying the Kirby pensions to the recipients.

Books, Boxes, Papers and Administration

The account books are still in existence from 1598, with the accounts usually being produced annually. Unfortunately, an account book is missing in the mid 1600s, in the period covering the Civil War (which began in 1642), the execution of Charles I and the Commonwealth of Oliver Cromwell (who died in 1658); so it is not possible to decide if the war had any influence on the working of the Governors in Wantage. The churchwardens' accounts give a hint that the royal army was in Wantage in 1643: some men were paid 5s for ringing the church bells "when the Kings Majesty came to Wantage"; two women were paid 4d for putting the shrouds on the bodies of some soldiers, and graves and burials of five soldiers were paid for by the parish. It was also necessary to pay to have the church cleaned "when the Kings Majesty's prisoners lay all night there". The accounts of the Wantage Town Lands begin again in 1680, long after the restoration of Charles II, when life had returned to normal.

Minutes exist from 1656, giving more details of the decisions arrived at and the work carried out by the Governors. It looks as though there may have been meetings held when minutes were not recorded, as there are times when a previous or a future meeting is referred to but no record of these meetings are in the books, or whole years are unrecorded when there must have been business discussed.

The original Act of Parliament stated that the accounts of the Town Lands should be seen and approved every third year by the Bishop of Salisbury. Over the years that followed, the accounts were sent to the bishop but judging by the information in the records, this was less frequently than every three years. The Governors started off well, after the first three years the bishop signed a certificate at the bottom of the accounts stating that he had examined them for each of the preceding years. Three years later, Gregory Webb the bailiff rode to London but there was no reason given and no signature of the bishop, so the accounts may or may not have been seen. After that there is no record of the accounts being checked in this way for many years, although as both minutes and accounts are missing at times, this does not necessarily mean that they were never presented. The next reference was in 1689 when a shilling was paid "for a horse for Mr Brookes when he went to carry the bookes of accounts to the bishop"; which would have been Robert Brooke, one of the Governors. There was no bishop's signature on these or the previous year's accounts, but the next year the accounts were signed by the bishop "at my lodging in Covent garden the 20th

December 1690" and the expenses incurred in sending the accounts for this signature were recorded with £1 spent on "procuring the Accounts to be perused and allowed by the Bushopp of Sarum" (Sarum being Salisbury); and one shilling "paid for carriage of the bookes to London". However, the bishop wrote that he had seen the accounts dated 1676 to 1690, so what happened to the books taken by Mr Brookes in 1689? If the bishop saw them, he had not signed them off. The next time there were just over nine years not three between examinations when the bishop gave the dates of accounts seen: this time he had examined them at St James Palace, April 1700.

Over the subsequent period of time, the intervals between inspections were three years, five years and four years so the bishop was seeing the accounts almost as regularly as the original Act of Parliament had stipulated. He signed as "Gi. Sarum", or Gilbert of Salisbury. There was then a longer interval of twelve years, by which time a man called Benjamin had become the bishop, and it cost five shillings to take the books to London and back. Another change of bishop, an even longer period of twenty six years between, brought the next inspection to 1750, when the books were taken by Thomas Brewer, the Wantage vicar who was one of the Governors. The books were examined four more times by the bishop, now Bishop John, until the last time an inspection was recorded in the accounts in 1789.

From the minutes and accounts it appeared that the Charity Commissioners then took over the task of overseeing the Town Lands charity. In 1838 ten shillings was paid for "the Charity Commissioners Report Book" and over the years the commissioners were involved when money was invested, as in 1871 when a garden was sold to Mr Dixon and the purchase price of £120 was invested in Consols (or Consolidated 3% Bank Annuities) with the Commissioners. Any income from charity investments was paid to the Governors by the Charity Commissioners, and was shown as such in the annual accounts. Before the Charity Commissioners became involved with holding the investments, the funds were invested in Consols but were held in trust for the Governors by a named person, who paid over the dividends twice a year. An example is given in 1769 when Mr John Giles (a Governor) paid to the rent receiver in February and July, "half a year's dividend on £117 10s 0d Consolidated 3 per cent Bank Annuity standing in the Name of Mr Thomas Hudson in Trust for the Governors of Wantage Town Lands", amounting to £1 15s 3d on each occasion.

The original seal of the Governors of the Town Lands.
BRO D/QW49

Any legal documents relating to transactions carried out by the Governors on behalf of the Town Lands had the official seal of the charity imprinted on them. The original Elizabethan seal was used until 1920, when a reproduction of the old seal was made for general use. The original is now kept at the Berkshire Record Office. In 1900, a Miss Lewis of Wantage had asked the Governors for permission to reproduce the design of the seal on china articles which could then be sold as mementoes of Wantage, but the Governors did not think this a good idea and did not give her their permission.

As well as the minute and account books, a few leases can still be seen but other items for carrying out the business of the Trust are no longer in existence. Much of the charitable giving was done 'by order' or 'by consent' between meetings and in 1716 a Book of Orders was bought for 2s 6d, which was probably where these orders were recorded or were forms to fill in to give to needy poor to enable them to obtain items from Wantage tradesmen. Property transactions took place in the form of leases to tenants of lands owned by the Trust, and when in 1726 two 'skynns' of parchment were bought for two shillings, this could have been what this parchment was to be used for, or it could have been for the accounts, as in 1729 a shillings was spent on "parchment to Ingrosse the Account on". In 1733, the Governors decided that a new parchment book was to be bought before the next meeting, and as the next annual accounts were in a new book this must have been the one bought. From the mid 1700s a day book and paper, various lots of printed receipts and hand bills were bought, five hundred or two hundred receipts being printed at a time. In 1820, paper was bought to make a book in which the cloth list could be recorded; a list of names of Wantage poor who were given small sums of money and clothing each year, but this book no longer exists.

Before the penny post started in 1840, postage was paid by the person receiving the letter, so the Governors' accounts tell us who was sending letters to them. In 1755, they paid threepence to receive a letter from the Sun Fire Office. As they were insuring buildings such as the school and the almshouses, these insurances must have been taken out with the Sun. Francis Clifford was given a pension by the Governors in the 1770s but seemed to be living away from Wantage as on several occasions there are payments made when he writes to the Governors about his pension: in 1776, "Pd. for a post letter from Francis Clifford about his pension - 3d". The postage for a letter from the Radcliffe Infirmary in 1808 cost two pence but by 1830 this had risen to five pence.

Money was also spent on keeping the Trust's documents safe. In 1632, a new chest costing 19s was made by William Armstrong to hold the documents, while Robert Keate was paid 26s 8d for the iron work and four locks and keys for the chest. It sounds as though it was a chest where four different people had to be present to unlock it, in order to keep the documents inside it safe. Just over a hundred years later, 5s 6d was paid for an oak frame for 'the chest'; perhaps it was the same chest. In 1751, a box to hold the book of accounts was bought, which as the book was sent to the Bishop that year could have been a travelling box. A tin case to hold the estate maps, iron handles for the Governors' box and a repair to the lock of the chest were items paid for in the second half of the 1700s. It is possible that the chest which Armstrong and Keate made in 1632 lasted until 1839, when the treasurer was instructed to purchase "an iron chest for depositing the books and accounts belong to this trust". This iron chest was referred to again in 1845 when it was noted that Mr Hayward, the treasurer, "has one of the keys of the Iron Chest in his possession." Whether this was referred to later as a safe, or whether the iron chest went out of use and was replaced by a safe, is not clear; what is known, however, is that by the beginning of the twentieth century, the "old iron safe" holding the Governors' deeds and documents was kept at the bank. By 1910, the bank felt it was taking up valuable space there and it was moved to the clerk's office, and ten years later it was decided to sell it as it was no longer used.

The date of the annual meeting when the accounts were presented varied over the years. To begin with, the year end was Michaelmas Day, September 29th. In 1752, the Government adjusted the calendar so that England was working to the same calendar as the continent. Up to that date, we had used what was known as the Julian calendar while the continent had used the Gregorian calendar, with the same date on the two becoming further and further apart owing to the Julian calendar not having leap years. By 1751, there was a difference of eleven days between the two methods of recording the date, and the Government in London decided to bring them into line, with an Act of Parliament being passed to make the Gregorian calendar the one used in Britain, the same as the continent. This meant England had to move the date forward eleven days, which caused a great outcry as some people thought it would mean they would die eleven days earlier, and there were reported mutterings of "Give us back our eleven days". The accounts of the Wantage Town Lands show them running from 29th September 1750 (Michaelmas day) to 29th September 1751, but in 1752 they end at 10th October, which is eleven days on from the previous date for Michaelmas. October 10th became known as old Michaelmas day, and the Governors took this as the year end for the next thirty years. The accounts were not produced annually for many years after this. Before the change in the calendar, each new year began on March 25th (Lady Day) but after the change, New Year's Day became the 1st January. From 1834, it was decided to produce the accounts from 1st January to 31st December, with the annual meeting held in either January or February of the next year and the treasurer for the year changing yearly. This year end continued from then on.

3
Repairing the Roads

Maintaining the highways was one of the responsibilities of the Governors set out in the Act of Parliament, for which they were to use the Town Lands income. Initially, ten shillings each year was given to "the surveyors of the highwaies" towards the upkeep of the roads in Wantage. A Highways Act of 1555 had made it necessary for each parish to elect a surveyor of the highways who would be responsible for the repair of the roads in that parish, the costs to be paid from local parish rates. So the Governors were not undertaking the actual repairs but were funding part of the cost of keeping the roads in good condition by handing over sums of money to the people responsible for this task in Wantage. After the first few years, the amount started to vary from year to year and some years the surveyor was named: in 1614, Edward Galland was paid twenty seven shillings towards repairing the highway for the previous year and forty shillings (£2) for that year, while William Anger was paid forty shillings in 1615. Edward was a Governor and William became one a few years later; it was not unusual for Governors to be elected to other official posts in the town.

In 1680, the Governors paid directly for work to be done, as well as giving a small amount to the surveyors, or supervisors, of the highways:

	£	s	d
To William Styles for six days work on hyeway	0	4	0
To William Oates 3 days work	0	2	0
To John Darlinge 3 days work	0	2	0
To John Vokins 2 days work	0	1	4
To Henry Styles 2 days work	0	1	4
To the Supervisors of the high Ways	2	0	0
For Fettchinge of a Load of Stones	0	3	0

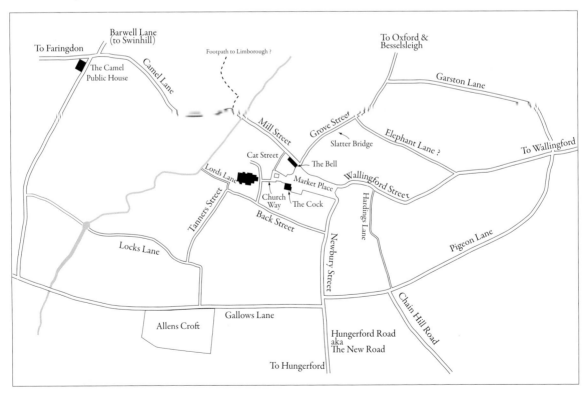

The approximate site of Slatter Bridge over Bryan's Brook, Grove Street.

From 1681 onwards, for many years, the surveyors of Wantage were paid a regular £5 each year. Grove and Charlton were both part of the parish of Wantage, and in 1686, it was decided to let the inhabitants of Grove have £3 each year towards repairing their highways, followed two year later by an agreement to give an annual donation of £2 to Charlton for the same purpose. These three sums of £5 to Wantage, £3 to Grove and £2 to Charlton were paid regularly each year until 1718, when Grove's money was increased to £3 10s per annum, while the inhabitants of Charlton were to give an account each year as to how they had spent their money. Charlton was not paid any regular sum after 1719, so perhaps they could not account satisfactorily for this expenditure. From then on Charlton and Grove were paid only very occasionally. The Governors had stopped including Grove and Charlton in their commitment to the highways on a regular basis and the inhabitants of these two hamlets would then have been almost totally responsible for the condition of their roads.

All the time the Wantage surveyors, or supervisors, were receiving an annual amount of money from the Town Lands, there was no information given as to what repairs were carried out, except once in 1689 when after making the usual £5 payment to the Wantage supervisors, the Governors paid £5 extra for two particular jobs. The road by Slatter Bridge was mended at a cost of £1; and £4 was spent on "patching the way before the Cock". It has been suggested that the Cock Inn was in the market square where Barclays Bank is now, and that Slatter Bridge, which could have been the local pronunciation of Slaughter Bridge, was where Bryans Brook crossed Grove Street, near the present day Clock House. However, this lack of information on what work was carried out on repairing the highways was to change. At a meeting in 1715, the Governors decided that a small group of the Governors would decide how the money given to the surveyors of the highways was to be spent each year in repairing "the common streets of the Towne". From that time,

The white building is thought to be the site of the Cock Inn in the Market Place

there were more details of which roads were being repaired, as the Governors were finding the materials and workmen to carry out specific work. During the following three years 1716, 1717 and 1718, the Governors spent a total of £30 12s on work on the roads and byways of the town, which on average was more than twice the previous annual donation to the Wantage supervisors of highways. One wonders if the Governors had decided to take the matter of repairs into their own hands because the streets had got into a parlous state through a lack of attention from the parish officers. There were four main places where work was carried out during those three years. Tanner Street, which is now Priory Road, had £10 13s 3d expended on it. Eight loads of stones were used plus three loads of Lambourne stones, and more than five loads of sand. Possibly 'stones' were flint stones used in road making, while the Lambourne stones could have been larger stones. John Kent and his labourers were paid £3 17s 8d for the work they did there, and John Stiles was paid £1 0s 4d for his work and that of his labourers.

Even more expensive was the work done at the Bell steps which cost over £12. Sixteen loads of Lambourne stones were used, as well as Garford stones and picked stones (flints?); along with two loads of gravel and twelve loads of sand. The cost of employing workmen and labourers was just over £3. As an approximate day's wage by then was a shilling, it had taken around sixty man days to finish the work at the steps. The Bell Inn

at present at the end of the Market Place by Mill Street was there by 1800 (see map on page 28), but if this was the Bell in question, where could the steps have been? As the footpath at the top of Mill Street, alongside the Bell, is on quite a steep gradient, possibly the steps were similar to the ones in the photograph below.

Grove Street was also repaired; using a load of 'causeway stones' among other stones, with the total cost for materials, the carriage of the stones and labour coming to £2 7s 3d. John Stiles and his labourers did

The type of 'steps' possibly laid in Mill St by the Bell Inn

the work in Grove Street as well as part of the work in Tanner Street. There is no longer a Camel Lane in Wantage, but an old map showed it as the continuation of Mill Street, between the mill and the present Camel Crossroads. Smaller repairs were necessary there, costing £1 1s 7d. There were eight men and boys involved with the work there at the beginning of

February 1716; Yewstis, Logrove (Lovegrove) and his two sons, William Belcher, John Farmer, Goodman Dowlinge and a boy all worked for two days. The pay for eight men would have been expected to be about eight shillings a day or sixteen shillings for the two days worked. As the money paid out for labour came to 15s 5d, this seems reasonable as Lovegrove's sons could have been adults and the boy would not be paid as much as the men. With two other small items of repair, in addition to the main work, this had been a busy and expensive three years for the Governors, but to the benefit of the town streets, and no doubt to the approval of the inhabitants.

Three years later, more work was needed on Grove Street. John Stiles was again employed as well as Joseph Painter and possibly William Keate. Only one load of stones was brought in to do the repairs, but this cannot have completed the necessary work there as the Governors then agreed to give the supervisors of Wantage £5 "provided they mend Grove Street". The responsibility of keeping the highways in good condition was proving expensive as another sum of just over £5 was "laid out upon the Highways" for that year. The following year Barwell Lane was mended and a small amount of work was done yet again on Grove Street. A load of gravel was bought as well as several loads of stones, but as the Governors were doing a lot of building work on houses at the time, the stone might have been for walls rather than roads.

Generally the accounts do not state where work was done, and even when the place was pin-pointed, it often means nothing to a modern reader. When work was carried out "at the highway against Mr Humphrey's house", the Governors knew where Mr Humphrey lived but we do not. Other work involved roads whose whereabouts today can be guessed at. The causeway to Grove, repaired for 13s in 1735, was most likely the road between Wantage and Grove; the highway leading from the downs to the town was probably the present Hungerford road; the way leading to the church would have been the little road from the market place to the

churchyard. As the work on the road from the downs and the work on Church Way had been carried out in the same year, 1737, and had cost a total of at least £14 12s 5d and possibly more if the eighteen loads of stones and labour costing £4 5s 6d belonged to this project, it was not surprising that the Governors were worried at the high cost of road repairs and the drain on their funds. In 1738 they agreed that not more than £5 in any one year was to be spent on repairing the highways of Wantage without the consent of three or more of the Governors. In the past, the rent receiver or treasurer at the time had the authority to give the go-ahead for any work he felt was necessary but now he would have to involve other members of the governing body when the expense of highway repair was greater than £5 in any one year.

A large undertaking to make a new road from the town onto the downs was carried out over about twenty years from 1750 to 1770, at enormous expense to the Town Lands charity. Bartholomew Tipping, who at the time lived at Woolley House on the downs, near Brightwalton, gave a donation of five guineas (£5 5s 0d) towards the expense of the new road; it would probably have been of benefit to him personally. The cost over the twenty years of construction was approaching £230, and may have been more as although many entries in the accounts refer to the cost being part of the new road construction, there are items which might also have related to this work but were not shown as such. There were many loads of stones and flints carried up onto the downs, as well as rubble, and the carting costs were high; being over a third of the total cost of making the road. At the other extreme it appeared that some of the men doing the work were only paid sixpence a day (half a shilling), although others were paid the usual shilling. Eustice received 4s for four days work "on the New Road" but James Wallis only got 2s for four days work, so only 6d a day for him. William Lamboll was paid 2s 6d for digging rubble for two and a half days, which must have been unskilled work, so payments cannot have been less for unskilled

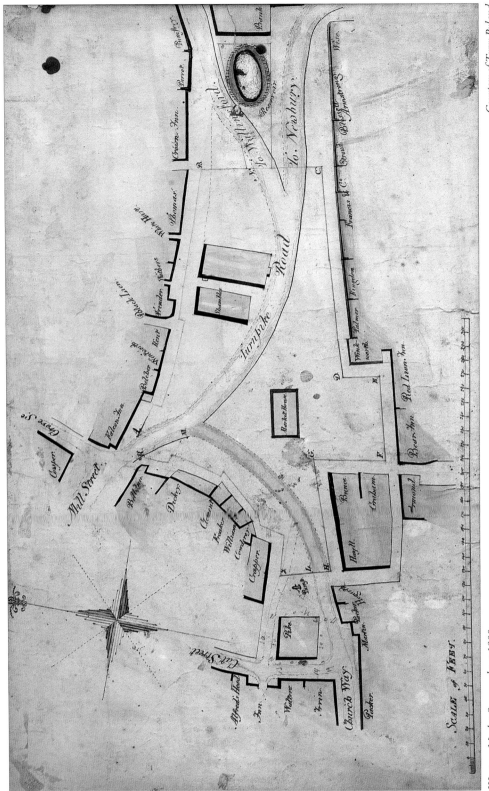

Courtesy of Terry Ryland

Wantage Market Square about 1800

work; perhaps men were paid 1s a day and boys 6d. Judging by another payment of 5s 3d for digging twenty one loads of rubble, it must have taken nearly a week to dig those twenty one cartloads. Assuming that 1s a day was paid for digging rubble, Edward Gregory who was paid 11s 6d for digging forty five loads of rubble and for spreading this as well, would have taken about two weeks to complete the task, and he had dug and spread four loads a day. One small charge for 1s 6d to mend a wheelbarrow used at the New Road reminds us that everything would have been done by hard manual labour; no mechanical diggers in those days.

Which present road out of Wantage and up onto the downs was the 'new road' is open to debate, as nowhere do the Governors set out explicitly where it was. There are two possible roads, the present Hungerford Road or Chain Hill. Both these roads existed before 1750, and it seems likely that the new road was not an entirely new way onto the downs, over land which had previously been fields, but was the upgrading of an old green track into a highway, using stones and gravel to give the track an improved surface which would be passable in all weathers. There are two clues which point to the present Hungerford Road being the road in question. A Governors' map of 1753 shows an area of land to the west of this road with the name of "Hedgewell" and near this is a strip labelled "piece of land purchased by the Governors for a way". During the time the new road was under construction, there were numerous references to it being the road at Hedgewell; and just before the work began on the road, four of the Governors were asked to make enquiries as to who were the owners of the land next to the road from Mile Bush to Hedge's wellhead (the place usually called Hedgewell), so that the land could be purchased or rented in order to mend the road. Later £9 12s 0d was paid for a piece of land leading from Hedgewell to the New Arch (whatever that was), so most likely the small strip shown on the map. A further piece of land "at Mile Bush" was rented from John Howell. There is no indication of Mile Bush on any of the old maps,

but an old definition of 'bush' is a thicket of shrubs: perhaps Mile Bush was a thicket about a mile from the town. There were certainly other lands on the 1753 map along the Hungerford road with the word 'bush' in their names.

The hill leading out of the hollow way to Hedgewell was to be paved, or 'pitched', provided Wantage parish would provide the stones needed for that, which was probably upgrading the road nearer Wantage. Some of the repairs to "the New Road from Mile Bush to Hedgewell" was carried out by a Mr Frogley: he was paid £23 for his work in 1753/4 when the total bill for the road work was £27 6s 0d; the only work on the road in 1756/7 was done by Mr Frogley when he was paid £11 6s 0d "for work and materials on the new road"; and when he died in 1759, his widow was paid the £6 3s 8d which had been "expended by her late husband in repairing the New Road from Mile Bush to Hedgewell". Mr Frogley rented Governors' land on the site of the present sports centre but he probably had a business involved with the cloth industry in Wantage, and the Governors were sub-contracting some of the road work to him, as a man with the ability and finance to organise the job.

From the accounts, it seemed that more work on the road was carried out some years than others, with several years when no work was done on it at all. Sometimes, the years when there was little road work taking place coincided with work being done on other property, but not always, so other calls on the Governors finances could not have been the only reason the work on the road fluctuated. A few men, like Robert Jennings, were involved over most of the project, working a few days or weeks at a time; others appearing only once. Some were labourers digging rubble, laying down flints and stones; while others, even one widow, were involved in supplying the transport. John Butler brought twenty two loads of stones and laid them on the road; Robert Jennings took five days to bring ten loads of flints and put them into Hedgewell road, he also brought twelve loads of stones; Mrs Skinner and

John Stone were paid for carting stones and flints, and Richard Akott and Thomas Armstrong took three and a half days filling up the ruts at Mile Bush. These examples were only a small indication of the loads of stones carried to the site and the work done there.

The Church Way from the church yard to Allen's Croft was needing repair in November 1760. Four

any attempt to do the repairs and the Governors commented that it was "very ruinous". They therefore decided that they would carry out the repairs, bearing the complete cost, "beginning at the Church Gate and from thence into the Town as far as shall be thought necessary." Thomas Barret supplied 2,424 building bricks, Miss Pinock delivered thirty two loads of sand

This was probably what a 'pitched' road looked like. The larger stones could have been the 'plank' stones or 'causeway stones' referred to when roads were repaired — put down to give added support and smoother running to cart wheels.

of the Governors were delegated to make sure the repairs were carried out. The part of Church Way between the market place and the churchyard must also have needed repair, as two years later it was agreed that if the churchwardens decided to put down new stones on Church Way between the town pump and the churchyard gate, then the Governors would pay them £2 towards the cost. A year later, this had not been done so the Governors then said they would pay the churchwardens £4 towards doing it. The next year passed and the churchwardens had not made

and three men worked hard for six days to surface the road with the bricks. The cost was nearer £6, if the cost of the beer supplied to the workmen was included; rather more than the £4 offered to the churchwardens to do the job. The work was described as 'pitching' the Church Way; this meant laying stones or bricks on the surface, not covering the road with tar or pitch. In this instance bricks were used, which was slightly unusual. Stones were the normal material, sometimes obtained from Garford pits, presumably the Garford near Abingdon, or from Lambourne; and flints in large quantities from the downs. The Wantage surveyors of the roads owned a stone pit on the downs just below the Ridgeway, where the youth hostel now stands, and they also had a gravel pit in Grove, which they would use for material for road mending.

At the time that the Governors were trying to encourage the churchwardens to deal with the road by the church, other work was being carried out on the town's streets. The road from the Bell Steps to the corner of Elephant Lane had to be mended, the Elephant being in Grove Street; so work had to be done from the Bell, across the top of Mill Street and a little way down Grove Street to wherever the Elephant pub stood. Posts were put up in Farringdon Street (Mill Street) in order to keep horses off the foot way. At the same time, a group of men worked for several weeks repairing the Mile Bush road (the new road), while others picked flints in the fields on the downs to be carted to the town to carry out the work on the town's roads. The men were being paid 1s 6d a day for the work picking flints and repairing Mile Bush road; this was more than usual but as it was from August to the beginning of October when it was done, it would have been harvest time with harvest bonuses available and perhaps higher wages had to be paid to encourage men to apply for this road work. There was co-operation between the Governors and the parish surveyors of the highways; when it was decided that the footpath leading to Limborough (the field on the hill where the convent stands) needed repairing, the Governors appointed five of their members to oversee the work but with the approval of the surveyors. However, they must have been very pleased when, before starting the work, they found out that they were not responsible for this footpath; it had always been under the care of the Lord and Lady of Wantage Manor.

The road between Allen's Croft and the churchyard, which was mentioned above, became news in the town in March 1777 when the Governors actually went out in a body to have a look at it. They had been told that someone had taken up the plank stones from the road leading to Allen's Croft and they were investigating the truth of this for themselves. What a plank stone was is a bit of a mystery but these were used on many occasions in connection with roads and bridges, so possibly large flat stones like those in the photograph on page 30. The Governors found that the stones had indeed been removed from the roadway leading to Allen's Croft and they ordered that "the same be laid down again." So it sounded as though the stones had not been stolen but just lifted to one side. They recorded that it appeared to them that someone was intending to alter the road and they made it clear that if at any time "the old road shall be stopt we do order that ... the same be opened again." It was not allowed to rest there. On March 4th they paid the town crier sixpence to cry that there would be a reward for the discovery of the man who took up the stones. He had not gone undetected, as on March 8th they paid 1s 6d to a man who gave them information as to who had taken up the plank stones. They did not say what happened to the culprit but the stones were put back and the matter seemed to be over; until on March 24th when the town crier was once more paid sixpence for crying that the plank stones had been taken up again! Unfortunately nothing else was recorded of the matter, so who did the deed and why they did it will never now be known.

Vandalism is not a modern phenomenon and the town crier must have been employed whenever the authorities wanted information on culprits. The churchwardens' accounts give other examples of this: in 1828 they paid twice in one month for "crying damage in the churchyard" as well as the cost of a warrant and 6s 10d to Mr Packer, who was the glazier, so possibly the damage had been caused by stones being thrown at the church windows. A few years earlier 8d was paid for beer given to the men who got the churchyard gates out of the brook, which sounds as though more high jinks had occurred around the church. Perhaps the churchyard was a meeting point for the youths of the town, as in 1849, 13s was paid out "for watching the churchyard at Fair Jubilee days."

Another lane between the church yard and the brook "commonly called Lords Lane" which is still there and has recently been renamed Betjeman Lane, was repaired in 1780 at the expense of the Governors. At the time there were entries in the accounts for eight loads of plank stones, pitching stones from Mr Alder and some gravel, but other work was being done at the same time so it is not possible to tell whether these items were for the work on Lords Lane or for somewhere else. Shortly after Lords Lane was put in order, a fairly extensive programme of work was carried out in Hardings Lane (or Ardings Lane as it was sometimes recorded) and in the road from Hardings Lane to the bottom of Chain Hill. Hardings Lane was the lane which runs from Wallingford Street, up the side of the present Post Office and Rowe's newsagents. Joshua Gooding, Richard Painting, William Gregory and others worked for several weeks there, using seventy four loads of rubble. Stones were used to repair the drains, but it seemed that only rubble was used on the road repairs this time. Repairs often went on for some time once they were started, although it is possible that this work was carried out when other work on the land was not available, or at a time of year when the weather conditions were suitable, which would mean the roads were repaired a bit at a time. In the case of Hardings Lane and Chain Hill, the Governors decided at a meeting in January 1782 to do the repairs, but it was not until the middle of May that work began, when it was reported that "Slatford begun Ruble cart". Slatford was paid £19 4s 0d for carting rubble, a large sum of money. Also in May, "Farmer Barnard begun carting with two horses and ended 29th June" but there is no record of him being paid. The following year, 1783, William Slatford began carting the rubble on June 2nd and the job was probably finished later that year. James Oakley worked as a labourer on Chainhill Road and Hardings Lane for fifty weeks less two days and ended working there on 23rd November 1783. He was paid six shillings a week, which was the usual shilling a day, with no work on Sundays. James Miles also worked there but only for twelve weeks, while two other men

joined them as labourers occasionally. Robert Chapman had been employed digging the rubble at eight pence a load, and he had dug forty two loads. Tools had to be sharpened and a shovel needed a new handle, which all together cost the Governors two shillings, while a new sledge hammer cost a further two shillings. By 1787, the road up Chain Hill was needing to be "put into good repair" once more, so the original repairs had not lasted long. James Miles and Robert Chapman were employed on this work again: this time pitching stones were used as well as rubble.

By the end of the eighteenth century, the Governors were offering to pay part of the repair costs for various streets if other bodies would carry out the work and pay the remainder of the cost. In 1797, Lords Lane from the churchyard to the brook was once more in need of repair, when the Governors decided that they would contribute to the expense if the town of Wantage would do the considerable repair necessary there. They also suggested that if the Lord of the Manor of Wantage, Samuel Worthington Esquire, and the inhabitants of the town would do the necessary repairs to the pavement in the Market Place and at the south end of Grove Street, where it joins the market place, then the Governors would pay part of the cost of those repairs too. There was no more mention of the pavements in the Market Place or Grove Street, so either this was not carried out at all or the Governors were not asked to contribute, although they did pay the surveyors £10 "for Pavement" in 1815; rather a long time afterwards. Lords Lane was not repaired at this time either but five years later, in 1802, the offer was again made that if the town would carry out the repairs there, the Governors would make a donation towards the cost and this time it was done, with the Governors paying £10 the following year towards repairing Lords Lane. Also about this time, it appeared that the Governors started occasionally paying a road rate for their properties. This would be paid to the supervisors of the highways of the parishes where the property was situated, and which possibly meant that the Governors were playing less of a part in carrying out road repairs themselves but instead were handing over the responsibility to the parish authorities and were paying the road tax that other landlords would have been expected to pay. These taxes were not paid on any regular basis however. In 1806 the Hanney road rate was £2 13s 6d, while in 1808 the Wantage and Grove combined road tax was £22 12s 3d. Quite often the highway rate was paid together with the poor rate, with only the total amount given: in 1811 the property tenanted by Mr Tame had a poor rate and highway tax of £6 19s 2d paid on it, while in 1813 the Governors paid a combined poor and highway tax of 10s 3d for a close of land "near Turnor's garden wall in East Challow"; Turner being Exuperious Turnor Esquire, who lived in the mansion at Challow. In 1870, a highway rate was paid to Wantage, the entry explaining that the rate had been set that year at one shilling in the pound; so for example, if a property was valued at £10, the highway rate would have been 10s. That year, the Governors paid rates of £1 7s 4½d for their almshouses and 13s 3d for the cottages they owned in the town.

Work was often done on ditches and water courses, as well as the roads. Hedgewell ditch was regularly given attention over the years. It appeared that there were springs by Hedgewell from where water flowed down towards Wantage. A modern OS map shows Edgehill Springs by the side of the Hungerford Road, about a mile from Wantage, slightly up the hill from Manor Farm, in the spot where Hedgewell spring could have been sited; this also gives further confirmation that the New Road constructed in the mid-eighteenth century by the Governors was the present Hungerford Road. Ditches alongside roads needed to be kept clear and functioning if the roads were to be dry and passable in wet weather, and the Governors made sure that this was the case with Hedgewell ditch. In 1668, they minuted that maintaining the stream and bank there would prove to be "a great preservation to the highwayes" and they set aside forty shillings a year for this purpose, the money to be paid to "some

fitting person who is to be accountable for the same." How long this sum continued to be paid out was not clear, although it did not appear to be paid for long. However, work at Hedgewell took place at frequent intervals and the Governors then paid men directly for doing this work. So for example, in 1689, three days work cleaning the ditch by Hedgewell cost 3s, work was done on a sluice there costing 1s and John Hyde was paid 15s 10d for thirteen feet of oak timber for the sluice and a day's work. In the early 1700s John Harwood was set to work weeding Hedgewell shoot, while Mr King did some more work on the sluice there. A few years later the ditch was scoured and the dam mended. With a sluice and a dam, there must have been regulation of the flow of water and it was probably one of the sources of water for the town, which would account for the frequent cleaning (or ridding as it was sometimes called) and scouring it underwent and the regular repairing of the sluice. Possibly the reference to a 'shoot' meant a man-made channel bringing water into Wantage. In January 1770, Hedgewell ditch was once more cleaned and the banks strengthened, and details were given of the men doing this work. They were named as Richard Panten (or Pontin), Richard Accot, Joseph Gilbert, Thomas Lay, Joseph Alder and Dick Keate. Dick was paid 6d a day but the others were well paid at 1s 2d a day; perhaps Dick was only a lad. The job took nearly a month to complete.

The ditch in Gallows Lane was attended to in the early 1800s. Gallows Lane was the name given to what is now known as Portway. At different times John Dry, Thomas Patience and Charles Holloway worked on the ditch, probably digging it out where it had become overgrown: on one occasion, Mr Daniel Trinder supplied half a load of plank stones. The trees in Gallows Lane were kept trimmed and the trimmings were bundled up for fire wood, or faggots. This was probably the case when Charles Holloway was paid 6s in 1808 for "doing Gallus lane and ditch": he had trimmed the trees in the lane and cleared the ditch, most likely taking six days to do all this.

New bridges or repairs to bridges were necessary at times. There was a bridge over Hedgewell Shoot ditch which was repaired by the Governors in 1760, at the time of making the new road to the downs. Other bridges were the responsibility of the Governors and in 1769 John Eustace was paid 5s 6d for doing some trenching work at the Governors' Bridge in the Town Ham, and at Tappings Stream, which was another part of the town often needing attention from the Governors. It needed work doing on it again in 1774, with "Hedgall" shoot bridge being attended to at the same time. The two bridges at Tappings (or Tappin) Stream and Hedgewell Shoot needed yet more work in 1781, as well as "the road between" which suggests they were not too far apart, although I have not managed to find where Tappings stream was. A new bridge had to be built over the brook at Grove in 1856, to give access to a meadow there leased from the Governors by Mr Belcher. If it was to enable him to get into his meadow, it would have needed to have been robust enough for a horse and cart to cross over at haymaking time, and also for cattle or sheep to cross when the meadow was used for grazing. It was stipulated that good materials must be used and the bridge was to be of one arch. Mr Hunt built this bridge for £10.

From the mid eighteenth century, other bodies gradually took over the upkeep of the roads in the area. The road through Wantage from Wallingford to Faringdon became a turnpike road in 1751 and a turnpike trust was then responsible for making sure it was kept in good repair, while a little later in 1771, another turnpike trust took over the upkeep of the road from Besselsleigh, through Wantage and on to Hungerford, part of which was the New Road recently improved by the Governors. The repair of these roads was then paid for from the tolls levied at toll gates and paid by people using the roads. In 1828, the Wantage Improvement Act was passed by Parliament, which appointed commissioners to deal with repairing the roads and footpaths in Wantage, as well as taking charge of the street lighting and cleaning. The part the Town Lands had played in keeping roads in repair was now being taken over by this new body, although the Governors carried out some road repairs during the few years following 1828. The highway leading from Miss Packer's house to the churchyard gates (Church Way from the market place) was in need of attention in 1829 and this was repaired by the Governors, stones being bought from Mr Plumbe at a cost of £16 9s 6d and their carriage adding another 4s to the bill: there does not seem to be any payment for labour though, so perhaps the new commissioners paid that part of the bill from the rates. The Governors told the Charity Commissioners in 1837 that, generally speaking, mending the highways had seldom been one of their main priorities and had never been carried out to any great extent. They certainly did not spend as much on the roads as on the grammar school or the poor. Church Street was given a face lift by Mr Tombs in 1841 at a cost of £39 4s 4d, but from that time on, the Governors no longer took any financial responsibility for the highways, apart from paying highway tax at irregular intervals.

4

Schools and Education

There was already a Grammar School, also referred to as the Free School, in existence in the Wantage churchyard, when the Act of Parliament relating to the Town Lands was passed in 1597. This grammar school could originally have been a school attached to a chantry chapel with the boys taught by the chantry priest, until chantries were banned by Henry VIII in 1545. There was mention of a chapel in Wantage, in addition to the church, in 1529; and John Leyland, who visited Wantage in 1540, wrote that he saw "two churches in this market toune in one chirche yarde, but the one is but a chapelle." At this time, a typical schoolboy's day would be spent learning Latin and sometimes Greek and Hebrew, and reading Cicero, Ovid, Virgil and Horace; this being the only means of moving into the professions, as Latin was needed for entry to the church, law, government or medicine. Science, maths, history and modern languages were not taught. The boys, usually sons of tradesmen, skilled craftsmen, yeomen farmers, merchants, gentlemen and landowners, spent their day sitting on backless benches for long hours, with breaks for breakfast and dinner but under the strict discipline of the master and with the rod used for any small misdemeanour. Pupils had to supply their own writing materials and would wear a belt with their inkhorn attached and carry a satchel for goose quills, penknives and books. Their games had to be suitable for gentlemen: no football was allowed but archery and bowls were acceptable.

The master of Wantage grammar school in 1597 was Mr John Wirdnam and he was paid £10 a year to teach the boys there. There was quite a turnover of

A sketch of the old school in the churchyard, 1816. Demolished 1850

masters at the school at this time, with Mr Wirdnam being followed by three other masters over the next six years, all being paid £13 6s 8d a year. In 1604, there was the first mention of a second schoolmaster who was employed to teach the 'petties', in other words the petits or the younger boys. He was expected to teach simple reading and writing in English, whereas the Grammar School also taught Latin. The masters at the Grammar School were usually ordained ministers and would have had a university education, so were paid more than the teachers of the younger boys. While Hugh Floyd, master at the Grammar School from 1605, was paid the £13 6s 8d a year, Thomas Otes (or Oates), the master teaching the younger boys, was only paid £5 a year. Hugh Floyd must have been ordained, as in 1613 he was paid an extra ten shillings for giving two sermons during the year. Thomas Oates also carried out extra duties, as for several years he was paid for writing up the accounts of the Governors, being paid a shilling most years for doing this. Whether this only involved making a fair copy of the accounts at the

end of the year, or whether he actually worked them out is not clear, but more likely he just copied out the accounts which had been kept during the year by the bailiff, Gregory Webb.

Some fairly extensive repairs were carried out at the schoolhouse at the time Mr Floyd took over in 1605. It appeared that at least part of the school roof was repaired, as slates, laths and tile pins were bought as well as a supply of moss which would have been put under the tiles, probably as insulation to keep the draught out. John Barnes was paid 29s 10d for "mozeing the schoolhouse", or in other words putting the moss in place. As there was no mention of any other schoolhouse for the 'petties', it is probable that, at that time, they occupied a room in the Grammar School; although later the English School, as the non-Grammar School was called, was in a separate building in the churchyard. A desk and seat were made in the schoolhouse about the same time that Mr Oates arrived to teach the petties, which might indicate that he was using a room in the Grammar School.

The site of the old Grammar School in 2011

The following year the glazier was paid for mending the schoolhouse windows, but this was a very regular occurrence; one wondered what the boys got up to at times. It was the custom at the time for boys to smash their schoolroom windows to celebrate the end of the school year. A report made by the Charity Commissioners in 1908, suggested that the boys "as the early accounts show, wrecked the windows ... annually in accordance with the fashion of the period". During the 1600s and early 1700s, bills to the glazier for mending the windows of one or other of the schoolhouses (or both!) were paid out on average one year in two, and some of the items for "repairs to school" might also have been for windows. After 1720, the windows had to be repaired less frequently and into the 1800s hardly at all, although there must have been a problem with windows being broken in 1812 when the Governors said they would pay to repair the glass in the windows at the English school where Ashur Packer was master; they would also pay for shutters to be fixed at the windows, but that in future the master would have to be responsible for the cost of replacing broken glass. This of course might be why the Governors' accounts did not show frequent sums paid to the glazier at this time; the schoolmaster was paying the bills. The glazier's bill in 1812 was for £6 3s 8d, a fairly large sum, so this might have been the reason why the Governors felt they had paid out enough to put right the boys' carelessness or downright vandalism. As well as windows getting broken very frequently, the door locks suffered plenty of wear and tear. A new lock for the "Schoolhouse dore" cost 2s 6d in 1624, while a few years later as well as a lock and key a new door was supplied too; to a study, so probably for the master.

Most years there were small repairs done at the schoolhouse but in 1615 fourteen bushels of lime were bought to carry out repairs there, along with hair for the plaster and laths and nails, so it appeared that new lath and plaster walls were needed in some part of the school. John Barnes carried out the work and as he was paid a total of 6s 5d, when a day's labour at

the time was usually charged at around 10d, he must have been busy for approximately eight days. Thomas Green was paid for new windows and hinges; and Edward Cox was once more paid for "mending the Scolehowse windows". Between 1617 and 1619 some very extensive building work took place, with earth being moved; timber and boards being bought as well as slates, stones, moss, pins, hairlime, laths and nails; and men paid for carpentry, glazing windows and other work. On one occasion the Governors bought seven loads of earth and 'donnge' (dung), which tells us that the lath and plaster walls being built had dung mixed in with the clay and hair for the plaster infill on the laths. There is no indication as to what was being built, but in 1624, there was a payment for "mending the schoolhouse windows which Thomas Oates teaches in", in other words the English, or petty, school. It appeared that there were now two separate schools, which was confirmed when in 1628 six shillings was paid "for mending the glasse of both Schoolhouses". The previous year, a chimney was built in the "new schoolhouse", which again points to there being a recently erected building for the English school. The work ten years earlier must have been the building of this English School, as it was referred to, for the younger boys, so from now on there were two schools, later references to them showing that they were both in the churchyard. Mention in 1775 of the schoolhouse being next to the Vicarage Yard and a comment that the drain leading from the English school through the Vicarage Yard was to be put in good repair shows it was most probably in the corner of the churchyard near the old Vicarage, as shown on the map on page 38.

Small repairs were carried out over several years in the early 1630s, first at the grammar school with nails and boards, bricks and hair lime being used. The costs each year were not large, even including the labour, ranging from around £3 for the year to £6 18s 1d in 1633. The grammar school master was paid £20 a year by then and the English school master £5, which puts the amount paid for repair work in context. During

1636 and 1637, it was the turn of the English school to have some major work carried out on it. John Barnes was paid for "slatting and walling the English Schoole"; materials charged for included "fower hundred and fortie slatts", three bushels of lime, planks and boards, as well as the usual glazing work on the windows. The 'slatts' were slates for the roof, and moss was also bought in to put under them. They would have been stone slates, and later in 1680 we find "work done about the Schole house and Ripping up the slatts and covering it againe" which sounds like work done on the roof once more.

Items were sometimes paid for which give a picture of the furnishing of the classrooms. John Webb was paid 2s 6d for making a frame "to hang hatts on" in the free school (or grammar school) and in 1630 a table there cost 23s; this was described as "a table bord and frame" so was a sort of trestle table, common in those days in homes and not just in schools. At several times, but not frequently, money was provided for books to be bought by the schoolmaster for the school, usually of the order of thirty to forty shillings. The master lived in the schoolhouse as well as teaching there and would have had his own furniture and household goods, but he also seemed to have had to provide some of the equipment for the classrooms, for which he would be reimbursed if it was left behind when he left. Mr Floyd was given twenty shillings by the Governors in part payment for his goods left in the schoolhouse, when he gave up teaching at the grammar school in

1618. Mr Oates, the teacher at the English school, died in 1630 and his widow had to move out but she was paid eight shillings for forms, benches and shelves which she had left in the schoolhouse; whether these were in her own part of the building or in the part where her husband had taught the boys is not clear. The Governors allowed her ten shillings a year as a widow's pension, which would not have supported her for very long but would have been a token of their goodwill. John Cooke taught for a year in the English school in 1631 but he did not get the refund of 8s 6d for his "deske with lock and key and wrytinge boorde and shelves left at the Englishe Schoolhowse" until 1639. Mr Keepe had built himself a study in the grammar school in 1633 and the Governors gave him £5 towards the cost of building it. In later years, this refunding of the cost of equipment in the schoolroom, which the master had supplied himself, continued. In 1843, when William Butler left the English school, he was refunded £4 5s 0d which the Governors considered was a fair value for the desks and other items he had furnished the school with.

In 1659, Mr John Heron, the master at the grammar school, was being paid £18 a year by the Governors. The following year, in May 1660, Charles II was restored as king, and at the next recorded meeting of the Governors in the August, they refer to the "happy restoration of the King's Majesty", which might mean that they had supported the Royalist cause during the Civil War, or only that they were making

The sites of the grammar school and the English school in the churchyard

sure they represented themselves to be on the side of the restoration now it was a fait accompli. They were discussing the position of John Heron as schoolmaster, and they suggested that he had come into the office of schoolmaster "by undue means" which had taken place "in the time of the late warr against the King", which implied he was a supporter of the Parliamentarians and was now a politically incorrect person to have as the schoolmaster. The Governors were about to rectify this and by "mature consideration" of the majority of the Governors had decided to replace John Heron with Mr Francis Slade the younger, at the same salary as Mr Heron. They also ordered that all former orders made by the Governors concerning Mr Heron were to be considered null and void. The vicar of Wantage at this time was a Francis Slade, so it is possible the newly appointed schoolmaster was the vicar's son. There was a gap of five years at this stage in the minutes, so what happened about the schoolmasters is not known. However, the next record in September 1665 referred to Mr Heron the schoolmaster having his pay increased from £18 to £20 a year, so not only had he not been replaced as schoolmaster, but he must have been giving enough satisfaction by his teaching to warrant an increased salary. It is not possible to tell whether Francis Slade the younger ever acted as the schoolmaster or not.

John Heron was still schoolmaster in October 1670, but because of poor health he had informed the Governors that he wanted to give up his post at the school. It appeared that he had recommended a Mr John Hunsdon to take his place, but the Governors had found out that John Hunsdon had paid John Heron to give this recommendation, and because of this the Governors ordered that neither of the men were to profit from the school, but that Mr Samuel Jennings, a Fellow of St John the Baptist College in Oxford, was to be chosen as the new schoolmaster, at £20 per year. Samuel Jennings remained as schoolmaster until April 1689 when it was revealed that he had "lately absented himself and neglected the care and management of the

school without giving any notice or reason" It appeared that he had left his wife behind as well, because she was asked by the Governors to give up possession of the schoolhouse when a curate at Wantage church, John Birch MA, was elected schoolmaster of the grammar school to replace her husband. Shortly afterwards Mr Birch was allowed forty shillings to spend on books for the scholars as he thought fit, and it appeared that some fairly major repairs were carried out at the school costing £25 14s 10d; even the small sum of a shilling for beer drunk by one of the workmen, Richard Winterborne, while working at the school, was included in the cost. A new schoolmaster often seemed to coincide with repairs at the school, so perhaps a new man would complain of inadequacies and the Governors would put matters right to please him. John Birch was only there for three years, as at that point the Governors dismissed him "for sundry reasons". They did not enlarge on what these reasons were but gave him about two months to quit the school and schoolhouse. By then he was the Vicar of Wantage as well as school master, so it must have been embarrassing for him to be asked to leave as this would no doubt be a talking point in the town. William Sloper (or Sloaper) took his place; he came from being schoolmaster a few miles away, at Drayton. Once more repairs were considered necessary, including the relaying of the floors. Mr Sloper did not have enough room to live in the school, so perhaps he had a large family. The Governors added £3 a year to his £20 salary so he could rent a house or rooms that would be more convenient for him.

The masters of the English school were not mentioned for many years, but it is possible that the Edward Silvester who was master in 1644 carried on teaching there during at least part of the Civil War, as the church burial records show that an Edward Sylvester died in early 1660: this man was the clerk and deacon of the parish, so it was feasible he was also the schoolmaster. There was no reference to the English schoolmaster or to this school after King Charles II's restoration, until 1699 when it was reported that the master, Mr Freer, had just died and Thomas Fewtrell was to "be admitted into the room in the Churchyard called the English School house" in his place. It appeared that Mr Freer might have been there for some years, although according to the accounts, the Governors had not been paying him, and there is no indication that they paid Mr Fewtrell either. The fact that the English school was referred to as a room, makes it sound very small. If the schoolmasters there were not paid by the Governors at this time, perhaps parents were paying to have their children taught to read and write rather than poor children being given this education at the expense of the Town Lands charity. The Governors were simply providing the schoolroom. From the church registers, it appeared that Daniel Freer and Thomas Fewtrell, like Edward Sylvester, were the parish clerks as well as being the teachers at the English school. After Daniel Freer died, his wife was awarded a pension of twenty shillings a year, which she received each year until her death fifteen years later. As mentioned earlier, Thomas Fewtrell also acted as bailiff to the Governors and it is possible he was a tailor as well, as a Thomas Fewtrell was paid regularly by the Governors for several years, for making various items of clothing for the poor. If so he was a man of many parts.

In 1683, a House of Office (a privy, or toilet) was put up for the grammar school boys at a cost of £4 17s 2d. As it was 'put up' and was not just a repair job, it sounded as though perhaps this was the first time such a building was considered necessary at the school. One wonders, if this was the case, how the boys had coped beforehand. The Governors had ordered that this house of office for the use of the school was to be erected "in a convenient place" in a lane leading to Low Bridge. As the school was in the churchyard, near the west end of the church, it is likely that the lane was the one now coming up from the brook to the steps by the war memorial (which used to be known as Lords Lane and is now Betjeman Lane), and Low Bridge was in the same place as the present bridge over the brook by the entrance to Betjeman Park. In 1700, Edward Butler

was paid for work done on the school privy house, while further repairs were necessary during each of the following three years, as well as the cost of providing a lock on the door. Over the next few years, the lock needed mending several times, on one occasion costing the rather large sum of £2 17s 4d. The boys cannot have treated it with much care; perhaps if the privy was some distance from the schoolhouse, a certain amount of fooling around took place there away from the eyes of the schoolmaster.

Lords Lane (now Betjeman Lane) where the grammar school 'house of office' was most likely situated

To return to the masters at the grammar school, Mr Sloper, who had started teaching there in 1693, was schoolmaster for fourteen years until, in 1707, he refused to take the Oath of Abjuration. This was an oath taken by clergy and public office holders, pledging to support the current British monarch (Queen Anne in 1707) and to repudiate the right of the Stuarts to the throne. On his death, Mr Sloper was recorded as being a cleric, so a member of the clergy of Wantage. His refusal to take the oath probably indicated he had Jacobite leanings and regarded James Edward Stuart, the son of James II, as the rightful king. The Governors were requested by Gilbert Lord Bishop of Sarum (Salisbury) to discharge Mr Sloper from "the care and management of the Grammar School" and to take away his salary and the extra money he was paid. He and his family were to move out of the school house within the following two months, but although the Governors obeyed the Bishop, they must have had a certain amount of sympathy for his situation as they decided to pay him £3 10s 0d per annum towards his cost of renting a house. This was paid to him for the next twenty years until his death in 1726. Although the next schoolmaster, Philip Barton, was officially appointed in April 1707, shortly after William Sloper had moved out of the schoolhouse, he must have been teaching there from the beginning of the year as he was to be paid back to St Thomas' Day at the end of December. It looked as though the Bishop had insisted that Mr Sloper be replaced immediately, even before the meeting that had given notice he was to leave. It is possible that, as the Governors were paying William Sloper a reasonable sum of money each year, after his dismissal, he may have been assisting with the teaching.

There was no mention of the English School after Thomas Fewtrell was installed as master in 1699, and it is likely that by 1711 there was no school operating there because it appeared that people, not connected with any school, were living in the schoolhouse. In September 1711, the Governors ordered that "the several persons now dwelling in the English School house in the Churchyard be removed ... with all convenient speed." They were however to be provided with somewhere to live at the expense of the Governors, so were not just being turned out to fend for themselves, which argues they were possibly poor people put into the schoolhouse by the Governors, when it was no longer being used as a school. We know one of them was Widow Evans, as at Lady Day 1712 she was paid her usual pension but the Governors gave her five shillings more because she had been turned out of the schoolhouse. This extra five shillings was paid to her for the next ten years until her death. After the people were turned out of the English schoolhouse, someone called Madam Barenburgh chose a schoolmistress to instruct twenty poor girls in reading and sewing, and this schoolmistress was to move into the schoolhouse. She was to live there for free but there was no mention of any payment for teaching the girls. Who Madam Barenburgh was remains a mystery. Money was spent on repair work done at the school when the new female teacher moved in, and the following year more work was done there, mainly on the roof, which had some slates and tiles put on but also a load of straw was bought and the thatcher and his assistant were paid to thatch the schoolhouse. It was quite a small area of thatch as the men only worked on it for two and a half days, so the roof was probably part thatch and part slates. No further mention was made about the girls' school or the schoolmistress. In 1715, the Governors made a decision to put ten pounds towards employing "a fitting person" to teach poor children to read and write, if their charity statute allowed this. It is not clear whether the poor children were to be boys or girls; and why the Governors were worried they might not be legally allowed to provide this service to poor children is a puzzle, as they had done so in the past. However, no teacher seemed to have been appointed; the only reference in the accounts to payment for schooling relates to a young boy. Two shillings was paid "for Inge's boy's schooling" in 1719 and the following year the Governors paid Widow Cooke four shillings "for twenty four weeks of schooling of Inge's boy". Nothing more seems to have been paid of the ten pounds they suggested putting towards teaching the poor.

Then in 1726, the Governors decided that the English schoolhouse in the churchyard was to be let to people approved of by the vicar at a yearly rent, so

41

there cannot have been a school operating there at this time. These tenants were to keep their part of the house in repair. So with rents being paid and repairs expected to be carried out by the new tenants, these people cannot have been paupers. There had been a family already living there, who were removed at the time the Governors agreed to let the schoolhouse to tenants paying rents. Perhaps Richard Attewell and his family were squatting there because it was unoccupied. The clerk was paid £5 17s 0d for ejecting Richard and his family from the schoolhouse, which seems rather a large sum, perhaps it had to be done by legal means involving fees. Tenants cannot have been a satisfactory solution to the use of the schoolhouse, because two years later, in November 1728, it was decided that the old schoolhouse should be repaired so that the building could become a school once more. More than just repairs were carried out: the building was later referred to as the newly built schoolhouse. At first, five thousand bricks were bought and three bushels of lime for the mortar; later fifteen hundred more bricks arrived on the site, several loads of earth and sand, six quarters of lime, and twenty three bushels of hair which would be used in the plaster on the inside walls. Tiles were bought for the roof, the carpenter and various other tradesmen were paid for work done there, including Thomas Dennis for iron work.

At the end of 1732, the Governors appointed Joseph Humphreys as the teacher at the newly built school. He was to live there rent free but was not paid a salary. When he was replaced by Mr Pratt a few years later, the Governors paid the new master fifty shillings a year (£2 10s 0d) for teaching six poor boys to read, write and cast accounts, so now some arithmetic had been added to the curriculum. Mr Pratt was to live in the newly built schoolhouse in the churchyard, rent free, provided he showed the Governors a certificate of his place of settlement. If he did not bring this he would not get any salary. A certificate of settlement showed where a person legally belonged; the village or town to which they could be returned if they fell on

hard times and needed to ask for relief. The Governors wanted to make sure Mr Pratt could not ask Wantage parish for help in the future if he did not belong there. After he had spent a few years teaching at the school, the Governors minuted at their meeting in October 1744 that Mr Pratt was not to be paid any salary until the following March "by reason of his ill conduct and carelessness in regard to his school." And if he did not then produce a certificate signed by at least two of the Governors to say that he had "much amended his conduct and been greatly more mindful of his school and scholars" his salary would not be paid any longer and he would be turned out of the schoolhouse. He did not leave but did not seem to be paid a salary either, just small odd amounts in the years that followed. Then in November 1752 the Governors decided it was time for him to go. They felt that he had "for some years past neglected instructing his scholars in the manner he ought to have done" and asked the clerk to give him notice to leave by the following Lady Day (March 25th), "unless his behaviour be at that time more agreeable to the Governors." As no more was heard of him, it is fairly certain he did leave. He had not really given satisfaction over many years and the Governors had put up with him for perhaps longer than they should have done. No-one replaced him for the next two and a half years, until Joseph Green took possession of the schoolhouse and was to live there rent free with a salary of £7 a year, a larger sum than any English schoolmaster before him, for teaching twelve poor boys, the boys to be nominated by the Governors. He, like his predecessor, was to produce a certificate of settlement. He only stayed a year but the following teacher, Mr Austin worked there for nearly twenty years.

The boys at the English school were not very young. In 1765 the Governors stipulated that no boy was to be under the age of nine when he started at the school and he could not stay longer than three years. The following year they changed the rules so that no boy was to be admitted under ten years of age and was to stay only two years. So it was unlikely that with such a short school life any of the children achieved more than the basics of the three Rs at the English school, but no doubt it was better than nothing.

The grammar school was not doing too well by the mid 1700s. In 1763, the Reverend Mr Goldwyer, who was in his second year as master there, agreed to take boarders at a lower price than before, by which the Governors hoped to increase the number of pupils and hence the school income. This was the first indication that the boys at the grammar school were not all local boys. Some must have lived further away from the town to make it worthwhile to board. Mr Goldwyer left the following year and the school was uninhabited for four years as the Governors could not get another master. To begin with they said the school would be left vacant until the school and the necessary house had been repaired. Later they advertised in the Oxford Journal and the London Evening Post on more than one occasion but with little success, as no person applied after the first advert. It was not until the end of 1768 that they finally appointed another master, the Reverend Mr Bailey, at a salary of £30 instead of £20, so perhaps before they had been offering too small a salary for anyone to be interested. However, when Daniel Robins replaced Mr Bailey in January 1775, he was appointed at the old salary of £20 per annum. He was paid this amount for eighteen years, but then the Governors decided to increase his salary to the £30 a year that had been paid before he arrived. They added that "in consideration of his faithful attention to the school" and because his salary had been so low, they would give him an additional present of ten guineas (£10 10s 0d).

As mentioned in Chapter 1, Mary Harbert (or Herbert), who died in 1763, left one hundred pounds to the Wantage Town Lands in her will, towards the cost of a school in Wantage. The Governors invested this money in a trust fund and decided to use the interest towards supporting a school for the education of twelve girls belonging to the parish of Wantage. The girls would attend the school for three years and would learn reading, plain working and marking. Notice they would not learn to write, unless 'marking' meant learning to write the letters of the alphabet; writing was often considered unnecessary for girls. They were taught reading so they could read the bible. The girls were to be between eight and twelve years old when they entered the school and the mistress would be paid fourteen shillings a year for each girl. This was quite a large sum as the total amount would have been £8 4s 0d a year, but she would no doubt have had to provide any school equipment out of that. Mary Brown was appointed the first school mistress and it was agreed that the benefactor's brother would be able to nominate one of the girls. The interest on Mrs Herbert's bequest would not cover the schoolmistress's salary so the Town Lands would make up the remainder. The first year the interest was £3 10s 6d so was nowhere near the amount the Governors said should be paid for the twelve girls. Mrs Brown did not always have as many as twelve girls to teach, her salary showed it was more often eleven or ten girls. At this point, the school mistress was being paid more than the school master (who received eleven shillings and eight pence per boy), which was unusual as men were always paid more than women for doing a similar job. It could have been because she had to provide accommodation. Where the girls school was situated was never mentioned. It was not in the churchyard with the grammar school and the English school, and must have been somewhere else in the town. As the Governors did not pay for the building or room where the girls' lessons were held, the schoolmistress's salary probably included the cost of the rent she had to pay. Mr Austin, the boys' teacher, may have had other employment at the same time as teaching, because in 1769 he was paid by the Governors for printing seven hundred receipts for them.

When a new schoolmistress was appointed in 1774, she was soon paid £8 8s 0d for teaching twelve girls for a year, while the new schoolmaster appointed shortly afterwards had taken on the position for £4 a year. When he took over as master, it left the previous master, Thomas Austin, "in distress" and the Governors gave Thomas £10 because of this. He was also paid two shillings and sixpence for doing more printing for the Governors. Ashur Packer, the new schoolmaster at the English school soon had his salary increased to £7 per annum and when he married three years later, his wife took over the teaching of the girls' school, although still at a higher salary than his. In fact he was not paid more than his wife until seventeen years later when his salary was increased to £10 per annum and then only if he took six more boys as well as the usual twelve. In the first seven years of their marriage, the Packers had five daughters, the first one dying just before her first birthday, but Mrs Packer taught the girls as well as coping with her increasing family. Ashur Packer had been the English school master for thirty seven years when he died, while Mrs Packer carried on teaching after she was widowed. It is possible that one of her daughters took over for a short while as a Miss Packer was paid for several years, with the payments once again being made to Mrs Packer the same year as a daughter, Ann, died. Mrs Packer continued until her death in 1834, when unbelievably the burial register gave her age as 88. Even if this was inaccurate, she was certainly over 75 years of age. It was never very clear whether the English school master lived in the school house or not, but as one of the towns-people was paid for an iron casement and a few other small iron items "at the house occupied by Ashur Packer" and "at the house rented by Ashur Packer" it sounded as though the Packer family rented separate accommodation and the schoolhouse was only used for teaching. Perhaps Mrs Packer taught the girls at the Packer home as this would have made it easier to look after her small daughters at the same time. The girls' school was definitely held at the teacher's home some years later; a report in 1837 stated, "It is necessary that a more suitable school should be provided for the girls, who are at present taught in a close small room, the residence of the mistress."

There were two interesting comments in the minutes while the Packers were teaching the poor boys and girls. In 1781, the Governors decided to impose a rule which stated: "If any boy or girl shall be absent from school a fortnight at any one time in the year (except in the time of harvest) that the Master or Mistress do immediately turn such boys or girls out of their school and that they have no further benefit in learning therefrom." The grammar school may have been included in this rule, it is not clear, but possibly only the poorer children were likely to be kept from school to help with the family finances, the grammar school boys would be more likely to be from the artisan class or above and less likely to be expected to work at a young age. It was interesting to see that even the Governors accepted the need for the poorer children to help at harvest time, or perhaps they realised they would not get parents to agree to send children to school when there was work available for all the family. In 1786, the parents of the children from the English school and the girls' school would have been informed of another notice given out by the Governors, which set out that if the master at the boys' school or the mistress at the girls' school wanted to keep any of their scholars behind at the end of the day as punishment, then the parents should not interfere or obstruct the punishment. If any parent did not keep to this rule, then their child would no longer be entitled to go to the school. It rather sounded as though some of the parents had been complaining if the children were kept in after school. Again it might have been because they expected their children to work after school. Mrs Packer was also asked to make sure the girls were trained in household tasks "that they may be better qualified to become good and useful servants."

About this time, 1789, the English school was in need of repairs and the Governors minuted that this should be done "with all convenient speed." William Noak was paid £10 17s 10d "for pitching and for mason's work at Mr Packer's School", so a fairly large repair bill, although what 'pitching' involved was not made clear, possibly, as with the repair of the roads, it involved paving with stones. From 1798, small sums began to be awarded by the Governors for "coals at the grammar school", usually between one shilling and two shillings a year, and not every year, so only a small contribution towards the heating; sometimes there were gaps of several years when there was no record of coal having been paid for at all. Many years later, Mr Butler who became the master at the English school after Ashur Packer died, was allowed twelve shillings a year for a fire in the schoolroom. He had started at the school with a salary of £15, which was £5 a year more than Ashur Packer had been getting, but by the time money was given for coal for the fire at the English school, he was being paid over £20 a year.

In 1806, the Governors made a donation of five guineas (£5 5s 0d) to the Sunday School, and the same amount was given in 1807, 1810, 1811 and 1826, but no other times. The Sunday School movement started in the 1780s, when on Sundays poor working people were taught to read the bible, initially adults as well as children. One of these schools must have been started in Wantage, which the Governors felt happy to support by occasional donations from the Town Lands funds. Another Wantage school made an appearance in Wantage in the minutes for 1823. This was a School of Industry for Girls of the town, no doubt where girls would learn housekeeping methods to make them suitable for employment as servants. Mrs Packer was still teaching at the Governors' girls' school, which had similar aims, so quite why a second school had been set up is not clear. William Beckett was one of the Governors and a solicitor of the town; the treasurer of this new school was a Mrs Beckett, so quite likely his wife. The Governors decided to make a donation of £2 to the School of Industry in 1823 and again in 1825, At the second agreement to donate to the School of Industry, there was an entry donating £2 to the Sunday School as well but this had been crossed out: it must have been decided only to support one of the institutions. In 1826, £2 was given to both the

School of Industry and the Sunday School, but also a £2 donation was given "to aid the Infants School in this Town"; another school had been set up, this time for young children. The infant school was given £2 for each of the next two years and was then not mentioned by the Governors again. The School of Industry had four more annual donations and then that also was mentioned no more. Either they were both short lived or the Governors decided they did not need financial help from the Town Lands.

In 1831, it appeared that the grammar school, at which nothing but the classics were taught, was not doing too well, as there was only one boy being taught as a Town Lands' scholar. The master, the Reverend Daniel Robins, was told that his salary would be reduced from £30 a year to £20 a year, and the £10 saved in this way was to be used to increase the number of pupils at the English school taught by William Butler and at the girls' school taught by Mrs Packer. Six extra boys and six extra girls were to start at these two schools and the Governors were to be able to choose one child for each school. Mr Butler was to be paid by the Governors for any writing or 'summing' books he needed for his pupils; in the past he must have bought these from his own money. Daniel Robins at the grammar school resigned when his salary was reduced, but was probably getting too old to teach anyway as he had been there for fifty six years, and he died soon afterwards. No master was appointed to replace him, no boys applied to be admitted and part of the school building was being used as an office for the Savings Bank in Wantage. William Wasbrough, the clerk to the Governors, drew up a document of comments on the Town Lands trust in 1836, in which he made suggestions for improving the organisation. Regarding the grammar school, he wrote that in the past many persons of the Town had received a good education free but that "the Governors have not shown the least anxiety to the great advantages of a Public School." He gave the impression that some of the Governors were not really in favour of a grammar school and indeed thought "Latin and Greek very unnecessary for the sons of tradesmen and shop-keepers." One of them had proposed just having a master to teach English, which annoyed Mr Wasbrough who commented that this Governor "thought himself very clever when he stated to his colleagues that this was within the meaning of the Act as Grammar must mean English as well as Latin Grammar." Although Mr Wasbrough suggested appointing another grammar school master, there was a gap of twenty years between Daniel Robins and the next schoolmaster there.

The English school, which seemed to be thriving as the grammar school declined, taught the boys reading, particularly from the Bible, writing and arithmetic; a few of the older boys at this time also learnt English grammar and the Governors paid £3 a year for the copybooks the boys used to practise their writing. The Governors could send twenty four boys to the school and the Baptist minister was allowed to send another eight or nine, paid for out of an endowment made by Robert Dowsett in 1770 to enable poor children of Wantage and Grove to be taught to read: this charity also sent four girls to a school in Grove. In addition to the boys paid for at the English school by the Town Lands and the Baptist charity, the schoolmaster was allowed to take private pupils whose fees were paid by their parents. At the girls' school up to eighteen girls were paid for by the Governors and the mistress could also take extra private pupils. The girls were taught reading, spelling, needlework and knitting and several learnt writing and arithmetic, which had to be paid for by themselves as this was an extra not covered by the Governors' fees. Both schools were open from 9 am to 12 noon and from 2-4 pm, every day except Saturday, which was given as a holiday as it was market day.

At the January meeting of the Governors in 1841, they were anticipating that William Butler the English schoolmaster would soon be retiring and they thought this would be a good time to put the boys' school "on a more efficient system", and suggested that the management of the girls' school would also be discussed at the next meeting later in the year. Unfortunately the next recorded meeting was two years later and the discussions about the two schools are therefore missing. Mr Butler had retired at the end of 1842 but was to be paid ten pounds as he had had to retire because he was physically unable to continue teaching. The Governors also paid him for the desks he had left in the schoolroom, which he must have provided. In 1847, the Governors were agreed that it would be a good idea to build a National School (a school belonging to the Church of England) in Wantage and that £25 of the salaries of the two teachers at the boys' and girls' schools run by the Town Lands could be transferred to the support of this school, as long as this could be done legally; they were not sure if the Town Lands funds could be used in this way. The vicar, the newly arrived Reverend William John Butler, had probably instigated the idea of a National School for the town. The following year, he proposed that the two schools belonging to the Governors in the churchyard (the grammar school and the English school) be taken down and the materials used in the new schools that were about to be built by subscription. So it appeared that money was already being collected to enable the National School, and possibly a new Grammar School as well, to be built. The vicar also proposed that the Governors' properties in the town, near the Alfred's Head Inn, which were in a dilapidated state, should be taken down and the materials from these buildings could then be used in building the new schools. The Governors thought they would need to take legal advice about this, so no decision was made at the meeting. At the opening of the National school, in 1850, the Governors' girls' school was discontinued and the mistress was pensioned off, being paid £8 a year until 1864. Mr Warner, the English school master was given £10 and dismissed. The boys and girls from these schools transferred to the National School and after that time, the Governors made no further contribution to the expenses of elementary education in Wantage.

By 1849, plans were under way for a revival of the grammar school. The town was planning to hold a jubilee

King Alfred's Grammar School, opened 1851. The schoolroom is on the left.

to commemorate the millennium of King Alfred's birth, and it had been proposed that a committee be set up to organise the rebuilding and enlarging of the grammar school as part of the celebrations. Some of the Town Lands Governors were to be part of this committee; Mr Ormond, the Wantage solicitor and one of the Governors, was asked to be treasurer of the fund that was being set up to pay for the building work on the grammar school, and every subscriber who donated three guineas or more to the fund would be given a copy of the Jubilee Edition of King Alfred's Works. The Governors agreed to contribute a hundred pounds to the building fund.

Judging by a long report in the newspaper, the Alfred Jubilee was a day to remember in Wantage. It started with a service in the church, followed by addresses given in the town hall by various eminent gentlemen. A procession then gathered in the market place and, with banners and bands leading, marched to King Alfred's well in Locks Lane, where a lecture was given on the life of King Alfred. An ox roast and "various rustic amusements" took place in a nearby field, which must

have been the entertainment for the hoi polloi, as at 3 o'clock a dinner for the ladies and gentlemen of the town was held at the Alfred's Head Inn. This was accompanied by numerous speeches and toasts, poetry reading and a performance by a Welch harpist. At 10 o'clock most of the party went on to the ball at the Town Hall, while fireworks in the town provided everyone with more fun and excitement. Perhaps surprisingly, the newspaper was able to report that "no disorderly conduct occurred to mar the pleasure of the day."

Enough money had been raised towards the building of the new grammar school for the Governors to start putting plans into action in early 1850. The school was to be built on part of a meadow belonging to the Town Lands, where the school still stands. A Reading architect who specialised in Gothic revival buildings, Mr John Clacy, was chosen and he drew up plans for the new grammar school, which it was hoped could be built for a thousand pounds. The plan was for buildings round three sides of a rectangle but initially the funds would only cover the cost of two of

The new schoolroom

the three sides. A contract was drawn up with Messrs. Hunt, Kent and Haines, a Wantage firm, to build this part of the school and master's house at a cost of £865. Bartholomew Wroughton, a large landowner living at Woolley Park on the Downs, and also a Governor, was requested to lay the corner stone on 29th July 1850, and he humorously observed as he did so that he was laying the foundation for two thirds of a school. As soon as more money had been raised, a further contract was entered into to build the remaining side according to the architect's plan, for an additional £232. The building firm agreed to buy the materials of the old grammar school in the churchyard for £80. The English school was taken down too and some of the materials used in the new grammar school building but not the material from the dilapidated buildings by the Alfred's Head, as initially suggested by the vicar. Extra costs arose, when the following year additions were made to the plans, which was something which seemed to happen when

any new building was under construction. It was decided to erect two privies, a coal house and a yard at the school; then steps at the entrance were considered a good idea; as well as attending to the drainage, which must have been somewhat essential!

At a meeting in May 1851, the school rules were drawn up (see Appendix 3) and the Reverend Edmund John Smith, MA and Scholar of Worcester College Oxford, was elected master of the new grammar school, at an annual salary of £50. He started work at the grammar school before there were any scholars, no doubt overseeing the furnishing and organisation. The Governors reimbursed him for desks and fixtures at a later date. In July and September, the Governors met to elect their first scholars. Twelve boys were chosen as free scholars, paid for by the Town Lands charity and a further ten boys were elected as £5 scholars; their parents would pay this amount annually for their son's education. (According to the rules, the Governors could have elected twelve £5 scholars.) The pupils at the school were to be taught Classics, English Grammar, Mathematics, Reading, Writing, Arithmetic and 'useful learning'. The rules allowed any pupils resident in Wantage to be educated in Latin grammar free of charge, except for the cost of books and stationery. Parents of all Governors' scholars were expected to pay for books. The following boys were those first scholars:

Boys elected Scholars on the foundation:

Walter PALMER	William READ
Arthur ROBINS	William BEASLEY
John SELL	Richard HOWSE
Henry LAY	Alfred Hurndall KEALL
Rice BENNETT	William HANNON
Robert PUMFREY	Charles MILSUM

Boys elected Scholars at £5 pa:

John HANNON	Edward Skinner KEALL
Oliver ROBINS	Charles Lovegrove BENNETT
Wm Godfrey LAY	William Charles WHEELER
Thomas PAINTER	John BETTERIDGE aged 12
Joseph LEWIS aged 11	Charles CURTIS aged 10

At the end of November 1853, Edmund Smith wrote a letter of resignation to the treasurer of the Governors. As he was writing from Oxford, at a time when he would have been expected to be at the grammar school in Wantage, he felt it necessary to explain why he was not where he was supposed to be.

"*My Dear Sir,*

I trust you will excuse me if I say that I find my present Salary as Master of the Grammar School inadequate to the position. The number of pupils attending it obliges me to maintain an Assistant Master at a considerable expence & the present high prices of provisions render the receiving Boarders very slightly remunerative. Under the circumstances I beg to inform you that I purpose resigning the Office of Master of the Grammar School at the end of the ensuing Quarter.

"*I may take this opportunity of stating that I have come over here to attend the Gaudy, a festive occasion certainly but also a time for College business which I should not be justified in neglecting. I trust therefore that you will give me credit for not absenting myself from my duties without sufficient reason.*

Believe me My dear Sir
Very faithfully yours
Edmund J Smith"

The Gaudy is an annual college event, when past students of a college meet for dinner, drinks, conversation and, if one is to believe Mr Smith, for business.

The Governors replied that they regretted they could not increase his salary and therefore they reluctantly accepted his resignation. At which he withdrew it. Later he had a boundary wall built in front of the school and was probably not very pleased when the Governors only allowed him £10 towards the cost of the wall rather than the whole amount. The total cost is not recorded. Although Mr Smith had withdrawn his resignation made at the end of 1853, three years later he once again gave in his notice and this time did not change his mind. The rules stated that the grammar school master should be a graduate of arts in an English university but the Governors were always looking for an Oxford or Cambridge graduate if possible: they advertised in the Times, the Guardian, and the Oxford and Cambridge papers in 1856 when Mr Smith left. Even though the news that Mr Smith had given notice had only just been received when a meeting was held at the end of November, and a new master was needed for the beginning of January, there were ninety seven applicants for the post, which must have said something about the number of unemployed graduates at the time, or perhaps being head of Wantage Grammar School was a very desirable position. Seven of the men were invited to come for interview and the Reverend Cornelius Hargrave Crooke BA, Curate of Milton in Berkshire, was chosen to fill the post, at first being paid the same salary of £50 per annum as Mr Smith but by 1861 this had increased to £80 per annum.

The rules set out that the master would be provided with his house and premises rent free but

The doorway from the old grammar school incorporated into the entrance to the new schoolroom

school for maps, gig house, door to potatoe (sic) house, extension of mound surrounding playground, paving stones from master's house to school"; for which Mr Smith was paid £57 19s 3d. The Governors owned a small piece of land next to the school and in 1860 they agreed to let this to the next master, Mr Crooke, rent free. He probably made this into a garden as the following year he asked to have a fence put up between the playground and the garden (the garden was most likely his own private one). The Governors said they would pay for the fence but Mr Crooke would have to make arrangements to have it delivered and to have it erected.

When the old grammar school in the churchyard had been pulled down, one item which had been reused was an old doorway, which had been moved to the new school site. In 1857, the vicar of Wantage, Canon Butler, asked to have it moved to the church. The Governors agreed as long as this was done at the vicar's expense and that he also had another doorway built in its place. As it is still situated at the entrance to what was the schoolroom, Canon Butler must have had second thoughts about moving it.

There must by this time have been more than the one teacher, as Mr Crooke was referred to as the headmaster and when Mr Smith sent the Governors his first letter of resignation, he reminded them that he was having to employ an assistant master. Any additional masters like this must have been appointed by the head master and paid for out of his income as there was never any mention in the minutes of the Governors being involved in appointing or paying other members of staff at the grammar school. It is also not clear as to how many paying pupils were taken into the school by the headmaster, as only the free scholars involved the Governors. Correspondence passed between Mr Crooke and the Governors when they decided to offer John Heater, aged nine, a place as a free scholar. He was already a paying pupil at the school and making him one of the free scholars meant that Mr Crooke had one less paying pupil. The Governors had

he would pay any rates and taxes. He was to keep the premises in good condition; the Governors would do all substantial repairs but the master was expected to provide any extras, even equipment needed for the school, although he would be reimbursed at least part of the value when he left. Mr Smith had paid for various items in the school and the Governors had these "fittings, buildings and fixtures" valued before agreeing to pay him for them. Mr Belcher the estate agent and auctioneer carried out the valuation, and the list of articles agreed upon was: "Bells, green door, cupboard near bedroom door, ditto under stairs, ditto corner of passage, chimney and grate in bedroom, door between pantry and cellar, shelves in ditto, back kitchen grate, large cupboard and screen in dining hall, grate in ditto, partition in assistant master's room in dormitory, papering & painting, corner cupboard in obviously not thought that through before electing him as a free scholar but when the master queried their decision, they agreed that John's father would have to pay as usual to the end of the quarter and said that in future free boys would only be admitted twice a year, at Christmas and Midsummer; and that if the boy was already at the school a quarter's notice must be given to the master. The master was expected to inform the Governors when any boy on the free list left the school, and also to hand over a list of the names of free boys each year at the annual meeting.

In 1863, Mr Crooke asked the Governors to provide an infirmary and extra classrooms for the school. They told him that they would consider the matter later but at the present time did not have the means to enable them to spend any more money on the school. Later that summer, he wrote again and they said they would "take the matter into consideration when the estimate and specifications of the proposed buildings are produced for the inspection of the Governors." They finally agreed to pay Mr Crooke a total of £170 in three instalments; £60 when the architect certified that work to that value had been completed, £60 twelve months later and £50 the following year, as long as the work was satisfactory. So the building work went ahead.

The grammar school had privies draining into a cesspit and there were obviously problems with this as the Governors looked into the drainage in 1866 and asked the Wantage firm of Kent to drain the cesspool. The headmaster, unlike his modern counterparts, kept pigs. These must have been adding to the sewage draining into the cesspit as the Governors told him that "if he continued his pigsty it would be necessary for him to provide for the draining." The following year there were still problems with the drainage and the Governors agreed to try an experiment by using earth closets for four months instead of having a cesspool. One of the Wantage doctors, Walter Barker, who was also a Governor, was to be responsible for keeping these earth closets 'supplied' (with dry earth?) and

Moules dry-earth closet improved version from 1875

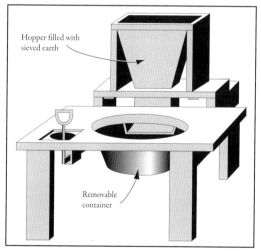

Another version of Henry Moules closet, first patented 1860

emptied. The experiment must have been successful as a little while after it had been carried out, Mr Partridge of the town was paid £20 7s 0d for work and materials for new earth closets; Mr Aldworth another tradesman was paid for putting up the roofs of the earth closets; Messrs Kent were paid for erecting "an earth house" which, at a guess, was to store the dry sieved earth used in these privies. In 1882 a shed was provided "for the reception of the earth from the earth closets", which could have been the used earth waiting to be removed; and a rubble road was built to this shed to make moving the earth easier.

By 1866, having only been in existence for fifteen years, the school was suffering some difficulties. It was agreed that Mr Crooke would be asked to attend a meeting of the Governors to "consider the present state of the grammar school and the small number of Governors' Scholars, with a view to an alteration and improvement in the present system." An inspector the previous year had found only three foundation scholars paid for by the Governors, three day scholars paying their own fees and twenty one boarders. There was obviously not the full number of free scholars attending, most likely because the school did not have a good reputation and parents were not taking up offers of the places for their sons. The meeting of the Governors with the master was held at the end of May and ways and means of improving the grammar school were discussed. It was decided that the Governors' scholars, the boys getting a free education, should be proposed for the Oxford and Cambridge Middle Class Examination, as well as making sure that their commercial education was of a good standard. As many of the boys were sons of tradesmen and shopkeepers in the town, probably expected to follow their fathers into the business, their commercial education would be as important, if not more so, than a classical education. Every boy applying for one of the places as a Governors' candidate, had to attend a Governors' meeting to be vetted, and once chosen he was not to be removed from the school without permission from the Governors. As for some time the number of free boys had been lower than the number specified in the rules, the Governors asked Mr Crooke to take two extra boys, to make up for this. Also while Mr Crooke was headmaster, "certain

complaints" were made to the Governors about the grammar school, and so the treasurer was asked to speak to him and get his version of events. Later it appeared that the complaints mainly centred on the number of half holidays the boys were being allowed, which was greater than the rules permitted. The master and the treasurer to the Governors usually arranged the dates of the main Christmas and midsummer holidays, but the headmaster was responsible for half day holidays. The boys were allowed five weeks holiday at Christmas; five weeks in the summer, which after 1868 was increased to six weeks; along with Good Friday, Easter Saturday, Ascension Day, Monday and Tuesday in Easter week, Monday and Tuesday in Whitsuntide week; as well as half day holidays on Wednesday and Saturday afternoons. Originally the Wantage Michaelmas Fair day was also given as a holiday, but this had ceased by 1868. Mr Crooke was giving holidays extra to these days.

After the Governors had discussed ways of improving the school with Mr Crooke, twelve boys were elected and were then examined by the Governors at the beginning of August, but only nine took up their places at the school. Their parents were recommended to provide them with college caps (the school was occasionally referred to as the college), and it had been suggested at an earlier meeting that parents of the free scholars would be asked to pay ten shillings in advance for books and stationery. The stationery was to include pens, penholders, plain paper, ruled paper, blotting paper, exercise books and copy books. From 1868 when the Governors re-wrote the school rules (see Appendix 3), it appeared that the twelve junior scholars who were chosen would pay £5 a year plus the ten shillings for books and stationery, with the Governors adding £2 10s 0d to this payment to the headmaster. These boys were not to be under eight years of age. When they became old enough to be senior scholars, they would become free scholars if the Governors felt they had done well enough at the half yearly examinations. Also about this time, the Governors began appointing a person not

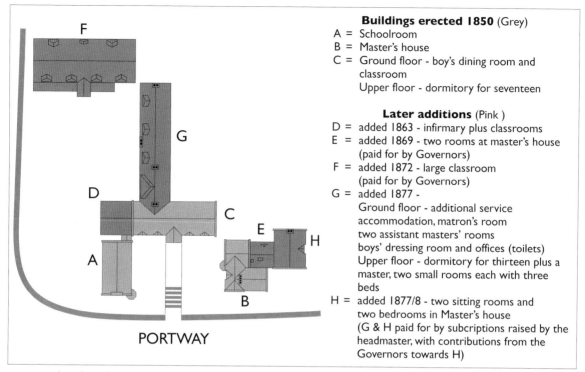

Buildings erected 1850 (Grey)
A = Schoolroom
B = Master's house
C = Ground floor - boy's dining room and classroom
Upper floor - dormitory for seventeen

Later additions (Pink)
D = added 1863 - infirmary plus classrooms
E = added 1869 - two rooms at master's house (paid for by Governors)
F = added 1872 - large classroom (paid for by Governors)
G = added 1877 -
Ground floor - additional service accommodation, matron's room
two assistant masters' rooms
boys' dressing room and offices (toilets)
Upper floor - dormitory for thirteen plus a master, two small rooms each with three beds
H = added 1877/8 - two sitting rooms and two bedrooms in Master's house (G & H paid for by subcriptions raised by the headmaster, with contributions from the Governors towards H)

PORTWAY

connected to the school to be the external examiner for these exams, who was paid around £5 for doing this. This was another change in the running of the school which it was hoped would improve standards. The examiners were mostly reverend gentlemen and usually either fellows or scholars of Oxford or Cambridge colleges. The Governors also made a donation each half year of between £2 and £3 towards prizes. Extra payments were made to the headmaster on the results of the examinations: £10 if a scholar passed with a first class certificate, £5 for a second class and £2 10s for a third. By this time, French and Science had been added to the curriculum and the scholars were to undergo a sound Religious Education.

The rules stated that the senior scholars elected by the Governors could not stay at the school after they reached the age of sixteen, except by special permission. A boy named William Saunders was a case in point. He had been elected, aged eleven, as a free scholar in February 1866 but had suffered a good part of 1867 from ill health, so much so that his father had asked for him to have leave of absence for the second half of

the Christmas term. He should have left the school in July 1870, on becoming sixteen, but was given special permission to have a further half year of schooling because of his long absences through no fault of his own, and he stayed on until the end of December. Another boy given permission to stay at the school after he became sixteen, was Frank Marlow who was academically outstanding. He was sixteen by the July of 1874 and was given permission to stay an extra term but when he did remarkably well in the Christmas exams, gaining four prizes and distinguishing himself in the Cambridge Exam for Middle Class Scholars, he was allowed to remain at the school until the summer holidays. William Talbot, was another boy given extra time at the school because of his abilities as well as his good character, staying for the Christmas term in 1875 when he would normally have left the previous summer. Arthur Nunney was allowed to continue as a senior scholar for an extra year as he had obtained a distinguished honour at the Cambridge Public Examination.

Another stipulation in the rules was that the free scholars must live in Wantage. In July 1870, George

Additional buildings. Above built 1872 (F on plan on page 53), below built 1877 (G on plan).

Dixon, the father of one of the boys at the school who had moved to Sparsholt, was told that unless he made arrangements for his son, William, to live in the town he would be disqualified from being a Governors' scholar. As William was twelve in December 1866 when he was elected a free scholar, he must have been coming up to the age of sixteen by the time the Governors complained of him living out of town, so perhaps his father simply removed him a term early. As well as living in Wantage, Governors' scholars were expected to show regular attendance; W.H. Liddiard had his scholarship removed in 1879 for not doing so, and in 1882, the junior scholarship of Richard Stonill, whose father was the station master at Wantage Road Station, was taken away for the same reason.

There were also suggestions made by the Governors as to how infectious illnesses were to be dealt with by the school. In 1870, it was decided that no boy would be allowed to attend the school if during the previous three months he had suffered from scarlet fever or any other infectious illness, or had lived in a house where there had been an infectious illness. In order to return to school he would be expected to produce a medical certificate saying he was clear of the disease. In May 1871, perhaps to the delight of the boys, the exams were not able to be held due to an outbreak of measles. When several cases of scarlatina broke out at the school in 1885, Mr Barker, town doctor and also a Governor, suggested that the foundation boys (the free scholars) should be given leave to remain away from school until the end of the epidemic. Why the suggestion did not apply to all the boys may seem rather strange, but the paying pupils were the responsibility of the headmaster, while the free scholars were answerable to the Governors if they were absent without permission.

The Reverend Crooke resigned his post as headmaster of the grammar school in 1868 and Henry Cook replaced him, at a salary of £80 per annum. At this time the school buildings consisted of a small schoolroom, a master's house and dormitories, all built round three sides of a small quadrangle. Soon after Mr Cook became headmaster, he decided that his accommodation in the school house was not satisfactory and asked for additional rooms to be built there. Mr Aldworth, a builder, was instructed to build two rooms onto the schoolhouse, at a cost of £85, and other work was carried out costing £45. Mr Cook had rapidly increased the number of boys from nineteen to seventy, so the classroom and dormitories must have been very crowded. In 1871, the Governors agreed to increase the school accommodation. This was expected to be a sizeable building project and it was decided to ask the Charity Commissioners if the Governors would be allowed to borrow a sum of money to do this, as they were expecting the cost to be higher than they could meet from the usual income of the Town Lands. One of the Governors was delegated to visit the Endowed School Commissioners in order "to represent to them the present condition of the Grammar School and its pressing need of enlargement." These commissioners quickly agreed for the Governors to erect new buildings at the grammar school and William Butterfield, the architect of Keble College in Oxford, was approached to design a school for a hundred boys at a cost not to exceed £1,000. By the beginning of 1872, the Governors had approved the position of the new building, a large schoolroom in the playground of the existing school, and had given Mr Butterfield the go ahead to prepare the specifications and estimates.

The Governors asked the Charity Commissioners if they could borrow the £1,000 needed for the grammar school buildings from the money that Mrs Burd had bequeathed to the Town Lands. This was agreed but the commissioners were not happy that the Governors wanted the loan to be repaid over thirty years; they felt twenty years should be a sufficient time. The final instalment of the repayment of this loan was made in 1892, so the Governors must have agreed to the Charity Commissioners' timescale.

Tenders for the building work were received and the Wantage firm of Wheeler and Gregory was chosen

"To the glory of God and the beloved memory of Henry Cook Headmaster of King Alfred's School in this town from 1868 to 1884 who died 3rd April 1885 aged 58. Also Jane Elizabeth widow of Henry Cook, who designed this window in memory of her husband and her younger son and died in her house of Highfield in this parish on 23rd January 1920 aged 85 ..."

to carry it out. They agreed to do it for £850 and a clerk of works was appointed by Butterfield to oversee the work. It was also decided to build a wall round the school playground and this seemed a good opportunity to widen the road by the school. The Commissioners for Improving the Town were consulted about this and they agreed to pay £20 for a strip of land to be taken off the playground and be added to the road. James Bunce of Hanney built the wall round the playground for a little over £120. A gateway was put in the wall to the playground and a path between the old and new buildings was paved.

Even after all this work, Mr Cook was not satisfied. In 1874 he wrote to the Governors regarding improvements to the building, which the Governors felt, perhaps understandably, were impossible to pay for out of their funds. Mr Cook persevered, bringing the matter up again a few months later. It appeared that by then he had prepared plans for whatever alterations he wanted. The Governors once more replied that they could not give him permission to make the improvements he wanted, but that they were happy for him to collect funds to enable him to carry out the improvements if he so wished. If he was successful, they might consider the matter again. By the middle of 1875, he had collected the impressive sum of £2,000 which he wanted to use to build new dormitories and to enlarge the master's house. The Governors were willing that he should proceed on condition that the plans were approved by Mr Butterfield and that Mr Cook guaranteed that the building work would be carried out according to these plans and specification. Also that each boarder should pay five shillings a term to the Governors to be used for repairs and insurance in the future. By the end of 1875, an architect, Mr Brook, was appointed by the Governors to make sure that Butterfield's alterations were carried out, and Mr Cook was given permission to start building as soon as he had guaranteed £1,000 to the treasurer.

However there was then, for some reason, a delay and the Governors finally approved the plans in

February 1877 and agreed to contribute £200 towards the cost of enlarging the master's house. They also agreed to reduce the suggested five shillings from each boarder to half that sum. When later in the year Mr Cook asked to have a passage in the school repaired at a cost of £6, the Governors said that they regretted that their funds would not permit this expense. That cost had to come out of his own funds. The Governors did, however, pay for painting the doors and windows at the school. Work needed to be done on paving the playground and the Governors consulted the surveyor of the roads, as being a person who would be able to advise them. A method was suggested and an estimate given for nearly £70 plus the cost of the labour, which the Governors thought too expensive. They felt £40 would be sufficient, of which they proposed to pay half, with Mr Cook footing the bill for the other half. As well as working to raise money to provide buildings to improve the school and setting out plans for their layout, Mr Cook also provided the playing field at his own expense. In 1871 the Governors agreed to let a meadow across the road at the front of the school to him and the accounts show that he paid ten pounds a year to rent this field. As it was later referred to as the Cricket Field, it was obviously for the use of the boys for games. Mr Cook was also allowed to provide a gate into the field (at his own expense).

During his time as headmaster, Henry Cook improved the grammar school so that it was in a flourishing and successful condition, but unfortunately he had to resign due to ill health at the beginning of 1884. He had taken time off five years earlier in order to have an operation, and his health had not been good since then. In his letter of resignation he wrote that he regretted he could not expect a pension but "considering what scant provision he had been able to make for himself and his family and the extent to which the value of the school property had been increased by his exertions, he trusted that at least the money he had put into the buildings might be returned to him." He indicated that he had spent up to £250 on the school buildings but when the Governors accepted his resignation they said that although they recognised the improvements he had made at the school, the funds of the charity would only permit them to refund him £200. He died a year later, aged 58 and his wife was given £150 towards the money spent by Mr Cook on the dining room and bedroom which he had added to the headmaster's private quarters. According to Mr Sugden, who was headmaster from 1919, Mr Cook's old boys subscribed money to build the house called Highfield, across Priory Road from the school, for the Cooks to live in after moving out of the schoolhouse. Unfortunately Mr Cook died before it was finished but Mrs Cook lived there with her sister, Miss Robins, who had also been a teacher. Mrs Cook was a portrait painter who had been commissioned to paint the Queens of Holland and Portugal. She designed the memorial window to her husband in the north aisle of Wantage church.

There was an unfortunate mix-up when the new headmaster was chosen. A short list of candidates had been drawn up and these men were interviewed. A Mr Muschamp was elected but it was minuted that if he declined the post, it was to be offered instead to a Mr Arnett. Mr Muschamp did refuse the job, but by then the treasurer had already told Mr Arnett that his services were not required. It appeared that the other short listed candidates were not suitable as none of them were given chance to take up the position; instead five other men were invited to come for interview and finally the Reverend William Pace Rigg was asked to become the new headmaster. He had no sooner taken up residence than it was found that the stove in the large schoolroom was worn out and the Governors suggested that he should provide a moveable stove at his own cost. He took over the rent of the cricket field that had been let to Mr Cook; the rent had now gone up from ten pounds a year to fifteen pounds but he let the grazing on the field for £8 a year, reducing the cost to himself. Perhaps only part of the field had animals in it, otherwise playing cricket could have been an interesting experience. Permission was granted

to construct a running path of tar and cinders round the sides of the field, so athletics must have entered the curriculum. He was given five pounds towards the cost of papering his dining room and bedroom, as Mr Cook's pictures had left marks on the walls, but he was told that the Governors were only agreeing to this as the damage had been done before he arrived: it was the custom for the master to be responsible for internal repairs while the Governors would repair the roof and external walls. A few years earlier, in 1877, a town water works had been set up and the master wished to have the school connected to the water supply. The Governors agreed to pay the cost of the piping from the force pump to the bedroom floors, but not the cost of the fittings from the water works to the school.

When Mr Rigg had been head for just over two years, the Governors began to hear reports of mismanagement in the school and a special meeting was held to which Mr Rigg was invited. It was suggested that the problem seemed to be a lack of discipline and he was asked to write out a report for the Governors to consider. His explanations suggested that there was more than discipline involved. He gave his word that he had in no way tampered with examination papers or conducted an examination unfairly, which threw a rather worrying light on his conduct; there would hardly have been complaints in the nature of cheating without there having been some substance to them. There must also have been problems between his staff and himself as he reported that as he had found the masters not suited to the requirements of the school, he had decided to change them. He commented that the system of leave that had worked successfully at his previous school was not suited to "the character of the boys he now had to deal with", so he had restricted it to its narrowest limits; which cannot have gone down too well with the local Governors as it implied Wantage boys were inferior to the boys he had previously taught. The Governors were not impressed by his explanations and decided they must insist on a radical reformation of the whole management of the school. At a further meeting between the Governors and Mr Rigg, he satisfied them that he intended to make alterations in management and discipline. A few months later, the boys of the grammar school asked the Governors' permission to take an extra week's holiday in commemoration partly of Her Majesty's Jubilee and partly "of the joyful event which had taken place in the household of their Head Master". The Governors agreed to grant the boys their request. A whole extra week's holiday seems rather excessive, even if there had been a happy event in the head's family; no doubt the boys could not believe their luck. Mrs Pace Rigg had just produced a baby girl, Edith Winifred.

Standards at the grammar school did not improve greatly. The report of the examiner the following summer was not very satisfactory and two years later, after the examiner's report had been read at a meeting of the Governors, they sent a letter to Mr Rigg saying they were disappointed, asking to see the examination papers and telling him that they were withholding their contribution to the annual prizes until they had had further discussions; although the usual prize money was later contributed by the Governors. Mr Rigg was sent a copy of the examiner's report and was asked to take greater care in teaching the subjects which were shown to be very weak. Luckily for him, the examiner's report the next year, 1891, was considered satisfactory.

In the summer of 1891, Mr Rigg decided that it would be a good idea to have a cricket pavilion in the cricket field he rented for the use of the school. The Governors were asked to contribute towards the cost and they agreed to pay up to £15, on condition that they saw the plans and approved them and that the building cost more than £35. Once it was built it was to become the property of the Governors but was to be kept in repair by the master. When the plans for the pavilion were shown to the Governors, they only asked for one change to be made; that the floor should be asphalted instead of being made of wood. By this time it was the autumn and the cricket season was over for that year. The Governors built a new wall between the cricket field and the road

and asked the headmaster to make sure that the boys, as well as any other person from the road, did not climb up and damage either the wall or the iron railing on top. But the wall must have proved to be an attraction to boys wanting to climb, as before long the Governors were bringing to the master's attention the fact that damage had been done to the ironwork on the wall.

By 1892, Mr Pace Rigg was paid £170 a year but out of this he paid two assistant teachers who received £60 and £30 a year; there was also a student teacher. There were at this time twenty five day scholars, nineteen of them Governors' scholars, all free as the £5 scholars had been abolished that year. Other day boys paid fees of £8 a year and the twenty four boarders paid up to thirty six guineas a year (£36 36s 0d, or £37 16s 0d). The headmaster took all the fees for his own use, but as the majority of the day scholars were on the Governors' foundation, most of his profit came from boarders. The numbers of scholars had fallen drastically since Henry Cook had been headmaster. The inspection in 1892 had found the buildings dirty and dilapidated and the asphalt in the playground in holes. Towards the end of that year, Mr Rigg had applied for the post of headmaster of Abingdon School and he asked the Governors for a reference. Considering the problems they had had over his poor management of the school and the standard of teaching there only a short time previously, the summary of the testimonial they gave him must have caused some raised eyebrows. They described him as a man of great ability, a good scholar and an able teacher, who was a popular headmaster amongst his pupils and exceedingly good in all athletic games. Perhaps they were hoping he might move on. It appeared that Mr Rigg did not get the job at Abingdon, as he was still head at the grammar school in Wantage the following March, but having been sent a copy of new proposals for the management of the school, he gave six months notice of his resignation.

The reference to his athletic abilities would explain his interest in the cricket field and the provision of the running track round its perimeter. While he was headmaster, the school held an annual sports day on the cricket field, the one held in 1893 being reported in the local newspaper, where the comment was made that "the Water Jump was a rather ugly looking affair, and some of the boys got, as they expected, a rather severe wetting, the width was nearly 18 feet."

Gradually legislation was being introduced nationally to improve the provision of education and to ensure that all children benefited from schooling. The Berkshire County Council set up a fund to provide technical education and in 1891 the Governors made an application to have a share of this. In 1892, the Governors discussed the recent legislation for providing free primary education and this was when they decided that the education of all the Governors' Scholars should be free. An alteration to the school rules was made, whereby it appeared that there were no longer to be twelve junior and twelve senior scholars; instead it was agreed to admit no more than twenty four boys over the age of ten, who were able to pass the entrance exam, which would be equivalent to Standard IV in a new education code. These boys would be taught all subjects in the school curriculum without paying fees. Boys from out of Wantage could now attend the grammar school as free scholars but priority would be given to Wantage residents.

About this time a meeting was held with a member of the Charity Commissioners to discuss a scheme that the Commission was planning to set up, to deal with the future management of the school. The scheme would provide for a separate foundation for the grammar school, which would no longer be part of the Wantage Town Lands charity. The school buildings and land would be made over to the education authority, the Town Lands would donate an annual sum of £220 to the school, and two of the Governors would be nominated as School Governors. The annual £220 became £200 when the meadow opposite the front of the school, which had been rented from the Governors by previous headmasters to be used as a sports field, was given to the school. Later, in 1928, the school bought the meadow in Willow Lane backing onto this cricket field, from the Governors, for £300.

Mr Rigg was offered the headship under the new scheme but as he then resigned and it was going to take some time to confirm the scheme, it was decided that the Governors would have to advertise for a new head rather than wait for the school governors to be appointed first. There were 195 applications for the post. Edmund John Piggott, the head chosen when Mr Rigg resigned, was the first head under the new scheme. He wanted to establish a science department and the education authority gave £150 towards a science laboratory and a carpentry room, plus a two year grant towards the cost of appointing a science master. The old schoolroom was converted into the science laboratory and the Town Lands Governors made a loan of £250 to the school to assist in initial running costs, this being paid back by 1914. The Wantage Town Lands Governors handed over responsibility for the grammar school to the School Governors in 1893, when more than four hundred years of involvement of the Town Lands in the running of the grammar school came to an end.

5

Helping the Poor of Wantage

One of the main reasons for the existence of the Wantage Town Lands charity was to give help to the poor of the town. This could be in the form of money, food, clothing or help with rent and other living expenses. People were mainly helped if they were old, widowed, sick, or with a large family and a small income. As far as giving money was concerned, methods of payment in money changed over the years. Initially a fairly small amount was given out each year: to a group of unnamed poor, usually between ten and twelve in number; with lump sums also given to the Wantage churchwardens and overseers of the poor, and Grove and Charlton churchwardens, to distribute to the poor in their parishes. The amounts were up to £1 each for the ten or so poor people, between £3 and £6 to Wantage, between £1 and £3 to Grove and amounts up to £2 to Charlton. There was also a somewhat puzzling donation each year to Farnborough parish, or as it was spelled at that time 'Farmeborowe'. Why this parish received money from the Wantage Town Lands is something of a mystery. There is nothing to indicate the reason in the Farnborough parish records and there was nothing in the Governors' accounts to explain why. There must have been a reason originally, but the donation had most probably been made for many years before the Act of Parliament regarding the Town Lands was passed in 1597, and the original reason was forgotten. This donation continued each year until 1668, when the Governors decided that the payments to Grove, Charlton and Farnborough should stop unless a reason for the payments was given by these parishes at the next meeting. By 1680, when the second book of accounts began, the only contributions made through parish officials were two sums of £3 given each year to the overseers of the Wantage poor to distribute, one at Easter and the other at Christmas.

There were now lists of one off donations to named poor as well as regular payments to 'pensioners'. Pensions were an agreed fixed amount given each year to someone needy, being paid to them at four times of the year, at Lady Day (March 25th), Midsummer, Michaelmas (September 29th) and either Christmas or St Thomas Day (December 21st). Many of these people were old or widowed, and there was one occasion, in the early 1680s, when a pension was given for a few years to a lame boy, William Acres' son. In the early days, the ten or twelve unnamed poor receiving a sum of money each year were the pensioners, as on one occasion the accounts showed that £12 was given "to twelve poor towards their pensions for a whole year". By 1680, the numbers of poor being paid pensions had increased dramatically: in that year there were 56 pensioners being paid a total of £52. Of these, 28 were men, 4 were women who were not widows, 23 were widows and there was one boy. There were also around ninety named people who were given money or clothing or other help, some because of sickness, others for no stated reason. Goodwife Savory was given 2s 6d "beinge very Antient and Poore"; William Oates was given 5s "he beinge Lame and his Family sick"; Old Butler was given four yards of cloth for a coat costing 9s 4d; and Widow Rogers was given 1s so she could buy some wood. The pensioners occasionally got extra help in this way but most of the one-off donations were to other poor of the town. After about 1700, the Wantage overseers were not involved with distributing any money from the Town Lands, although they would still be responsible for the money raised from the poor rates in the town; instead larger sums were given out at the Governors' annual meeting as well as the donations throughout the year to paupers for various emergencies. By 1720, it appeared that Town Lands' money was distributed at vestry meetings, which were the parish meetings where business concerning the town was discussed and decisions made. Later still, around 1780, sums of money were given out at the same times that the Governors distributed linen and money from Mr Brooke's charity.

Perhaps because some of the Town Lands' money was distributed to the poor after vestry meetings, when poor relief funded by the Wantage poor rates was also agreed on, some paupers benefited from both sources. At a vestry meeting in 1730, a fifth of the poor awarded financial help from the poor rates were also Town Lands' pensioners. And over that year, casual assistance was given by the Governors to others on the vestry list; nearly half of the paupers on the list getting some benefit from Town Lands' charity. These however were only a very small proportion of the individual handouts given over the whole year by the Governors. There were 97 people and their families helped in some way by the Governors that year, some of them only once but others many times, with one widow helped on fifteen occasions. Of the men who signed the vestry minutes, one was a Town Lands Governor and two others were elected as Governors shortly afterwards, so there was another common link between the two sources of relief, in the men involved in helping the poor from both organisations.

To return to the pensions, from 1680 names of pensioners were given and over the next years it is possible to trace who had pensions and for how long. Some people continued to receive pensions for many years, so were either not old when they first received them or lived to a ripe old age. Most got 5s each quarter, or £1 a year, although there were a few payments varying between 1s and 7s 6d a quarter. Numbers gradually dropped from then on, as did the total amount of money paid in pensions, as can be seen from the chart below. Individual payments also decreased; by 1740, most pensioners were getting 10s a year rather than £1. The lowest point was around 1765 with one year when only one person was given a pension. From then on, the number of pensioners rose again and so did the individual amounts given: in 1800 the majority were paid £2 a year, the others £1 a year. The end of the eighteenth century and the beginning of the nineteenth was a time when there was a growth in population and a rise in food prices due to poor harvests and the Napoleonic wars, which prevented food being imported, leading to increasing poverty for many. In 1802-03 in Berkshire, 20% of the population was on poor relief. This was perhaps why the Governors paid out more and more in pensions over

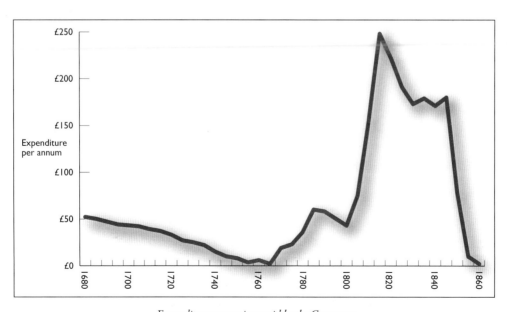

Expenditure on pensions paid by the Governors

the first twenty years of the nineteenth century. From £43 total pension money in 1800, the amount had risen rapidly to a peak of £248 in 1815.

The minutes show that pensions were allotted, increased, decreased, or discontinued after discussion at the Governors' meetings; the pensioners for the following year being chosen at the main annual meeting. In 1722, it was decided at a meeting that the pensions of Widow Sorrill and Widow Burchall were to be suspended as both women had married 'out town men'; in other words their new husbands did not belong to Wantage, so the women were not now eligible for help from the Town Lands, whether their husbands could support them or not. Pensions were sometimes paid for a short period when a person was in need of temporary assistance: in 1665, Robert Keepe was to have a pension of 5s quarterly "because of his present distress" and this was to be paid until further notice. The same year, Edward Robbins, who was a smith, so probably still working but in financial difficulties, was to be given 10s a year towards his rent, and this was also to be paid quarterly until further notice.

People living in the almshouses in the early 1800s were also given quarterly pensions, until in 1848 it was decided that instead of quarterly pensions, these almspeople would be paid weekly. People who did not live in one of the almshouses but who were given the quarterly payments, continued receiving this money but these pensions were gradually phased out as pensioners died, with quarterly pensions finally stopping around 1865. The weekly amounts paid to the almspeople increased over the years, particularly when the money from Cless's and Whitfield's charities were incorporated into the weekly payments instead of being given separately. When Lloyd George introduced old age pensions in 1908, some of the almspeople were eligible for this state pension. To claim it a person had to be a British subject over the age of seventy, to be of good character, not on poor relief and not earning over 12s a week. From the beginning of 1909 a person who qualified was paid 5s a week or 7s 6d for a married couple. The Governors reacted by reducing the pensions of those people who were eligible for a state pension by 2s 6d a week, at the same time paying 5s instead of 4s 6d to those not eligible. Then, as we have seen earlier in Chapter 1, from 1940 Kirby pensions of 30s a month were paid to people in Wantage who were not inmates of the almshouses.

Having dealt with pensions in some detail, we can look at some of the reasons that people through the years were able to obtain help from the Governors. Many of them were recorded as being 'in want' or 'in distress': these were people who for one reason or another were destitute at that particular time. In 1826, Sarah Goff who was a spinster, was given the quite large sum of three guineas (£3 3s) "on account of her reduced circumstances". Illness caused many to have to ask for help, and that will be investigated in more detail later. Even if a person had work, sickness or an accident or simply having a large family to cater for could mean that the family income was not sufficient to meet the needs at the time. So in 1669, Richard Gyles, who was a Wantage butcher, was to be paid 20s for "the relief and maintenance of him and his family"; and in 1776, Edward Evans, who was a hempdresser, was given £1 "being in distress". Sarah Tripp, on the other hand had to be helped because she had no work, when she was given sixpence in 1735.

As well as being given small sums of money for everyday expenses, or items of clothing, on many occasions people had their rents paid by the Governors or were given a contribution to the cost of their rent. In 1640, the Governors paid Arthur Webb 10s for Bartholomew Hind's rent for a year: Bartholomew must have been renting a house or a room belonging to Arthur Webb and because he was not able to pay him, the Governors had stepped in. Notice they paid the amount directly to the landlord, rather than give it to Bartholomew to enable him to pay the rent, perhaps he was not very reliable. In 1691, William Cobb was given 2s 3d towards his rent, but as shortly after this he was given sixpence because he was sick, illness probably was the reason he could not meet his rent commitment at the time. Non-payment of rent could result in becoming homeless, and the Governors were able to prevent this happening to James Allen in 1711 when they gave him £2 "to prevent his being turned out of his habitation".

There were times when a person had not paid the rent so had had some of his goods confiscated by his landlord to cover the amount owed. On several occasions the Governors paid to retrieve goods which had been taken for this reason. In 1732, they paid out £1 to recover John Oates' goods which had been taken when he was unable to pay his rent, and in 1758 they gave Joseph Painter, a labourer, £1 7s 6d to redeem his confiscated goods. They also gave Joseph an extra £1 towards the support of his family "he being sober and industrious": people were always more willing to help the deserving poor rather than the feckless and lazy members of society. A slightly different slant on the problem of non-payment of rent occurred in 1783. John Hunter owed Thomas Woolford rent, which he could not pay, and some of his goods were confiscated and sold to raise the money needed. However, more goods were sold than was necessary to pay Woolford, but as Hunter also owed the Governors money for property he rented from them, they took £2 1s 0d from this surplus to cover what he owed them. His annual rent to the Governors was £7 17 6d, so he was not a poor man, just someone who had found his cash flow had dried up. Goods were confiscated in more modern times when rent was unpaid. The Governors dealt with such a case in 1898, when they had let one of their cottages in Mill Street, opposite the almshouses, to a family of flower hawkers, who had locked up the cottage and gone away from Wantage for some time. When several months had elapsed without the family returning, and without paying any rent, the door of the cottage was forced open, the furniture was sold and the cottage was re-let to another tenant.

Repairs to houses belonging to people who could not afford this extra outlay were sometimes paid for by the Governors. Widow Silverside needed repairs doing to her house in 1733, and the Governors paid for this, which included a bill for 18s 10d for the masons, labourers and materials. When Alice Carter's house needed repairing a few years earlier in 1729, she was given 10s towards doing it. Alice must have been living hand to mouth as that year alone she was given seven payments of 1s 6d to help her out. The house was probably in need of constant small repairs, as she was given another 10s in 1734, and a further 2s 6d in 1737, both these payments towards the house repairs. It is not possible to guess what work was done on Widow Silverside and Alice Carter's houses, but in 1712, Peter Wilkins' house needed repairs to his thatched roof. Judging by the bills paid by the Governors towards putting his house in good condition, it sounded as though it had not been given a completely new thatched roof at the expense of the Wantage Town Lands, but probably just enough work done to make it watertight. The cost of the straw was only 2s 6d, so not a huge amount was used. The thatcher and his assistant were paid 3s 11d, which amount included the cost of the 'sprays' used. As a dictionary of 1730 gives the definition of 'spray' as 'a bough or twig', I think the sprays were the hazel spars used to hold the straw in place on the roof. A small amount of other work was done at the same time by Joseph Kent, a Wantage builder and bricklayer. As later that year Peter Wilkins was given a shilling because he was in want, and had been given other small amounts previously, he was obviously someone who would not be able to find the extra money to repair the thatch on his roof when it was leaking, or pay for other necessary work.

On a few occasions, people had travel paid for them by the Governors. We know why Edmund Gregorie, the cobbler, was given twenty shillings to pay for a journey in 1606, as the accounts state it was "to go to Devonshire about his land". Intriguing! If he owned land as far away as Devonshire, why was he living in Wantage and why did he need the Governors to pay for him, unless the twenty shillings was a loan. John

Wright was given 5s 4d to go to Oxford in 1614, a more understandable destination, although we do not know why he went. People travelling up to London could have been going there to work: there were openings for people to go into service in London. Widow Greene was given five shillings in 1631 "to carry her to London", and Widow Biddingfield was given £1 when she went in 1688; being widows, these two women would need to support themselves and it is possible that better paid work had presented itself in London, rather than in Wantage, or they may have had family there who would look after them. In 1711, Robert Stone had carried Moses Harwood and his family to Brentford and been paid 7s 6d for doing so. It is likely that Moses could not find work in the Wantage area to support his family and his place of settlement (the place where he belonged) was Brentford, and he was being removed back there so that he and his family did not become a charge on the Wantage poor rates. Goodwife Savory made several journeys at the Governors' expense, but we are not told why. During 1641 and 1642 she was paid eight shillings to take her child to London, and later eight shillings more to take her child to Oxford. Then in 1643 another eight shillings was given to her when she went with the child to London again.

Loans of money were quite often given by the Governors, not only to the poor. When money was lent like this, the person asking for the loan would sign a small document promising to pay the money back. For example, a note pinned to a page of one of the waste books (which were the working account books) gives the following:

"I do hereby promise to pay to the Receiver of the Governor's Rents or to his Successor in Office the Sum of Five Pounds which the Governors have lent me on my Note of Hand this 24th day of April 1775

Sarah Williams

Witness E. Towsey Junr."

Edward Towsey was one of the Governors at the time. Robert Darling, a butcher, borrowed £10 in May 1827 and he had to pay back half of this on midsummer day, the following month; with the other half to be paid back at the end of September on Michaelmas day, so a loan for only a short time. Some quite large sums were borrowed and in these cases the person borrowing would be expected to pay interest on the loan. William Masemore, one of the Governors, had borrowed £50 and when he died his executors had to repay the amount still owing. The Governors could be sympathetic when they realised a person was struggling to manage; there were one or two instances when they did not press for a loan to be repaid if there were mitigating circumstances. In 1756, Thomas Walker had taken out a loan of £5 with the Governors, which he was finding impossible to repay, so it was decided at a meeting that the Rent Receiver, who would normally have collected the repayments, was "to give up Thomas Walker's note of hand for five pounds he being poor"; his debt was being wiped out. William Nias, a carpenter who had worked for the Governors at times, died in 1782 and his wife carried on the business for a short time. William Hale wanted to set up in business as a carpenter but had not got the necessary capital, so in 1784 the Governors lent him £7 7s 0d "to purchase part of Mrs Nias' stock in carpentry" to help him out. There was no indication in the accounts, over the following ten years, that he ever paid this back.

Money was sometimes given, rather than lent, when tradesmen needed some cash to keep their business operational. Giving a small sum of money was probably better than having someone become dependent on the poor rates because their business had failed. In 1711, Phillip Doe was given £2 "to goe on with his trade" and Richard Darling was given £1 "the better to manage his trade"; while in 1760, Stephen Bigg was given £5 "towards putting him in a way of business". Butchers and shoemakers seemed to have more trouble making their occupations pay than other tradesmen, if the number of these people helped by the Governors is anything to go by. Richard Gyles, in 1671; Richard Clement in 1712; and Edward Coldicatt in 1813, were among several butchers over the years who needed help from the Governors to prevent their businesses coming to grief. When another member of the Gyles family was given 5s towards buying a sheep in 1716, he could also have been a butcher with the sheep providing meat to be sold in his shop. The shoemakers were often given money to buy leather, or the Governors bought the leather for them. In 1741, two shoemakers, William Wells and John Puzey were given a few shillings each to buy leather, but in 1750, Thomas Whiting was paid £1 5s 0d "for leather given to James Butcher and Alexander Alder, two poor shoemakers". The mid-1700s must have been a bad time to be a shoemaker in Wantage; as well as the three men mentioned above, Rivers, Noke and x Humphries were three other shoemakers given leather in 1750. In 1752 a hide of leather was given to John Mills and another half hide to him in 1756; while in the 1760s, shoemakers William Wilkins, Thomas Smith and "Waring the shoemaker", were given money and clothing because they were in distress. Even into the 1800s, shoemakers receiving help still figured in the Governors' accounts: in 1812 John Talbut, a shoemaker, was given £10 "to assist him in his business", and a further £5 was given to him in 1827 for the same reason.

However, one shoemaker found other ways to make extra money. He was William Wells, but unlikely to be the same man as the William Wells mentioned above. The case of this William Wells, a shoemaker, had come before the court of quarter sessions at Newbury in September 1740, because he had been keeping a disorderly house in Wantage "for his own Lucre and Gain". It was reported that men and women of "evil name and fame" had frequented this house both night and day "Drinking, Tipling, Whoreing and Misbehaving themselves unlawfully". Perhaps not surprisingly, although called to attend at court, William Wells had not put in an appearance and had disappeared from Wantage. Which is why he was unlikely to be the same William Wells who was helped by the Governors the following year. There was a large number of Wellses in Wantage, several called William.

Tools were given on several occasions, or money to buy them, again helping to keep a person in work supporting themselves. In 1711, Goody Mathewes was given 1s to buy a hoe; in 1734, the Governors paid 3s for a spade for Robert Titcomb; and in 1713 William Wells (another one!) was allowed to spend 8s on tools at the Governors' expense. On a few occasions, even horses were paid for when they were needed for the successful operation of a business. In 1832, Joseph Stroud, who was a fishmonger, was given £4 towards the cost of purchasing a horse. Joseph needed his horse to pull the cart in which he collected the fish he sold. We are not told what occupation William Champ carried out, but he also needed transport and when the wheels of his cart needed repairing, the Governors gave him 40s towards the cost of this.

A modern pair of cards for hand carding

From 1680 onwards, there were regular entries in the accounts showing that a great deal of help was given, mostly to women, to give them the means of working at spinning, one assumes in their own homes in Wantage. Pairs of cards were supplied, these being two wooden-backed brushes with handles, used to brush the wool into smooth bundles with the fibres all lying the same way, ready for spinning. A pair of cards could vary slightly in price but usually cost about 1s 4d, the amount the Governors were paying labourers for two days work at the time.

17th Century woodcut of spinning. Spinning wheels like this would have been used by Wantage women before about 1741.

Spinning wheels were also provided, or a woman would be given a small sum towards the cost of one. In the late 1600s, a spinning wheel cost about 2s 6d but the cost had increased to about 4s by the 1740s. In 1730 nine wheels went to various women, one being a widow, five being wives of named men, one a girl and two probably single women, so the spinners were of all ages and conditions. The wheels the women of Wantage were using before about 1741 were probably ones where one hand was used to hold the wool being spun while the other hand turned the wheel. In 1742, the Governors recorded that they had given 'foot wheels' to three women and in the years following, foot wheels were given in fairly large numbers. These would have been wheels worked by using a foot treadle, which left both hands free to hold and work the wool. Possibly this method was quicker; certainly it appeared that the old wheels were being replaced by the new in many instances. There was even one year when wheels were given to men in Wantage, when in 1747 seven wheels were given to men as well as thirteen to women and two to children, but that was the only time men appeared to be spinning.

It also appeared, at least for a short time, that the Governors, having given women the opportunity to spin, then bought back the spun woollen yarn, as for eleven years from 1680, they paid "severall poore people" each year for spinning at the rate of one penny for a pound of spun wool. The amounts paid each year were relatively large, averaging £14 7s 3d a year, with the largest amount being £20 12s 6d in 1691. The weight of wool that had been spun was also large: £14 7s 3d was the payment for spinning 3,360 pounds of wool, while payment of £20 12s 6d meant that 4,950 pounds of wool had been spun that year. After 1691, spinners were no longer paid by the Governors but as spinning wheels and pairs of cards were provided for another hundred years, until 1790, the poor women of Wantage were still spinning but must have found another outlet for the sale of their yarn. A clue might be the entries in the accounts in 1752, when the Governors paid "for spinning woollen as by agreement to Mr John Frogley's spinners" and also made payments to spinners working for John Gough, William Hazell and Cornelius Darling and others. It appeared that the women were spinning for various masters, probably men who supplied them with the raw wool and collected and sold the spun yarn.

A staged photograph with an old treadle spinning wheel. The 'foot wheels' given to Wantage women after 1742 would have been similar to this.

Why the Governors paid the women that year and the next is a mystery as no explanation was given in the minutes. In these entries, the women were only being paid a halfpenny for spinning a pound of wool, which could have indicated that they were being provided with the wool by the masters; while earlier, when paid a penny a pound, they may have been buying in the wool themselves; or the masters may have been paying them half, with the Governors funding the other half of their earnings. Over the one year 3,409 pounds of wool had been spun. The women doing the spinning for Cornelius Darling were named and paid individually but the other spinning masters were paid lump sums for their spinners. Three of the named women had spun a minimum of between 50 and 192 pounds of wool - possibly more when they were not named. The following year most of the payments were combined and given as lump sums to the masters, with 1,744 pounds of wool having been spun in total. These were the only two years when payments like this were made, to women working for various men of the town. The only mention of the Governors giving a loom to a woman is when Widow Goff is given one in 1724. Perhaps, as in the north of England, it was normally the men who wove and the women who spun. Spinning seemed to come to an end in 1790; or at least the provision of wheels and cards by the Governors ended then. Whether the requirement for woollen yarn in the Wantage area dropped, or whether the Governors decided that the men running the outworkers could take responsibility for making sure wheels were available to those workers, is not recorded. Entries regarding spinning wheels simply stopped in the accounts, and the minutes do not appear to give a reason. However, a trade directory published about this time, lists four clothiers (men who produced cloth from the raw wool) and a worsted maker in Wantage. Two of the surnames of these men, Goff (Gough) and Hazell are the same as two of the spinning masters in 1752 and they are also the men who were manufacturing the foul-weather cloth, which will be mentioned later. So cloth making was still an important activity in Wantage and

the fact that the Governors had stopped providing the poor with the means of carrying out spinning does not indicate an end to this means of obtaining a living in the town.

Payments were made to the poor on a few special occasions: when James I became king in 1603, on the death of Queen Elizabeth I, the Governors laid out 5s 4d on "the same day the Kings Majestie was proclaimed"; and a further 5s was given to the poor on his coronation day. This could have been spent on drink or some other form of celebration for the poor, or may have been small hand-outs to mark the occasion. No other coronations appeared to be celebrated by the poor in this way until that of George VI, when, as mentioned in Chapter 2, the almspeople were given extra for their weekly allowance.

There were occasional out of the ordinary occurrences, where the Governors felt that they could help to alleviate hardship. In 1603, a poor man was given 3s 4d to "burie one that dyed upon the Downes". The poor man could have been a traveller, not a resident of Wantage so not able to ask for the burial to be funded from the poor rates of the town, and probably the dead person was a member of the poor traveller's family. In 1808, John Herbert, a gardener, had been at church one Sunday and while he was there a thief had broken into his house and robbed him. The Governors agreed to give him £3 to replace the household items he had lost in the robbery. Maybe they felt more generous because he was at church at the time. Widow Perry was only given 2s in 1711 when she was robbed, but perhaps she didn't lose as much as John Herbert. Bad weather occasionally called for extra support for the poor: in January 1683 the Governors gave sums of money to several poor people because the weather was very cold, and in 1753 they gave a total of £5 3s 0d "to sundry poor persons in the severe weather". When Thomas Humphreys' harvest failed in 1761, he was given £1 1s 0d to help compensate him for his loss.

Fire was always a problem in towns, and there were a few times when people of Wantage were helped by the Governors because they had lost homes and goods when fire had broken out. James Stevens was given 20s towards his "losse by fire" in 1643. In 1688, there was a fire in Back Street, which is now called Church Street and runs parallel to the south side of the

Hand operated fire pump in Wantage museum

Market Place. At the time of this fire, the Governors gave sixpence to the Watchers. These could hardly have been people standing watching out of interest; were they people appointed to watch the buildings after the fire had been extinguished, until it was certain that it would not flare up again? Or they could have been members of the Watch, the men who patrolled the town making sure everything was safe. Did they spot the fire and give the alarm? The following year, the accounts showed that Augustine Harwood had been given a bed and a sheet to replace ones that had been burnt; perhaps Augustine smoked in bed and caused the fire. Although if that had been the case, he may not have been given new items to replace his burnt ones. In 1702, John Brookes, one of the Governors' tenants

was 30s in arrears with his rent: the following year the Governors wiped out this debt because John had suffered losses in a fire, which effectively gave him 30s towards his fire damage. In 1806, £5 5s 0d was shared between several Wantage inhabitants who had suffered losses in a fire in the town.

The first mention of a fire engine in Wantage is in the churchwardens' accounts of 1704, but even when this was operational, it was very primitive, little more than a pump. An earlier reference to fire fighting in the town occurs in 1669 in the Wantage baptism register, where an entry informs us that "the two Fire Hooks with new Poles brought in Church". These would have been used to pull down burning thatch when a roof was on fire, in the hope of preventing the fire spreading. In 1772, it was agreed at a meeting of the Vestry that the parish would buy a third fire engine, using a subscription of fifteen guineas (£15 15s 0d) from the Sun Fire Insurance, and levying a rate on the townspeople for the remainder of the cost. The bill for this new engine came to £44 16s 0d and a leather hose to use with the engine was also bought at the same time. A few years later, more leather pipe was needed as well as twelve leather buckets. In 1835, the Governors discussed making a donation towards the cost of a fire engine in the parish of Steventon, where some of the Town Lands were situated. At the meeting, it was decided to give £2 to the churchwardens and overseers of Steventon, who were asking for subscriptions, but when the accounts were published at the end of the year, the amount given had been reduced to £1.

People were expected to help one another and sometimes were given financial assistance to do this. In 1625, Edward Morris was given 10s for "keeping Robert Wryte half a year": this probably meant giving him lodging, as he could not have fed and clothed him as well for that sum of money, and about that time the Governors gave Robert some clothing each year. In 1671, Richard Arrowsmith rented a house from the Governors and he was told he must either make room in this house for Lawrence Ely and his family to live there too, or he must give Lawrence 20s so he could rent a house elsewhere. Richard refused to obey this order and also refused to pay his own rent to the Governors, so the following year they tried to eject him from the property. Perhaps the house was considered too large for the Arrowsmiths to live there alone. However, things seem to have been sorted out, as a few years later Arrowsmith was given 2s "for harbouring Talbott's wife and children". He had had another family wished upon him. The Arrowsmiths must have been expected to take lodgers over many years; as in 1712, Thomas Wilkins was given the choice of either being paid an annual pension of 20s or having a room in the house belonging to Widow Arrowsmith. Elizabeth Kent was given a pension of 20s a year in 1709 "so long as she allowed Susan Freeman house room but not longer". So Elizabeth's pension was really payment for the lodging she was providing for Susan in her house.

One person whose keep was paid for over many years was Magdalen Shepherd. No comment was made in the accounts as to why Magdalen needed looking after but it is possible she was handicapped in some way, as she seemed unable to look after herself. The parish registers give the basic details of her family, with various spellings of both her names. She was the sixth child in a family of seven born to Leonard and Dorothy Shepherd who married in 1584, Magdalen being born in 1597 (her baptism name was recorded as Madline). Both the parents died in 1620, and it is after that date that the Governors took charge of Magdalen's welfare. Before that her parents must have cared for her, whatever her problems. She seemed to be looked after by a succession of people. The first mention is in 1621 when Smythe's wife was given 16s "for keeping Shepheard's daughter". The following year Downe's wife was given 4s and the Governors also gave 14s 4d "to Maudlyn Shepheard for her relief". She was regularly given clothing: in 1624, "for a payer of Shooes and a paire of Stockinges for Marlyn Shepard 2s 4d", as well as smocks costing 4s 10d and

'cloathes' costing 8s 6d. By 1625, she was in the care of Richard Strowde; he was paid 20s for keeping her that year, and it appeared that he had agreed to care for her long term, as in 1627 the Governors recorded paying "for placing Marlyn Sheapherd during her life with Richard Strowde". Each year after that Richard received 10s for her keep, on two occasions the money was paid to his wife; for example in 1633, "to goodwife Strowde towards the keeping of Magdelen Shepherd which her husband stand bound to keepe". The Strowdes looked after Magdalen until 1634 when her sister Johane (baptised Jone and three years older than Magdalen) was paid for keeping her. Then, later that year Magdalen died, by then aged thirty six, and the entries relating to her in the Governors' accounts came to an end.

Margaret Lond and her father appeared in the Governors' accounts over several years. The first time Margaret's name appeared, in 1615, she was about twenty three years of age. That year she was given money on two occasions and clothing as well; a 'wascott', or what we would call a jacket rather than a waistcoat. Two years later, the Governors gave 5s "to Margarett Lond to go to the Ospitall". So she was needing treatment which could not be given by a medical man in Wantage. At that time, the Radcliffe in Oxford was not in existence, so it is possible she had to go to London, as there were hospitals treating the poor there, or to the free hospital in Bath where Wantage poor were sent on other occasions. Then in 1620, her father fell ill: the Governors gave 10s "to Margaret Lond in her father's sickness"; but the extra money did little good as shortly afterwards the Governors paid for his shroud, so he could be buried decently. Margaret was given money the following year, but it must have been decided that she was going to be a drain on the funds and it would be a good idea to move her to another place: in 1623, 3s 8d was given "to Margarett Lond to be rid of her". From that time she disappeared from the Wantage records, whether she moved somewhere locally or got work in London, we shall never know.

Helping the Poor in Sickness

As illustrated in the cases of Magdalen and Margaret, sickness or disability caused the need for financial assistance, from the very early days of the charity to the beginning of the nineteenth century. The first person helped in this way was Mother Hill, who was given two shillings "in her great sickness" in 1603; while the last person mentioned in the accounts was William Lovesey who was given £3 in 1814 "on account of his long illness". The poor would be unlikely to have savings to carry them over a period when they were not able to earn an income, so each year men sick and unable to work were listed as having had money given to them by the Governors. It was not only the man of a family, or a widow on her own, who qualified for help, though; a wife who was ill or incapacitated for any reason could not contribute in any way to the family finances, and a sick child, or indeed any sick family member, might need medicine which would cost money. So women and children were as likely to receive help from the Governors when they were ill, as working men. To illustrate this, in 1642, William Head was given 12d because he was sick, Widow Stalworth got 6d as did Thomas Thatcher's wife, and Goodwife Rogers got 12d for her sick child. Small amounts of money would be given for other reasons besides ill health: the blind and the lame, or those who had injured themselves also needed assistance, and got it. John Glover was given 2s 6d in 1644 because of his lameness; Goody Andrewes, who was almost blind, received 6d in 1704: and William Crane hurt his hand and was not able to work in 1721 so was given 5s.

Some years it appeared that large numbers of the Wantage inhabitants were ill, but this may have been due to the person recording the accounts giving more details of the reasons for giving help to the poor. Assuming that this was not entirely the case, it seemed that the end of the 1600s and the beginning of the 1700s saw most illness in the town, with relief being given by the Governors. Some of the years with an apparently high incidence of illness had smallpox epidemics, which could have accounted for many of the sick. In 1687, among other recipients, John Keepe's wife was given a shilling "when her children were downe with the small pox"; the Symond family were "visited with the small pox" and were helped out with £2. The following year, there were twenty one positive records of smallpox, with two men, two women, fifteen children and two families with the disease. There was

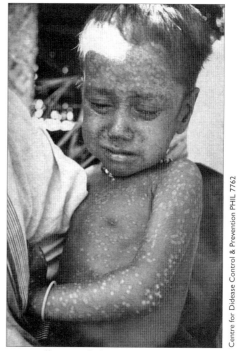

Centre for Didease Control & Prevention PHIL 7762

Smallpox was disfiguring and was often fatal

then no mention of smallpox until 1698, when the sick numbers rose and seventeen individuals or families were ill with smallpox. Small outbreaks occurred in 1702 and 1703, with a more serious occurrence in 1704 when there were ten families with members ill with smallpox. From then on there were a few mentions of the disease but the Governors' accounts did not indicate any more epidemics in Wantage. As these instances only relate to the poor who were being given relief, there were likely to have been many more cases of smallpox among the other inhabitants, and at the time of the larger outbreaks, there were probably a great number of people suffering at the time. The smallpox outbreak of 1698 coincided with a higher than average number of burials in the town. On two other occasions, a large number of burials occurred in years when the Governors were giving relief to many sick people, but apart from these three years, there did not seem to be a correlation between the number of sick poor given assistance and the burial numbers in Wantage.

In 1780, there was the first mention of people having their children inoculated to prevent them getting smallpox. In March of that year, William Savory was lent 15s by the Governors to pay for inoculating his five children, so each treatment must have cost 3s. In June of the same year, Thomas Sly was given 21s for inoculation, so probably seven children in his family; followed by the Governors giving two other families the money to pay for inoculation. No other payments were made for this by the Governors but there could have been families who paid their own bills to have it done, and any children who had had smallpox would be naturally immune and would not need inoculation. The three year old daughter of Lady Mary Wortley Montague was the first person to be professionally inoculated in England, in 1721, as her mother had seen it carried out in the Ottoman Empire. Inoculation involved making a small cut in the arm and introducing the matter from a smallpox pustule into the cut. It was regarded as safer to inoculate children than adults. Parson Woodward of East Hendred had his children inoculated in 1755. His wife and servants were sent from home for six weeks to prevent them catching the disease and his two children only had the smallpox slightly after the inoculation. By the early nineteenth century, vaccination was available using the matter from cowpox instead of from smallpox pustules, which was safer. There was no indication that the Governors paid for any vaccinations, which were however free to paupers after the formation of the Wantage Union in 1835.

Apart from smallpox, there is little indication as to what diseases may have caused epidemics in Wantage, when many were ill. Typhoid and typhus would be likely to occur at times due to poor sanitation, polluted water supplies and overcrowding in the houses: typhoid is caused by drinking unclean water and typhus is carried by lice. Typhus may have been the cause of illness when the Governors recorded in 1798 that there had been a malignant fever in the town, when they provided the sick people suffering from it with porter and wine costing the rather large sum of £10 12s 1¾d It must have been imperative to prevent someone entering Wantage who was believed to be carrying an infectious disease. In 1637, the Governors paid £2 10s 0d to Nicholas Baron who had brought a law suit "in defence of the Towne" against a man called Carter to prevent his entering Wantage "in the sicknes tyme". Carter was either suffering himself from something like the plague or had come from a place where it was raging, and the Wantage inhabitants did not wish to catch whatever he might have brought with him. Some of the sick children recorded over the years were likely to have illnesses such as measles, whooping cough or scarlet fever, which could have caused epidemics amongst the young of the town, but in only one case was this given, when we are told that in 1710 Henry Perry's blind daughter had the measles. An outbreak of some childhood illness may have caused the deaths of several children in the early part of 1722, when Peter Martin made small coffins for Robert Titcombe's child, Richardson's child and Skinner's child: it is possible to tell that the children were small as the cost of these little coffins was between a third and a half of adult ones. Richardson's wife was also given a contribution towards burying her child. Again, we only see the tip of the iceberg in the Governors' records; many other children in Wantage could have died at the time, but were not poor enough to receive help from the Town Lands.

There are a few other instances where the Governors recorded what a person was suffering from. We are told that John Umpton had cancer in 1712 and was bedridden: he was given total relief of six shillings over five different occasions during the year. At that point he was probably rather ill as he did not survive long into the following year, when the Governors paid four shillings to bury him, and his widow was given a shilling. Earlier, George Cottrill had also had cancer as 2s 6d was paid out in 1686 "for the cure of George Cottrill's cancer". Widow Holloway suffered from fits so was probably an epileptic. Her husband Richard had done odd jobs for the Governors but the Holloways sometimes needed the occasional shilling to help them make ends meet, particularly when the family had smallpox in 1704. By 1710, Richard collected a quarterly pension of 2s 6d but he died around 1711, and it was soon after the time of his death that the Governors began recording fairly regular fits which necessitated widow Holloway (or Goody Holloway as they sometimes called her) being given relief. By 1713, she was also paid a quarterly pension of 2s 6d, but she cannot have had enough income even with this help as that year she had extra money given to her on eleven occasions, usually a shilling but on two occasions more than that, three of the times recorded that she was ill and four of the times mentioned her having fits. Her daughter was also given help, including a pair of shoes. The mother lived until December 1719, when Peter Martin was paid six shillings for making her coffin. The following April, her daughter left Wantage and went to London, perhaps to work there as a servant.

At other times, it is possible to guess what complaint a person might have been suffering from. When in 1687, Thomas Grundy was "taken speechless" and later was referred to as "being helpless", it rather sounds as though he had had a stroke. Over the following years he was paid regular amounts of a shilling, until in 1693 the entry in the accounts showed "Thomas Grundy given a shroud — 3s 9d" and widow Grundy was paid a shilling. He had survived his stroke, if that was what it was, for around six years. Old Dowley had also probably had a stroke when in 1712, "being speechlesse" he was given a shilling. In 1732, Peter Marlin's wife was paid 2s for curing a boy of the itch and a few years later Mary Mackrell was also

cured of the same complaint. The itch was the name used for scabies, caused by a mite burrowing under the skin, and was very contagious. When men were given a truss, it was most likely that they were suffering from a hernia, probably caused by heavy lifting in their employment. The Governors ordered one to be given to John Richardson's son in 1770, costing 10s 6d.

Then as now, accidents happened to both adults and children. Widow Patient's son broke his arm, for which he received 2s 6d, while Widow Farmer's girl broke her rib and got 1s. Men had accidents at work and needed help until they had recovered and could return to work: Thomas King was hurt by a cart in 1682, Old Parsons was gored by a bull in 1687, and Benjamin Kent was injured by a piece of timber falling on him in 1738. Men working away, whose parish of settlement was Wantage, could expect assistance if they had an accident where they were working. In 1782, Joseph Green was working at Deptford in Kent and broke his leg. He wrote (or someone wrote on his behalf) to the Governors and he was sent £2 2s 0d to support him while he was unable to work. It was not clear why he asked for help from the Governors rather than Wantage parish, as it would normally be the poor rates of the parish that would be used in a case like that.

Medical practitioners were working in Wantage from the time when the Governors' records began. In 1615 Oliver Stevenson, a Surgeon, was awarded 26s: the reason is not given but it would have been for treating the poor in some way at the request of the Governors. The entry in the accounts in 1633, "For curing of Arnold's leg — £3" was most likely being paid to another surgeon, but he was not named. It might have been Mr Anns, who was paid 20s three years later "for phisick and surgerie hee applied to Nicholas Angier and his wief". Dr Elias Clarke, who amputated Elianor Alder's "infirm hand or arm" in 1669 was one of the Governors, who treated several poor patients over the years at the expense of the Town Lands. He was paid for Elianor's amputation, but when he claimed 50s extra for the 'physick' he gave her, the Governors decided that they would only agree to pay part of this, the rest would have to be paid by the overseers of the poor of Wantage. In 1696, it was minuted at a Governors' meeting that they would pay him £3 "towards his paines and charges in the cureing of Thomas Stronge, John Keepe and Thomas James". The doctors' bills were generally much larger than the amounts paid out in relief to the poor, but then they were professional men, even if they did not have modern expertise. One shilling was the most common amount given to a pauper for relief: Doctor Wenthill received 5s for treating Joane Talbott in 1707 when she had had an accident, £1 10s 0d was the cost of curing Robert Bradshawe's child's eye, and in 1712 Mr Lockton was ordered to be paid 10s for curing Goodman Perry's finger. As well as individual people having their ailments attended to, some of the doctors were available for the poor throughout the year, always needing permission from the Governors on an individual basis of course. The bills for medicines, or 'physick', for the poor the three consecutive years of 1735, 1736 and 1737 was £2 1s 9d, 13s 7d and £3 9s 11d; while in 1738, Mr Seymour was paid £5 for attending the sick poor for a year; and in 1740 Mr Cooper received £8 for medicine and surgery. Several people were treated for broken arms and legs over the years, one assumes this treatment was carried out by one of the medical practitioners, although when Old Parsons was given 2s 6d in 1687 "to pay the bone setter" one does wonder if this was a surgeon or just a person in the town who put bones back in place when poor people had accidents. We have seen above that Dr Clarke amputated a hand or arm, which of course would have had to be done without anaesthetic, other than alcohol to make the patient less aware of the pain. Another amputation was carried out in 1698, which might also have been done by Dr Clarke. This was the amputation of John Durnam's leg, for which John was given sixpence worth of "tape when his leg was cutt off", which was probably to bandage up the stump. He may have been given alcohol before the operation,

but he was definitely given it afterwards "to ease his wounds"; in fact he was given three quarts of brandy. That initial amount was not enough and he was given more brandy on five other occasions, which along with the first amount totalled nine quarts, or eighteen pints, in all. The poor man must have been suffering badly.

In Wantage, as in most places in the 1600s and 1700s, there would have been women who, although not medically trained, were skilled in aspects of healing, but they do not appear in the Governors' accounts. There were, though, examples of women who would nurse their neighbours when necessary. An example of neighbourliness can be demonstrated by the care given by three women when Widow Sadler lay dying in November 1643: Widow Slatter, Mary Gryffin and Goodwyfe Webb sat with the sick woman, or 'watched' her, no doubt easing her sufferings if they could; and when she had finally passed away, they laid out her corpse and wrapped her in her shroud, being paid 18d by the Governors for their care. A similar case occurred in 1689 when John Thorne died, although the Governors used rather unfortunate wording, paying for "stretching him out" as well as for his shroud and for burying him. When Len Marshall was ill, with no family to look after him, Thomas Smith's wife took care of him. There were many cases like this, some could have been friends, but all would have known one another. Goody Humphreys was given money by the Governors in 1695 "for tending Goody Roe in sicknesse"; in 1712, Widow Burchall was similarly rewarded "for looking after the Widdow Butler when ill"; and when Constance Lay was poorly in 1738, Martha Staite was rewarded for caring for her. Occasionally members of the family were given a small payment for nursing a sick person. Caring for a relative probably depended on whether or not there was family able to do this, with room in their homes to accommodate the sick or needy relative. Johane Harwood was paid 6s a year when she looked after her sister in the 1620s, and Goody Stroud was given 2s in 1738 for looking after her brother, Clement, as at the time he was helpless. People were most likely to need help from family or neighbours when they were ill, and the Governors were willing to pay for this care if necessary. Where a nurse was mentioned, the person referred to was probably a woman who earned her living by nursing the sick. In 1689, a nurse was paid to tend Thomas Butcher's wife for three weeks at 5s a week, and in 1731 a nurse was paid 10s for looking after Whithorne when he had smallpox.

Childbirth was one occasion when, unless there were complications, the woman would usually be attended by female family members or a local woman with a reputation for acting as midwife in such situations. There were no payments made to such women by the Governors, but as occasionally the poor would be given some relief money in this situation, it would be possible for them to give some of this to the midwife who had helped. In 1691, William Patient's wife was given 2s 6d "at her lyeinge in" and Mary Bell received 5s. William Patient's wife seemed to produce children fairly regularly, as following the payment just mentioned in 1691, another was made in 1693 and a third one in 1696. The third time she only got 1s but was given a sheet as well. Money was not always given: this was the case in 1712 when Richard Darling's wife was "lying in with two children", so presumably she had had twins; she was given a waistcoat (a jacket).

On at least one occasion, the successive entries in the accounts tell the story of the family. In 1687 John Symond's wife was given £1 to pay the man midwife, so she must have had more than usual difficulties during the birth of her child as the 'man midwife' would have been one of the Wantage medical men. In later years a man midwife might have used forceps but it was too early for this procedure when John Symond's wife had her baby. The next entry recorded in the accounts was a payment to John Symond for a shroud for his wife, while Richard Robbins made a coffin for her, which indicated she died soon after the birth. But then things got worse; a tiny coffin and shroud were supplied for

John Symond's child, so the baby had died too, with later in the year another entry for a shroud for Symond's girl and a shroud for John Symond himself. The family were rapidly following one another to the grave. Sadly there must have been more children, because soon after the father died, clothing was made "for John Symond's children". Over the following years, clothing and shoes were given to the Symond children and it appeared that there were two boys and one girl who remained as orphans. The children must have been boarded out with families in Wantage, although it appeared that they were not kept together and were also moved around, as over one year, the Governors' accounts mention one of the boys living with Robert Keepe, and then later refer to "Symons boy that is at Arnolds" and at the same time "Symons boy that is at Durnams", as well as "Symons wench" being given assistance. One of the boys may have been apprenticed in 1692, as that year the Governors apprenticed five poor children, and after that only one boy of Symonds is mentioned when clothes are given to him. The last mention of a boy is in 1693 and of the girl in 1694. They had perhaps by that time grown old enough to go into service, or to earn their livings in other ways.

As we have seen, the surgeons living in Wantage carried out small operations, doing amputations and setting broken bones. Perhaps surprisingly at such early dates, people also went to hospital, although there was no hospital in Wantage until the late nineteenth century, apart from the infirmary at the workhouse a little before that. Even as early as 1616, there was a reference to Edward Downe being given four shillings by the Governors to go to hospital in London, and Margaret Lond who was given five shillings "to go to the Ospitall" has previously been mentioned. In both cases, no explanation was given as to why these people needed to go to hospital. Later that century, in 1689, Thomas Butcher was given ten shillings "when his wife was at Reading under Cure". Unfortunately the Governors did not say where she went in Reading and what she was being cured of. In 1835, Robert Burchall's

The Radcliffe Infirmary 1863/5

boy went to a London hospital, the reason given was that he was to be "cutt for the Stone", probably kidney stones, which could be a very painful condition. For this visit, the Governors paid out £3 10s 0d: the cost of the operation as well as the cost of the journey and living costs in London, which would have been a big expense for an ordinary family from Wantage. Whether the amount given by the Governors covered all the costs or only part of them it is impossible to tell. Another hospital to which patients from Wantage were occasionally sent was Bath; in 1616 John Humfry was given £1 "to go to the Bathe". James Stowell went to Bath hospital in 1774, John Moulden in 1776 and John Baggs in 1782. Each of these last three men was given 'caution money' of £3; quite what that was for was not explained but as some or all of this money was returned when the man returned from Bath, it could have been given him as money to fall back on in an emergency. Why these men went to Bath is not explained, most likely they suffered from ailments which it was thought would be cured by taking the waters there.

When the last three men went to Bath hospital, the Radcliffe Infirmary had not long been open in Oxford. It was operational by November 1770, and in December 1770 the Governors paid their first subscription to the infirmary, which enabled them to send any poor from Wantage for operations or treatment at the hospital. Subscriptions were also made to the Royal Berkshire Hospital from 1877: this hospital in Reading had opened in 1839 and had been extended in the 1860s. Both these hospitals were for the sick poor. The Radcliffe had rules which stated that patients must behave with decorum, attend chapel and refrain from swearing or playing cards; patients were also expected to help with the nursing, the cleaning and the laundry. One assumes it was the female patients who had to help in this way, and that they were recovering at the time and no longer suffering from the complaint for which they had been admitted in the first place. Two people were sent to Oxford in 1778, Rebecca Burchall and John Green's son were both given clothing when they went, no doubt in order to make them presentable as inhabitants of Wantage. Visits to hospital for medical treatment were not always successful: in 1786, the Widow Rud was allowed £1 by the Governors so she could bury her husband at the infirmary; in those days this was probably a fairly common result of a visit to the Radcliffe, or indeed any hospital.

The Governors were often called upon to provide what was necessary for a pauper's funeral. Several carpenters over the years made coffins, prices varying according to size: in the late 17th century the adult ones were around 6s: this amount was spent on a coffin for Goody Pethers in 1688, while when John Symond's child died the previous year, the coffin only cost 2s 4d. Shrouds were provided as well as coffins: in 1602, four shillings was paid "for a shrowde and money to bury Warnar into the earth"; a shroud for a boy in 1688 cost ten pence; while George Cottrill, mentioned above as having cancer, was given a shroud which cost 2s 6d when he died in 1687, as well as a coffin costing 7s and 1s 6d towards burying him. In the earlier years, shrouds were given by the Governors more often than coffins and possibly some of the poor were not buried in a coffin. When Goody Fynche died in 1698, she was given "a shroud of cotton having no coffin". Cotton at that time was a cheap woollen cloth, not cotton as we know it today. By the early 1700s coffins were usually given by the Governors when a pauper died, sometimes being distributed in quite large numbers over a year: ten were supplied to paupers who had died in 1728, eight the following year and ten again the year after that. In 1714, the Governors "gave old Phillips a large Shroude": perhaps even then there were a few obese people in Wantage. Legislation in 1678 stipulated that, in order to support the wool trade, corpses should be buried in woollen material, not linen or hemp, with a fine of £5 for not using wool. One assumes that the Governors made sure that the shrouds they supplied kept within this new law, as for example in 1704, when they paid for a coffin and "wool to make a shroud" for Henry George. After 1735, wool was mentioned in a way that suggested it was used as loose wool rather than

by making a shroud from the wool. So in 1736, The Governors "payd for wool instead of shrowds for three persons", and in 1740 they supplied "ten coffins and wool" at a cost of £2 16s 8d. From that time on, shrouds did not seem to be used any longer when burying bodies, or at least the Governors did not supply them.

Food Given to the Poor

Bread was the staple diet of most people in England, certainly over the time the Governors of the Wantage Town Lands were assisting the poor, from Elizabethan times through into the early twentieth century. As seen earlier in Chapter 1, two of the benefactors of the charity, Robert Payne and Thomas Willis, who left legacies to the Town Lands, had stipulated that part of the income from their gifts was to be used to provide the poor with bread. For many years, it appeared that £5 4s 0d was spent each year on Willis's bread and £4 6d 8d on Payne's. The bread seemed to be in two sizes as, by 1745, the Governors began to refer to it as 'penny loaves' and 'threepenny loaves'. In 1742 the Governors spent £4 6s 8d on "one years twenty penny loaves", so it appeared that Payne's legacy provided the penny loaves, with twenty being given out each week. If Payne's bread was the penny loaves, then Willis's money was being used for the threepenny bread and would have provided eight threepenny loaves a week. The bakers who provided the bread were often named; in 1760 the accounts had the following entries:

"Paid John Hulcup for baking the penny bread from Apr. 13th to Oct. 5 inclusive (26 weeks) £2 3s 4d
Paid Mr Winterborn for the threepenny bread from Oct.10th 1759 to Oct.10th 1760 (52 weeks) £5 4s 0d"

As there were the same number of loaves each week, one wonders how it was decided who got them. The original bequests had asked for the bread to be distributed to the poor in the church every Sunday after the service, so it was obviously given to people who had attended church; probably a great encouragement to the poor who might have stayed away. But if there were a fixed number of loaves to give out and more poor people than that attended church, who decided on the lucky recipients? The Charity Commissioners were told in a report made in 1837 that "the bread is given away from a list of the most deserving objects in the town, made out by the Governors". Rather a strange way to describe people, but it answers the question as to who chose them.

The fact that some paupers probably only went to church to receive handouts is shown by a comment in the vicar's diary in 1853. The overseers of the poor of Wantage would be giving help to the poor in this instance, not the Governors. The vicar was commenting about a man who at the time was in the workhouse. He wrote that "When he is out of the house, he comes to church on Sundays but never in the week except when soup, meat or bread are given away." At least this man went to church once a week without an ulterior motive, unless of course he was on the Sunday bread list.

The same amounts of money each year had been spent on the bread for nearly eighty years through the 1700s, but there must have been extra income from Willis's lands by the end of the century, for in 1794 the Governors decided that the rent on the lands Willis had bequeathed would provide four extra threepenny loaves each week. They would be "in addition to those that are distributed every Lords Day" and would be given to "four poor persons who constantly attend Divine Service". And then in 1802, some of the common field lands in East Challow and Letcombe Regis, where Willis's lands were situated, were enclosed and the rent from his estate was considerably increased by this move. A decision was made by the Governors that they could now afford to provide more bread to the poor each week. There would be no penny loaves, only 26 threepenny and 12 six-penny ones. The annual bread bill, which had been under £10 since Thomas Willis made his bequest in 1714, now more than tripled to £32 10s 0d each year. This remained stable until the 1830s, when there was a gradual increase, with the annual amount spent on bread in 1836 being

£54 14s 1d and in 1840 being £74 16s 3d; seven bakers supplying the bread in 1840. By this time, the Poor Law Amendment Act of 1834 was operating, whereby able-bodied men and their families could not get relief on the parish without going into the workhouse just outside Wantage. Perhaps the Governors felt moved to give out more bread to enable the poor in Wantage to stay in their own homes when they were finding it difficult to keep their families on their wages. The bread up to this time had been referred to by the cost of a loaf, penny loaves etc, with no indication as to what was the weight of a penny loaf. When a report was made to the Charity Commissioners in 1837, it explained that at that time a four pound loaf, known as a 'quartern' loaf cost sixpence. At a meeting in 1846, it was decided that in future the bread given out at church on a Sunday should be in the form of quartern loaves, and that some scales and a 4lb weight would be bought and kept in the church to weigh the bread, in order to make sure the bakers were not giving short measure.

In 1851, the Governors agreed that although people living in the almshouses would continue to receive bread each week, no new poor recipients, who were not almspeople, would be put on the list, so gradually the numbers would decrease. Then in 1854, it was decided that instead of giving each of the occupants of the almshouses a weekly four shillings and loaf of bread, new almspeople would be paid entirely in money and would get 4s 6d. The existing almspeople would continue to be given money and bread. Ten years later, bread was still being distributed but the annual bill had decreased by about half. It was then agreed to give the non-almspeople, who were still getting bread each week, sixpence instead of a loaf. The last recorded payments for bread were in July 1866 when Mr Pinnell was paid for supplying seventeen loaves each week at 6½d each, and in January 1867 when J. Clarke was paid £13 4s 11d for a six month supply of 'weekly bread'. At the same time as this, the fifteen almspeople and two others were given 6d a week instead of the weekly loaf, in addition to their 4s weekly allowance.

Very occasionally there were other donations of food to the poor, besides the charity bread. For example in 1631 and 1632, two men were paid for fetching corn for the poor; and in 1805 seven sacks of potatoes were bought at six shillings per sack, which must surely have been for distribution to the poor. As we have seen in other chapters, when the Governors had men working for them, beer was sometimes given out as an extra to the wages. Men working at felling trees or putting up fences, fetching sand or mending the roads could be rewarded with an allowance of beer. The sick who were looked after by the parish were often given 'extras' of nourishing food or drink, which in some cases was porter or spirits, and it was possible that the Governors did the same when they were assisting sick paupers, although the only record of alcohol being bought was in 1816 when 11s was paid for two bottles of wine, and this might have been for something other than a poor person, as it was for a Mr Stroud, which would have been a rather polite way of describing a pauper.

Clothing Given to the Poor

One of the necessities of life is to have warm clothing and, at times, this was one of the main items given out by the Governors to the poor. Sometimes the entries in the Governors' books were rather vague: in 1616, Richard Vokins was given 20s "towards the appareling of his children" and in 1638, Mathew Winboult was paid 18s 2d for "the makinge of the poore folkes clothes" without any details. The accounts, however, often gave information as to what articles of clothing had been distributed and how much the individual items had cost. So in 1695, among various donations of lengths of cloth or garments for unspecified people, we learn of the particular items of clothing which were given to forty two people. Solomon Webb was given a coat which cost 12s 7d for the material plus 1s 6d for making it, Richard Dowley's girl had a petticoat (this was probably what we would call a skirt) which

cost 3s 9d, John Huck's shirt was 3s and Jone Keepe's gown was 8s 11d. Altogether that year, thirteen coats were given to the poor, along with twelve shirts, three pairs of breeches, a waistcoat (which would now be called a jacket), a suit, seven gowns, two aprons, three petticoats, two smock frocks, thirteen shifts, a pair of shoes and a handkerchief. We are even told what material some of the items were made of, with the two smock frocks being made of fustian (a coarse thick twilled linen cloth) and Jone Keepe's gown was made of lynsey (a cloth made of a mixture of linen and wool).

Various other types of cloth were listed, some which we no longer use; lockrome and dowlas, broad frize and kersey. Materials with the same names as ones known today, such as serge and canvas, could have been different then. In 1634 Goff's boy was given a length of canvas for a shirt: present day canvas would be much too stiff and uncomfortable for shirts, canvas in the 1600s was a coarse, poor quality, linen cloth. Often material was simply given as 'cloth' without specifying what sort of cloth, or 'lynnen cloth' and 'woollen', both of which could have been heavy duty or light weight. Where the accounts were given in minute detail, even buttons, thread, tape and binding were listed. From the mid 1700s, a material called 'foulweather' or 'fowlweather' cloth began to be given to the poor, which from its name must have been some sort of waterproofed material to keep the wearer dry in wet weather. This cloth was more expensive than some of the other materials of the time, costing 2s 8d a yard whereas kersey cost 1s 7d and serge cost 1s 2d a yard. A trade directory published in the early 1790s, gave the information that there was in Wantage a "manufactory of foul-weather cloth, superior to any in the kingdom, carried on by Messrs. Hazell and Goff". So this specialised foul-weather cloth was obviously a locally produced material. The first mention of it in the Governors' accounts was in 1740, when a foulweather coat was given to Gillin's boy, so by the time the trade directory reported that it was made in Wantage, it had been produced there for over fifty years. Other people were given this waterproof clothing besides the poor helped by the Governors. The vestry minutes for Wantage record in 1740 that the overseers of the poor for the town were to pay for a "great Foul Weather Coat" for Thomas Whiting "to protect him from the Inclemancy of the Weather". Thomas was the town bellman who rang the curfew bell each evening.

The clothing given could be items we know today, or ones worn in the past which are no longer part of our wardrobes and with names which mean little to modern people. Shoes and stockings, shirts, coats, gowns and breeches meant the same four hundred years ago as now, although the breeches and coats would have been of different styles to those worn today, and twenty first century women would feel restricted if they had to wear long gowns every day. However, we no longer wear 'a pair of boddyes' or a 'coyfe'. A pair of bodies was rather like a corset; sleeveless, low-cut, usually fastening at the back and stiffened with dried reeds or whalebone. It could sometimes be worn on the outside of other clothing and would then be woollen, lined with linen. A coif was a white head-covering to hide the hair. Butcher's daughter was given a pair of stays in 1760; an item not worn by women today but which would have been well known to our Victorian grandmothers. Men and boys are not seen in smock frocks for work these days but they were worn by farm labourers at the end of the nineteenth century as well as in the 1600s. In 1688, John Keepe's boy was given a frock and in 1700, Jonathan Hyne received a frock and a pair of breeches from the Governors. Breeches were usually made from cloth, but not always: in 1738, six pairs of leather breeches, costing 4s each, were bought and handed out; and in 1743, a pair of beaver breeches, costing 5s, were given to John Stevens' son; this material would probably be a felted mixture of wool, hair and fur from animals such as rabbits; thick and hard-wearing. Smocks worn by women in the early 1600s were later called shifts and were the under garments worn by women, while men wore shirts. Marlyn Sheppard was given two smocks in 1624, but

in 1695 Hugh Clement's girl was given two shifts and a petticoat when she went out to service. As will be seen later, children were often given clothing when they started work as servants or were apprenticed.

Through the years, the Governors' accounts tell us the names of some of the people in Wantage who had shops and businesses supplying the inhabitants, including the poor at the Governors' expense, with items of clothing or lengths of cloth. In 1769, four men, John Spicer, Robert Simpson, Mr Butler and Mr Eldridge had supplied linen at a total cost of £26 6s 5d; and in 1809, six men, Mr Graham, Mr Mattingly, Mr Thomas, Mr Aldworth, Mr Simpson and Mr Winkworth were paid a total of £99 9s 0d for a similar service. We also learn who were tailors, making coats and gowns for a living; which women did sewing to earn their keep; and who some of the shoemakers were. In the early 1600s, Mathew Winboult, who had a shop in the Chantry House, was a tailor making many of the clothes for the poor, and in 1718 John Lord, a tailor, was to be employed in making "the greatest part of the poor's clothes". Not as many women as men were paid for making clothing but there were several over the years: in 1716, Widow Burchall made seven small garments, and in 1760, Sarah Oakley was paid for making gowns for the poor. Shoemakers made regular appearances in the accounts: Thomas Chaplyn was given a pair of shoes in 1614, which had been made by Thomas Clement; Thomas Farmer was paid "for all shoes dilivered to the poore folkes" in 1637; and James Rogers was paid for making shoes for the poor in 1760.

In the early 1600s and again at intervals through the years, the Governors sometimes gave out material for lining coats or gowns, which would probably be similar to the use of lining today. For example in 1688, Widow Kimber's daughter was given "lyneinge to her coat", in 1701 the Governors paid for "trimming and lyneing for the poores cloathes", while in 1713 "some coll'd (coloured?) linen to line the children's gowns" was bought. However, in 1680, Hugh Snadham was paid for making various items of clothing, including "a pair of Lyneinges" for old Widow Pinnock, which does not sound like the modern understanding of the term 'lining'. This was the first mention of people being given pairs of linings as part of the Governors' clothing donations. In 1690, Symon's boy was given a "pair of stockins and lyneings", while in 1698 Umpton's boy was given a shift and a pair of linings. Pairs of linings were not a common item of clothing given by the Governors and apart from Widow Pinnock, all the recipients were men and boys. These were linings for breeches and could be removed and washed. Pairs of drawers (like underpants) were occasionally given out, only this was also not very common. Linings and drawers were probably the same thing. In 1680, cloth was bought to be used to make shirts and drawers; in 1696 Jonathan Hyne was given a pair of drawers; and in 1753, Evan Morgan was paid to make two pairs of flannel drawers for Lay's lame son. Men wore drawers in the seventeenth and eighteenth centuries as did French women but not women in England, they remained knickerless until the late eighteenth century. When Henry Knapp wrote the accounts in the late 1600s, he referred to giving 'changes' to men and women, boys and girls. Possibly these were changes of underclothes — shifts and shirts — as the first time someone was given a change was in 1682, before Henry Knapp was in office, when the rentgatherer recorded that someone was paid 1s for "making 2 chainges of her Linnen for a wench that lives at King's".

A variation in the number of items of clothing and cloth recorded each year could probably be due to the different men writing up the details. To begin with there was little mention of clothing, but it is possible that the sums of money given to named people was really given in cloth or clothing rather than cash. In 1624, when Edward Galland became rentgatherer instead of John Snodham, clothing suddenly became listed in great detail; but when the rentgatherer changed again six years later, the detail stopped until Thomas Aldworth took over that duty, in 1634, and records of the clothing was given in detail once more.

So we learn, in 1634, that Goff's boy was given one ell and a half of canvas for a shirt at 1s 2d per ell; he also got a hat costing 10d and a pair of stockings costing 1s 3d, both items provided by Robert Arrowsmith, who probably had a shop in Wantage. The same year, another lad, Stallworth's boy, was given a length of cloth, a length of canvas, two dozen buttons which cost 2d, two pairs of 'stockins' and a 'hatt'. In 1689, the accounts listed a hundred and four items of wearing apparel or lengths of cloth, with other entries paying tradesmen for making some of the clothing; in 1690 there were a hundred and forty five items; in 1691, with a different person acting as rentgatherer, only thirty one items were listed, although there was a large bill for "cloth delivered to several people". In 1693, one item gave "cloathes for the whole year as appears by a bill of particulars" which came to £12 19s 6d; most of the clothing had been included in one entry without giving names of people or what garments they were given.

It appeared that the Governors were worried that the bill for clothing was becoming too great, and were trying to reduce it, when they minuted in 1693 that in future no clothes or cloth were to be given to any poor people without the consent of at least two of the Governors. However, by working out the average spent on clothing and cloth during the three years before and after this decision was made, we can see that if the Governors' intention was to spend less on clothes, the plan had not succeeded. The average spent before the 1693 meeting was £22 a year and the average after was £26 10s 0d. The cost had risen slightly rather than becoming less. Another decision made at a meeting of the Governors, in 1698, again gives the impression that they were trying to prevent too many of the poor asking for material for clothing. It was agreed that any cloth given out to the poor would be of a dark blue colour, which was probably to make it obvious to other inhabitants of the town when a person was wearing charity clothes. The Governors also decided that this blue cloth would be bought from Wantage clothiers, as long as they could supply it as cheaply as material from elsewhere. That same year, nearly 77 yards of 'blew cloth' was handed out to the poor, along with 179 yards of 'blew kirsey'. Kersey was a coarse woollen cloth. Each year from then on, blue cloth and blue kersey were bought, initially the cloth being bought from John Baker in the town; the kersey from Mr Romans who was probably not a Wantage trader, as carriage was paid on top of the cost of this material. By 1800, the annual cost of cloth for the poor was £52; by 1809 nearly £100 a year and by 1812 over £110. The cost remained reasonably steady over the following years, and by 1840 was still around £100. In 1837, the Governors reported to the Charity Commissioners that the previous year they had given away lengths of dowlas (a coarse linen cloth) and coarse calico (a cotton cloth) to nearly three hundred families, which they considered to be about the average for a year; in all giving a total of 1,491 ells of cloth. The cloth was generally distributed at the beginning of summer, to provide the poor with clothing for the harvest. An ell was 45 inches, so the amount of cloth given away was 1,864 yards or 1,704 metres.

As was mentioned earlier, the Wantage overseers gave a waterproof coat to the town bellman. In a similar way in the late 1700s and early 1800s, the Governors gave great coats, not only to the poor but also to Wantage officials. In 1809 a great coat was given to William Owen, a poor Wantage labourer, but in 1813 great coats were given to Michael Crane and William Welladvice who were the town watchmen. William Owen got a second great coat in 1815, at the same time as William Savory, the Governors' servant. In 1830, the Governors decided that in future, only six coats would be given each year and these were to be given to individuals by the town Governors. The coats were paid for by the funds of the Town Lands, so the Governors must have chosen the recipients but not paid for the coats themselves. The six great coats were always given to six deserving married out-door labourers. And then in 1840, it was decided at the annual general meeting that this custom of the Governors choosing six recipients for great coats would be discontinued.

People needed clothing, which was why this was one of the Governors most regular ways of ensuring that the poor were looked after. But when a person was desperate for some ready cash, he might obtain it by pawning his belongings, even something as necessary as his clothing. Pawn shops must have existed as early as the 1600s, as in 1684 George Cottrill was given 2s 6d by the Governors to retrieve his clothes from pawn. Two years later George was being treated for cancer, so possibly at the time he pawned his clothes he was unable to work and was short of money. The fact that the Governors helped him to recover the clothing must mean that they considered him a worthy case and not just someone who was profligate and unreliable. He was getting a quarterly pension of 5s at the time, so was regularly being helped financially. Some years later, in 1771, Ned Stiles had put his coat into pawn and this time the Governors paid 9s to get it out but did not give it back to Ned; it was given to Charles Smith instead, another pauper. Each year tailors were paid for making coats for the poor, so most of the coats were new ones; but not all. In 1769, 8s 6d was paid for a second hand coat for Frank Martin, and in 1789, 5s was paid for Bartholomew Gregory's coat which was then given to William Champ. Bartholomew had just died, the parish burial register noting that he was a pauper and was very old. For several years previously he had been given a pension of £2 a year and the coat in question had been given to him by the Governors three years before he died.

By 1820, the Governors had a list of people, who each year were eligible for money and clothing when distributions were made. This list was called the Cloth List and was kept up to date and regularly revised at meetings. In 1849, it was decided that couples would have to have been married for more than two years before they would be given cloth. In 1866, Edward Ormond suggested that the cloth list be abolished, although by now the money paid out under this heading had decreased to between £30 and £40 a year from over £100 in the early 1800s. He was over-ruled but he suggested the same measure again the following year. In 1869, this was once more brought up at a meeting. Walter Barker proposed and Edward Ormond seconded the suggestion and this time it was agreed by the other Governors. That appeared to be the end of giving out cloth and clothing to the Wantage poor.

Helping Poor Children

The Governors assisted many children over the years, either by apprenticing them or by helping them financially when they started work. By serving as apprentices, youngsters were given a start in life which enabled them to support themselves in a trade when they became adults. They were then less likely to become paupers needing financial help from charities or their parishes. Sometimes a payment was made to the person taking the apprentice: John Webb was apprenticed in 1608 and the Governors paid 40s to his new master when this took place, although we do not know who the master was or what trade John was to be trained in. In 1704, the Governors paid 40s when Mathews' boy was apprenticed to William Patient, as well as paying an extra 5s for having his indentures drawn up. What trade the young Mathews was going to learn with William Patient was again not given, although as the Governors paid 10d for a leather apron for Mathews, and there was at the time a William Patient in the town who was a cooper, it is likely that young Mathews was going to be trained to make barrels.

In other cases, the father probably paid for a son or daughter to be apprenticed, but the Governors provided some of the clothes they would need or a small sum of money: in 1685 the rentgatherer paid 20s towards clothing Leonard Willis' girl when she was apprenticed; in 1695 Sexton's boy was given some serge material, shoes and money; while Thomas Butcher's boy was given a suit and a coat. When a young person became an apprentice, the relationship between this child and the master or mistress who was going to

take on the training would have been made legal with a set of indentures stating what was expected of both parties. In a few cases, the Governors paid for these legal documents to be drawn up and written out, as we have seen above when Mathews' boy was apprenticed. On another earlier occasion in 1641, Edward Sylvester, the schoolmaster of the English school at the time, wrote out the indentures for two lads, Oaklie's boy and Estmond's boy, charging the Governors 1s for each.

Many more boys than girls were apprenticed by the Governors, but some girls were given the opportunity to be trained in this way. In 1621, Green the weaver was paid to take on Walter's daughter as an apprentice and to teach her the necessary skills to become a weaver. In most cases where a boy or girl was apprenticed, there was no indication as to where the master lived; most likely they were Wantage tradesmen or craftsmen. Occasionally, however, the person taking on the apprentice lived further afield. Some were from one of the villages outside Wantage: John Tapping, in 1619, was placed with Mr Keate of Lockinge; in 1636, William Tayler of "Bushipston" (Bishopstone) was paid to take Thomas Estmond as his apprentice; in 1700, Widow Alder's son Richard became an apprentice at Hanney, and the same year Finche's boy was apprenticed to William Miles of Charlton. Others went further afield still: in 1621, John Burchall became the apprentice of John Hill of Donnington, near Newbury; a boy named Ryvers was placed with a tailor in Oxford in 1640; while over the years, boys were sent to Abingdon, Henley, and London to learn a trade. Apprenticeships were usually for seven years and the few references in the Town Lands' records to the length of an apprenticeship all gave a seven year period.

The Governors apprenticed the two sons of their bailiff in 1718. Peter Martin was given £4 towards apprenticing his sons John and Peter. There was no mention of providing them with clothes, so their father must have had to find the money for that. As well as being bailiff, Peter Martin was most probably a carpenter, but in 1726, eight years after the sons were apprenticed, a John Martin was paid by the Governors for doing work and providing wooden boards at the free school, so it is possible that this was Peter's son, having recently finished his apprenticeship, and that he had trained as a carpenter. Later in 1733, a John Marten was paid for making some coffins, which would again point to him being a carpenter like his father, if this was Peter's son. An interesting agreement, which the Governors set out in more detail than most others, related to a blind boy. In 1745, it was decided that if Richard Ebrall, Mr Ebrall's blind son, could raise some of the money needed to have him instructed by an organist, then the Governors would add £5 towards his fees, provided the majority of the Governors approved of the organist who was chosen by Richard and his father. There was no mention of him being apprenticed, just that he would be instructed to play on the organ. It was suggested that the organist could be "at Oxford or elsewhere" and that the Governors' money would be paid into the organist's hands and to "no one else nor for any other purpose". They were making sure their donation was only used for the organ lessons.

Instead of being apprenticed, some children were put out to service, which one assumes meant they were being taken on in households as servants of various kinds. In this instance, there were more girls than boys, although quite large numbers of both. Again some were likely to be working for local people but others were travelling further afield, mostly to London. Out of just over a hundred children placed in service in the seventeenth and eighteenth centuries, at least twenty two went to work in London; perhaps surprisingly more girls than boys. Some children going into service, who were possibly orphans, appeared to be clothed by the Governors even after they began working, probably while they were still minors, as was illustrated when in 1716 the Governors ordered that "Jones, a poor parish boy now in the service of Mr Charles Lush be allowed 10s for cloathes". More often, the youngsters were only given clothes by the Governors when they first left home to go into service. In 1769 we learn that

they gave John Richardson's son £1 "towards clothing him for service", and in 1688 Dowley's boy was given a shirt when he went into service. The girls too were given clothing; at the same time that Dowley's boy got his shirt, Widow Kimber's daughter was given two smocks (undergarments) when she went to London and Mary Farmer was given a smock and some linen, when "shee was placed forth". The travel expenses to go to London were often paid too: in 1640, Godfrey's daughter was placed in work in London, being given money, perhaps for clothes; and the carrier who took her on his cart from Wantage to London was given payment for the journey, and an extra amount to cover the cost of her food on the way. One wonders how jobs were arranged in London for the boys and girls going there. The general impression is that the children were going to prearranged employment, and it would have been most unlikely that youngsters would have been sent off to the capital in the hope of finding a situation once they got there. William Lay's daughters had already got work promised when they left Wantage in 1769, as the Governors gave money "to pay their carriage to London, they being hired there". One boy who went away from home, but not to London, was George Kent's son Joseph who, somewhat surprisingly for a boy living in Wantage, went to sea in 1750. He was given a pair of breeches, a pair of shoes and a pair of stockings.

The ages of the children being either apprenticed or found employment as servants were never given. Mostly these children were referred to by their father's name, or their mother's if the father was dead or not around. Some were mentioned by their own name, and using these children it was possible to find their baptism dates in the majority of instances, as they had been born and baptised in Wantage. From this it was possible to calculate an approximate age at which they had started apprenticeship or work. The ages ranged from a couple of thirteen year olds to a few eighteen or nineteen year olds. However, the majority were between these ages and the average age of the 28 children in the sample was approximately fifteen and a half for both those apprenticed and those going to service. There did not seem to be any very young children of seven or eight being apprenticed, which happened in the industrial north in the eighteenth and early nineteenth centuries, and which was more to cut the cost of poor relief than to give useful training to the pauper children. Although the Governors seemed to be treating the poor children of Wantage more ethically, the reason many of them were sent out of the parish to places like London could have been because there was more work on offer there, but equally might have been because in that way the children would gain settlement away from Wantage and would no longer be the responsibility of the rate payers of that parish if a need to claim support arose later in their lives. An Act of 1691 set out that a child gained legal settlement in another parish after 40 days apprenticeship there, and working for a year in another parish also gave legal settlement in that parish.

One small group of children given help by the Governors were orphans. In 1621, the Governors gave 18s "to three poor fatherless children and to her who kept them". In cases like this, a neighbour would often be paid for the children's upkeep if she would take them into her home and look after them. In this particular instance we are not told who the children were or who was looking after them, but at other times, this information is given. In 1634, "Stallworthe's wench" went to live with Goodwife Downe, who was given money to provide her with clothing, including underclothing, shoes and stockings. There was no mention that the girl was an orphan, and Mrs Downe was also paid £1 to take the girl on as an apprentice, so she might simply have been teaching her a trade. Five or six years later, the girl went to London to work and as she was referred to as "the wench latelie dwelt with goodwief Downe" rather than as Stallworthe's daughter, it was most likely she was an orphan. Mrs Downe seems to have taken on another child, a boy this time by the name of Painter. She was given sixpence to make him a shirt and he was provided with a hat,

and money for Mrs Downe to buy him a primer so he must have been of school age. The cobbler was paid for mending his shoes and Mrs Downe bought him stockings on two occasions. When, in 1641 and again in 1643, he was sick, Mrs Downe was given money for taking care of him. Symon's boy needed looking after in 1698, not because he was an orphan, but because his father had run away and left him: he had been taken in by Goody Smyth who was given 2s towards his keep.

Another small group, usually mentioned separately, are the illegitimate children. A single mother trying to support a child very often had difficulty managing, with no man of the house earning. Not many of these children were helped by the Governors, as the town's overseers of the poor would be mainly responsible. Perhaps the Governors stepped in where a previously respectable woman needed extra help. In 1683, Mrs Jackson was paid 2s 6d for taking "One that has a bastard" into her house and giving her and the child lodging there. Various items of clothing were provided for children born out of wedlock over the years. When an unmarried woman found herself pregnant she was supposed to inform the local JP and name the father so he could be made to provide for the child. At a vestry meeting in Wantage church in 1741, the overseers of the poor were ordered to take Faggott Giles's daughter who was "now with child" before a Justice of the Peace to find out from her who had fathered the child. If the father had not been named before the birth, the midwife at the birth would press the woman to reveal his name.

In 1740, a shilling was given by the Governors to William Harding's bastard child. So in this case the supposed father was known. The parish registers enable us to find out the story of the people involved in this case. William 'Arding' was born in Wantage in 1693 and two and a half years later, a girl named Jane Spoaks was also born in the town. So the two would have grown up knowing one another. Jane married Thomas Toby in 1720 and they had four children, but when the youngest was a year old, in 1732, Thomas died, leaving

Jane with this little one and three other children aged ten, seven and four. Soon afterwards 'Widow Tooby' was given 5s by the Governors. Life must have been a struggle for her, but around December 1736, possibly as Christmas was celebrated, Jane, now aged forty, met up with her lifelong acquaintance, William Harding. Unfortunately, the friendship became a little too close and the following September a baby boy, Richard, was born to Jane. She had been a widow for nearly five years, so no-one was going to be convinced the baby was her husband's. The entry of the baby's baptism, two days after his birth, is as follows: "Richard Toby, son of Jane, a vile whore". The good church people of the town did not approve. The Governors, however, felt moved to help Jane and several small payments were made towards the support of the baby. These are sometimes recorded in the accounts, mentioning Jane by name; "gave to Jane Tooby for Harding's Bastard Child 2s 6d", and sometimes just referring to the baby by the father's name, "William Harding's bastard child 1s". Almost all the payments were made in one year, 1740-41, when Jane was given money on sixteen occasions, being a total of 19s. Possibly baby Richard had been supported by his father for the first few years of his life but for some reason William Harding had stopped paying: he may have moved away from Wantage. However, there was a further twist to the tale. In 1742, Jane Toby and her two youngest legitimate children, Jane and Jonathan, now aged 11 and 14, were moved by the overseers of Wantage to Daventry. The most likely explanation was that this was where her former husband, Thomas

Toby, came from originally. Daventry would be his place of settlement — the place where he belonged — and on marriage Jane would have taken on his place of settlement, as would their children. The Wantage overseers, not wanting to support the family, simply moved them from Wantage to Daventry, where legally they were entitled to poor relief. A rather sad little story, only too frequent in those days. Jane and her two children were moved miles away from Wantage where they had lived all their lives, to a place where they knew no-one, while five year old Richard had to stay behind in Wantage, as bastard children took the parish where they had been born as their place of settlement. It is not possible to know whether he ever saw his mother again before he died in 1748, soon after his eleventh birthday.

By the mid nineteenth century, no names of people receiving help in any way were recorded and it appeared that the day by day donations to the poor as they needed help were a thing of the past. Apart from the weekly payment to the inhabitants of the almshouses, the only assistance seemed to be that given under the headings of 'cloth bills' and 'bread bills', both of which had ended by 1870. From 1834, poor law unions had been set up to deal with giving assistance to paupers under national regulations supervised from London, and as able-bodied paupers were not supposed to receive relief of any sort unless they went into the workhouse, it was perhaps more difficult for the Governors to justify giving help in the community, except to elderly people in their almshouses.

6
Property Belonging to the Wantage Town Lands

In late Elizabethan times, when the Wantage Town Lands charity was set up on a proper legal footing, the Trust already held land and houses in several places in the Wantage area, as well as in Wantage itself. As we have seen in Chapter 1, other land and houses were acquired over the years that followed, having been donated by various benefactors or bought with money left to the Trust. There are also examples of the profits of the Town Lands being used to buy properties: land in Kitchwell in Wantage (to the south of Portway, near the present Sports Centre and by the footpath to Letcombe Regis), which had belonged to Mr Robert Pinnock, a Governor who had recently died, was bought by the Governors in 1751; in 1771, the Governors paid £32 10s 0d for a house in Grove Street which had belonged to Nicholas Clement, which they then repaired and let for £2 a year; and in 1798 Thomas Beck's house, also in Grove Street, was bought for £60.

All the properties were let to tenants and it was these rents which provided the main income of the Trust and allowed it to fulfil its charitable purposes. There were two types of leases agreed with people renting houses or land from the Governors. One was a lease for a fixed number of years, most commonly for 7, 14 or 21 years, although in the first half of the eighteenth century it was not unusual for leases to be made out for 10, 11 or 12 years. The other type of lease was a lease for lives, which usually named three people and continued as long as the people named were alive. A lease of this type was agreed, in 1840, between the Governors and Samuel Plumbe of Wantage, a clothier, or maker of cloth. The lease was for three cottages in Mill Street, near the Brook, and was for 99 years or three lives, the lives being for Samuel Plumbe himself, aged 75, his daughter Martha aged 29 and his grandson Samuel aged 14. It was possible to change the lives in the lease: when William Talbott originally took out a lease on the house called Silverlocks, he had incorporated the names of two of his sons as lives in the lease. In 1660, he appeared to have remarried and he exchanged the names of his sons, Edward and Alban Talbott for the names of his wife Katherine and her daughter Martha Cottrill, as well as John Keepe who did not seem to be related to him. He was able to do this but had to pay a fine of £10 to the Governors for the alteration to the lease. Fines were the usual payment made on top of the rent when an alteration was made to a lease, or a new lease was taken out. When Samuel Plumbe renewed his lease in the cottages in Mill Street, above, he had to pay a fine of £45, and when Alexander Frogley died in 1713, while renting the cottage at the top of Grove Street, Samuel Stevens paid a fine of £3 to take out a new lease for it.

In 1795, the Governors decided that in future no leases for lives were to be taken out, and two years later they decided that the length of future leases would only be seven years. However, neither of these decisions was kept to, with leases continuing to be granted for lives or for 14 or 21 years; until in 1853 when Mr Morland, the tenant at the King Alfred's Head, and Mr Savory, the tenant at the Shears, both wanted to insert fresh lives into their leases, it was unanimously agreed at the Governors' meeting where this was discussed, that they would grant no more leases upon lives. The decision was obviously kept regarding the Shears lease and no new lives were allowed to be added, although the lease ran until the last person named in the old lease died in 1881. When that happened, the lease passed back into the Governors' hands and the Shears was advertised to let on a yearly basis, which meant an increased yearly rent from £1 1s 0d to £35, a much better deal for the Governors.

Each lease set out details of the land or cottage being rented. In 1665, Henry Aldworth was granted a lease for land in Grove; as well as the tenancy of a small enclosed meadow and 26 acres of arable land, his lease granted him use of the common pasture land in Grove "according to the customs there", where he was allowed to graze six horses, ten rotherbeasts (horned cattle) and eight score sheep (a score is twenty), so this must have been a large area. Many leases had covenants written into them which set out what a tenant could and could not do. Mostly these covenants stipulated that the tenants were not to plough up meadow land. So in 1756, when John Symonds was offered the lease on two acres of meadow in Grove, he was instructed "not to plow or convert the same". In 1797, the Governors minuted that in future, tenants would be fined £20 an acre if they ploughed up land, quite a large sum of money. Although most tenants were instructed not to plough up land, there were instances of permission given to do just this. In 1728, when Thomas Alder took out a lease on some land in East Challow, he was "to have liberty to plough a Close called Coopers Close conteyning about one acre" during the first seven years of the lease and then he was to lay it down with grass seed, so was putting it back as it was when he took it over. Robert Wilkins who also rented land in East Challow was given permission, in 1720, to plough up a close there for five years as long as he paid a fine of fifty shillings. Stephen Barr renewed his lease, in 1732, for the land he was already farming and a clause was put into the new lease that he could plough three and a half acres of Wick Green at Grove but the other part of the land he rented at Wick Green was to be laid down to hay, grass and hop clover.

Other instructions were put in leases: Edward Restall's new lease for twelve years, granted in 1733, had a covenant that in the last year of this time he would grow beans on a third of this land and would "howe the same twice in a husbandly manner". Several tenants were required to plant beans at the end of their tenancy, possibly because beans fix nitrogen in the soil, and this would mean the land was left in good condition. The reason may not have been understood at the time, but it had been known for many years that beans and other pulses improved the fertility. Perhaps for similar reasons, John Price, who rented land in the Ham in Wantage in 1751, was not to plant the land with oats the last year of his tenancy. In 1882, John Castle agreed to feed and mow the meadow land in Barwell Lane, in Grove, on alternate years; so he too was expected to keep the land in good condition. The Governors kept a close watch on how well the land was being cared for and fertility was an important issue. John Boote was allowed a rebate of half a year's rent in 1762 because he put pigeon dung on his land for the benefit of the next tenant. And in 1854, Mr Lay was told that all the manure produced on his farm must be spread on his land. The general expectation was that a tenant would leave the land and any other premises in a state of good repair at the expiry of the lease.

During the mid 1700s, several of the new tenants were told not to 'cross plant' their arable land. I could not find any reference to cross planting, but cross ploughing took place when the land was ploughed up and down in one direction and then again at right angles. So cross planting probably was similar, where the seed was drilled in rows in one direction and then this was repeated at right angles. A seed drill had been invented earlier that century by Jethro Tull, a Berkshire gentleman, and drilling the seed in rows in the fields gradually replaced the old method of scattering the seed by hand by a man walking up and down the field with a bag of seed. Perhaps, crossplanting was carried out by farmers trying to increase the yield from a piece of land, and it was felt this method could lead to over production and take too much goodness out of the soil in one harvest. Even into the twentieth century, clauses could be put into a lease to ensure that the land was cultivated correctly and kept in good heart. In 1919, John Simmons' executors, who after Simmons died had taken over the farming of the land he had leased on Manor Road in Wantage, attended a meeting of the Governors to discuss the state of this land. They were asked to give the Governors a report on their crop rotation for the previous seven years and it was then decided to draw up a new lease, with a clause setting out in detail how the land was to be cultivated, making sure that proper manuring of the land was carried out.

Rents were mostly due at Michaelmas (29th September) and Lady Day (25th March) and it is possible that there were designated times when the rents were to be paid, with tenants expected to come into Wantage to pay them, rather than the rentgatherer touring the countryside to collect them. In 1665, the rent of a property at Grove was to be paid on Lady Day and Michaelmas Day "at the Schoolhouse porch in Wantage Churchyard", so the school porch was possibly where all rents were paid at that time. This porch had had work done on it in 1634 when Robert Barber was paid for "pitching of the Scoolhowse porche and finding stuffe to doe it". There was no other record of where rents were to be paid until 1782, when it was ordered that rents would be received at the Alfred's Head Inn each year on the Monday evening after 10th October. The tenants would be given fourteen days notice of the meeting and would be expected to attend and pay their rents up to the following 5th April. (October 10th and April 5th were the dates which the old quarter days, Michaelmas and Lady Day, had moved to, when the calendar changed in 1752). The rent receiver would be there to collect the rents and it sounded as though there would be free drinks supplied. This only lasted for seven years. In 1790, the Governors decided that these evenings were to be discontinued as the expense caused was "altogether unnecessary". No mention was made as to where rents were to be paid instead. In more modern times, some weekly rents for cottages in Grove Street and Mill Street were collected by one of the tenants, who was given a small discount for doing this, and other rents were paid over at the solicitor's office where the clerk worked. From the 1930s, the clerk was responsible for collecting all the rents, but by then only a few buildings in Wantage and the almshouses belonged to the Governors, the other property having been sold.

A type of rent known as a quit rent was both collected and paid out by the Governors in several instances each year. Quit rents date back to medieval times. Tenants of the lord of the manor had a duty to give a fixed amount of their time to work on the lord's land. By paying a quit rent to the lord each year, they could be excused this duty. The rent continued to be paid on this land, often into the twentieth century, by which time its original purpose had been long forgotten. Also as time went on, it appeared that a quit rent could be imposed where a person encroached slightly on their neighbour's property; as was the case in 1834, when Charles Holloway built a shed which encroached on Governors' land. A party of the Governors went to examine the offending shed and decided that if he paid a one shilling quit rent each year, the shed could stay. The shilling a year was paid until the 1880s, when Charles Holloway not only gave up the small piece of ground next to the Governors' Pound Croft (the land in Portway opposite the school) where the cart shed had been built near his bakehouse, but he also pointed out to the Governors that the shed had been pulled down several years previously, and told them that he was no longer prepared to pay the annual shilling. A similar case occurred in 1836, but here the encroachment was actually built on the Governors' property in Newbury Street, when Mr Brown erected a summer house in the garden which he rented from the Governors. He was asked to pay a quit rent of 2s 6d a year. Forty years later, Mr Jotcham leased the house where Mr Brown had lived earlier; the offending summer house and a dog kennel were removed and so the payment of the quit rent was discontinued. Even a telegraph pole on Governors' land meant they could claim a shilling quit rent each year from the Postmaster General, and when Wantage Urban District Council ran pipes from the swimming pool in Mill Street under Town Lands' property, to discharge water into the brook, they had to pay a quit rent of 5s each year. Some quit rents were paid for many years without any indication as to the reason, possibly these were some of the ones going back a long time. Queens College, Oxford, paid 10s a year from the end of the sixteenth century right through to the nineteenth century, although by then it had increased to £1 a year; but with never a mention as to why they paid the Town Lands this rent, and by 1908 it appeared that no-one knew of the origin of this payment.

As well as collecting quit rents, the Governors also owed quit rents to other land owners. In 1598, they paid quit rents to the Dean and Canons of Windsor, to My Lord of Bath, to William Anger and for the almshouse: again no reasons were ever given. The three manors in Wantage were also paid quit rents by the Governors but not every year: in 1689 payments of quit rents were recorded to "the steward of the Mannor of Wantinge" and to "the Lord of Pryershold"; in 1692 the quit rent was paid "for the Mannor of Bryants". Some of the rent collectors simply lumped the ordinary rents and the quit rents together in the accounts, but others listed them separately. There were never more than a few, both collected and paid out, and the sum was quite small in both cases. By the late 1800s, the Governors began to take measures to get rid of quit rents, which must have been more of a nuisance than a benefit to all parties. In 1875, the treasurer was asked to apply to the Charity Commissioners for permission to sell the quit rents due to the Governors. People owing them would pay a lump sum larger than their yearly quit rent and this would cancel out the legal duty to pay the rent in future. Quit rents due from the Governors were also negotiated. In 1890, Mr Burton who was lord of the manor of Childrey and was owed an annual quit rent from the Governors for some of their land in East Challow, was offered a sum equal to twenty years rent, for which payment the Governors expected to cancel the need to pay in future.

Each year there were usually some tenants behindhand with their rents; William Hinde was still owing half a year's rent of 15s at the end of 1636 but seemed to be the only person in arrears; at the end of 1689 there were eleven tenants who were not up to date with their payments, with a total debt of £34. Some owed more than a year's rent, in fact one man, Kinge, owed ten and a half years. Generally speaking, through the years there were always some people owing rent but the numbers did not vary much, usually being in single figures. The Governors kept a fairly close rein on arrears and passed several resolutions over the years setting time limits for payment and warning tenants that they would be prosecuted if arrears were not paid off quickly. If a tenant owed rent money for too long, the Governors would sue or would confiscate some of his goods to cover the debt or would insist that the tenant give up his lease. In 1730 the clerk was asked to take legal proceedings against Clement Stroude, John Symonds, Stephen Barr, Edward Restall and Farmer Heddin to recover their respective rents unless they paid within a month. It was minuted at a meeting in 1755, "Unless Mr Gregory do forthwith pay his arrears of rent the Clerk do immediately make a distress in his goods etc for payment of the same": in other words he would have goods confiscated to the value of his arrears. And in 1672, Henry Alder was told he must pay his arrears of £24 9s 0d within the following two months or he would be turned off the land belonging to the Governors. Not only did eviction apply to land, a person could lose his home if he did not keep up with the rent: in 1814 John Dry was told that if his arrears were not paid within the following week, he would be served notice to quit the house he rented from the Governors, being given six months to find other accommodation.

One person who caused problems over several years was George Roe, who rented land at East Challow. In January 1816 he was more than two years in debt and it was decided to take legal proceedings against him to recover the £59 5s 0d he owed. A year later nothing seemed to have been done and it was once again decided to take legal proceedings against him. Later that year the Governors sold grass from the meadow that Roe had occupied, in Whitemead at

Challow, and leased this land to Henry Banting at £10 per annum. So Roe was no longer renting the land and running up increasing debt; it only remained for the Governors to recover the arrears owing. He paid off some of the money; by 1820 only £14 2s 0d was owing but the Governors decided once more to sue him. They were not successful; and in 1826 they minuted, "the arrears of rent due from George Roe appear to be irrecoverable" and agreed that these arrears were to be removed from the accounts.

In this particular case the debt was wiped out because the Governors realised it was no use pursuing the matter further, and there were other cases where similar bad debts had to be accepted as ones that would never be recovered. However, there were also occasions when the Governors agreed to allow money owing to remain unpaid and be removed from the accounts, due to misfortunes of the tenants. In 1741, it was agreed that all arrears of rent due from Thomas Stiles, George Kent and Thomas Crane "in regard to their poverty with incapacity of paying it be forgiven them and that the same be crost out of the Book of Accounts". George Kent's name cropped up again in 1764, when he had unpaid rent of £15, which he was forgiven. Thomas Stiles, a baker, was excused payment in 1736 when he was 'pooerly', and again in 1745 when he was ill once more and unable to pay. Stiles and another tenant's arrears were crossed off the accounts in 1751 "being both Dead" and also both insolvent; so it was no good the Governors trying to recover anything from either of them. Poverty and insolvency were the main reasons that arrears had to be forgiven, although when Richard Goff was insolvent in 1811, the Governors said that they would accept payment of 5s in the pound to pay off some of his debt of £31 18s 5½d. The same year John Taylor gave up his lease and was forgiven all his arrears: he was also given £20 by the Governors, as he was in extreme poverty. Thomas Church was usually very reliable and had rented his house from the Governors for many years, when he

began to find difficulty in paying the rent in 1866. The Governors decided to let him continue to live there rent free "in consideration of his long tenancy and poverty and punctual payment" and to let him off paying the arrears on the property. Thomas had lived at the top of Grove Street since 1840, and had first been in arrears in 1864, when the Governors were thinking of turning him out of the property if he did not pay, and when they also carried out repairs to the house. They had obviously re-considered the matter and realised he was worthy of help.

Other reasons were given for leniency to tenants who owed the Governors rent money. There was a fire at the property of John Brookes in 1702 so the Governors allowed him a rebate of 30s; and in 1707, 40s arrears were removed from the account of Mephiboseth Freeman "in regard of his extraordinary badd Cropp this harvest". Mephiboseth was again allowed a rebate on his rent in 1723, as by then he was lame and poverty stricken, so finding it difficult to make a living. He died and was buried in Wantage in 1726. The Governors were sympathetic to Mephiboseth when they knew he had had a poor harvest and this sympathy was shown to other tenants, at times when farming was proving to be going through difficulties. In 1818, three tenants were given rebates for the previous year because their crops had failed, two were farming in Swinhill at Grove and the third in Town Close at East Challow. During the 1820s farming was facing a bad time in the area and this led to several of the tenants having difficulties. The Governors appreciated this and tried to assist by giving rent reductions. In September 1822 they minuted: "Upon account of the low price of Farming Produce, we agree to allow Mr Daniel Trinder 10% on his year's rent due Lady Day 1821 and 20% on his rent due Lady Day 1822". The accounts show that a total of seventeen people were allowed a 10% discount on their rents for 1822, with similar reductions continuing up to Lady Day 1824. And in 1830, one of the tenants was given a rebate "on account of the pressure of the times on Farming Produce".

Towards the end of the nineteenth century, farming went through a longer period of difficulty in many areas, due to bad weather, imports of cheap corn, falling wool prices and animal disease, which led to many farmers either failing or selling up. Once again the Governors understood the problems and helped their tenants by reducing some rents. In 1879, they minuted that "in consideration of the present agricultural depression", Mr Martin would only be asked to pay £50 rent instead of £62 10s 0d, Robert Stroud would pay £15 instead of £20 for the two meadows in Challow he rented, John Simmonds' rent for land in Grove was reduced from £31 10s 0d to £28 and it was agreed that Mr Jackson could pay £14 rent instead of £16. The same year, two other tenants informed the Governors that they were giving up their land, and over the 1880s and into the 1890s this pattern of reduced rents and tenants quitting the land continued. It must have been a worrying time for the Governors, as they saw the Town Lands revenues decrease and tenants give up their leases. In 1881, a letter was received from John Lyford asking for a reduction in his rent for the cottages with land and other buildings at Hanney, but this was refused. He asked again in 1885 and the reason for the refusal was explained: money had been spent on repairs and more repairs were probably going to be needed, so that it was felt it was not possible to give a rent reduction. In 1887, Mr Lyford gave notice he was quitting the property; and then in 1891 there was a fire and the Hanney cottages burnt down. Luckily they were insured and the insurance money enabled a house and sheds to be built in their place, at a cost of £180. When, in 1887, Mr Jackson, who had already had his rent for a meadow near Manor Road in Wantage reduced a few years earlier, asked for a further reduction and gave notice he was about to quit at Christmas, the Governors agreed to reduce his rent, if he would remain. They did not want to lose any more tenants. There was a similar occurrence in 1895 when Richard Woods, who had been paying rent for land at East Challow, first gave notice to quit and then offered a rent of half his previous one. The Governors initially turned this down and advertised for a new tenant. When there were no takers, Mr Wood's offer of reduced rent was accepted. This sparked off a reaction from several other tenants at East Challow. Mr Simmons gave notice to quit but after some haggling, reminiscent of an Arab souk, it was agreed he could reduce his rent by £5. Another East Challow tenant, Robert Stroud, was not so lucky in his request to a reduction and continued to pay the same rent as before. By May 1896, Richard Woods was no longer a tenant at East Challow and the Governors had to accept an even lower rent for that land. Throughout the 1890s, negotiations by tenants for lower rents continued. In 1901, the clerk to the Governors commented that, "Rentals which formerly amounted to nearly £1,000 have now, by agricultural depression, sunk to £540 per annum". The £1,000, however, seems to be somewhat of an exaggeration, just over £600 being a more likely figure about the mid nineteenth century when rents reached a maximum.

The income from rents fluctuated over the years, most probably depending on the changing value of land and the state of farming at different times. Land became more valuable at the time that the common fields were enclosed, as will be seen later in this chapter, leading to increased rents; when farming went through difficult times, rents decreased. The Governors would have done their best to carry out their stewardship with skill, to enable them to raise the maximum possible from their estates, in order to benefit as many of the poor inhabitants of Wantage as they could. When land was let or leases were renewed the Governors would consider whether or not they could increase the rent from the sum they had been paid before. In 1738, three of the Governors were given the task of letting land at Grove, that had previously been rented to Stephen Barr, "at the best improved rent that can be gotten for the same". Farmer Hobbs took the lease at a rent of £21 10s 0d per annum, whereas Barr had been paying £25. It looked as though the Governors had got a worse deal

Cross Tree Cottage, East Hanney.
Built in the late nineteenth century after the original thatched cottages and other buildings on the site burnt down.

rather than a better one. However, it is often difficult to be sure whether the same conditions applied when trying to compare rents paid by consecutive tenants, and when this transfer of land is investigated in more detail, it appears that there had been changes in the lease which probably accounted for the drop in rent. The main difference was that Farmer Hobbs was now expected to pay the church tax and the poor tax on this land, which Stephen Barr had not had to do. And where Barr had been allowed to plough up three acres of grassland if he wished, Hobbs had a clause in the new lease strictly forbidding him to plough any land except that which was already under the plough.

In the reign of William and Mary, a tax on land and property was introduced to pay for the French wars. After 1693, each county appointed local commissioners to supervise the assessment and collection of this tax. It is possible that because the Town Lands were a charity, the Trust was exempt from paying; certainly there was no record of any amount being paid by the Governors or their tenants before 1714. The two estates acquired that year, Gentlemans Mead in Stanford and land in East Challow, were not exempt from tax and from then on land tax was paid on these two properties. An entry in the accounts for 1724 gives confirmation that the original Trust land was probably exempt from land tax; as the clerk was to be allowed his costs "for attending the Commissioners of the Land Tax three tymes for preventing the Governors Estate at Grove being taxt to the King's Majestie". Tax continued to be paid on property acquired later, including two houses in Grove Street. The amount of land tax was set each year by the commissioners, until 1798, when it was decided that landowners could redeem having to pay the tax by paying a lump sum, which then released them from the annual payment; and it appeared that the Governors decided to do this for the land and houses they paid the tax on.

Other taxes as well as land tax were paid. When the land was bought at Stanford-in-the-Vale, the Governors paid the taxes on that land; there was Church Tax (which would be the tithe), Poor Tax, Constables Tax and 'Trophy money', as well as the Land Tax mentioned earlier. The poor tax would be the money paid to the parish for support of paupers, while the constables tax was also paid to the parish towards the cost of the constables who were responsible for keeping law and order there. 'Trophy money' is a mystery: another strange tax mentioned was 'Gaol money' paid on the Challow land in 1722 and also paid regularly by the Wantage churchwardens. According to these churchwardens' accounts, this tax was for the relief of the poor prisoners of the Kings Bench and Marshalsea prison, although it has also been suggested that it could have been for the upkeep of the county jail. The properties which had been part of the Town Lands from earlier times had all taxes paid by the tenants: many leases had a clause, similar to that in Richard Sheppard's lease of 1726, which stated that the tenant was to pay the taxes to the church, the poor and the highways. The Governors occasionally paid these taxes for the tenants. After the Wantage Improvement Act was passed in 1828, properties in Wantage town paid a Lamp Tax to fund the street lighting and the Governors had to pay this for their town properties. Water rates were paid once properties were connected to the town water supply.

Sun Insurance fire mark as applied to buildings in the 18th century

Fire insurance, taken out originally with the Sun Fire Office, was paid on the workhouse in Grove Street from 1744, but later more of the Governors' houses and other buildings were insured against fire. This proved to be a good thing on at least two occasions, when there were fires at the Steventon and Hanney properties. Extra insurance was also taken out during the wars: insurance against war risks and aircraft risks in WWI and extra war damage contributions on town properties insurance in WWII.

Land belonging to the Town Lands

What is known as the open-field system was practised in a broad area down through the midlands and including Berkshire from early medieval times. In each village or small town, a few large fields belonged

Undulations left by ridge and furrow ploughing. Each ridge was one of the strips of land in the open field before enclosure.

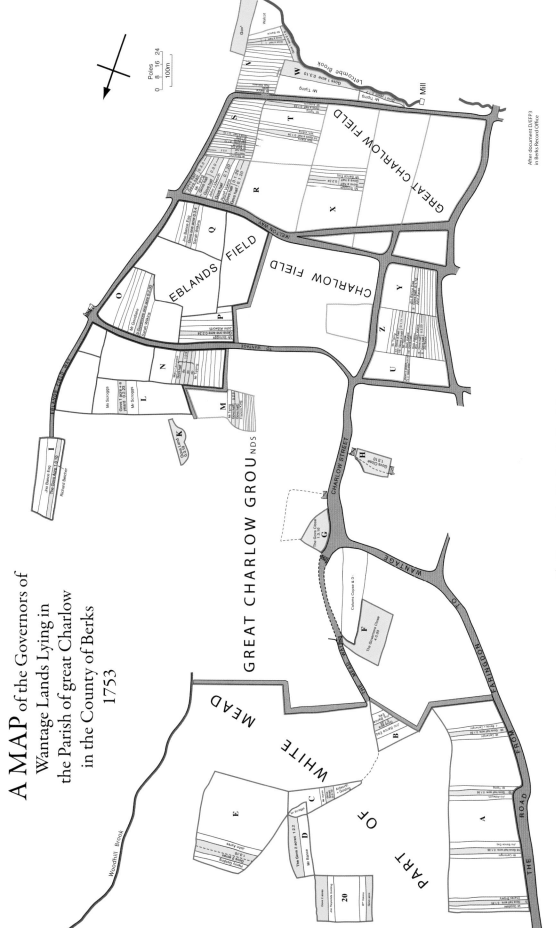

A MAP of the Governors of Wantage Lands Lying in the Parish of great Charlow in the County of Berks 1753

Poles
0 8 16 24
0 100m

The Governor's land in East Challow before enclosure

After document D/EFP3 in Berks Record Office

to the whole community and the inhabitants were allotted strips in different areas of these fields, which ensured that the good and the bad lands were shared out fairly. There was common grazing land for the animals and everyone involved had to cooperate in regulating the system. It meant that a large number of the inhabitants had some land to cultivate in order to support their families. Much of the land belonging to the Town Lands was originally in strips in the open fields. A person leasing land from the Governors could quite easily have land spread over a large area, in several small pieces. For example, when Henry Alder of Grove took out a lease in 1662, the land he was about to rent from the Governors was as follows: 2 closes (small fields) near Barwell, 4 acres (4 strips each measuring about an acre) of arable land in Lymborowe, 5 half acres of arable in Charlton fields, 4 acres of arable in a field in Grove called Norton and 2 lots of three yardlands (a variable measure of land) in Stubb...field in Grove next to the Green. So he was renting seventeen small pieces of land, scattered around Charlton, Wantage and Grove; for all of which he paid a rent of £12 5s 0d a year.

The map of the Governors' land in East Challow (page 95) made in 1753, demonstrates how dispersed one owner's land could be. The furlongs (parts of the large fields) edged in red show arable land, those edged in green were pasture and the total land owned by the Governors, although spread over most of the parish, only measured just over 32 acres. Sometimes it made sense for two landowners to exchange strips of land in order to concentrate their holdings in a few areas, rather than have them scattered evenly over the fields, and the Governors were no exception in employing this tactic. In 1672, Adam Mason of East Challow asked the Governors if they would be willing to exchange one of their strips of land in that parish for land of equal size belonging to him and his son. It was decided that three or four of the Governors would look at the two plots of land, and if they felt the exchange would "cause no inconvenience to the Town Lands" they were

to agree to the exchange. If several strips belonging to one person could be exchanged to produce a larger block of land, it made sense to enclose this with some sort of hedge or fence, forming a 'close' which could then be cultivated or grazed without the owner having to cooperate with others. East Challow gradually enclosed part of the fields in this way, by agreement between landowners, during the seventeenth century, and the Governors benefitted when, in 1659, they agreed to exchange some of their strips in the open fields for two enclosed closes.

These early enclosures were carried out by agreement amongst the village inhabitants and other owners of the land, such as the Governors, but during the late 1700s and early 1800s, a large number of parishes were enclosed by act of parliament, usually

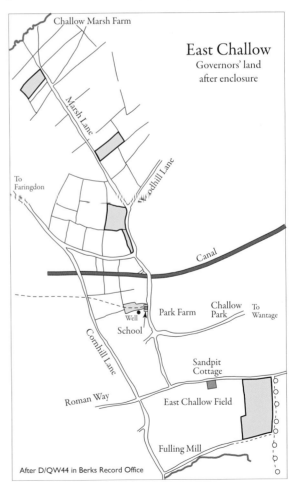

East Challow
Governors' land
after enclosure

After D/QW44 in Berks Record Office

instigated by one or several big landowners. In these cases, a survey of the land was carried out and each individual was allocated a similar acreage to the land they formerly possessed, but in a block or blocks rather than in dispersed strips. Landowners could increase the value of their land by enclosing, as it could then be cultivated more efficiently. When East Challow was enclosed by act of parliament at the beginning of the 1800s, rents on land there increased and, as mentioned earlier in Chapter 5, the Governors were able to increase the amount of bread given away each Sunday, which was paid for from the rent money on land at Challow left by Thomas Willis.

Between 1760 and 1850, there were 5,400 parliamentary enclosures carried out in England, which shows how popular this had become. Although larger landowners were enthusiastic about enclosure, small tenant farmers suffered by having their rents increased immediately rather than phased in gradually and by not having enough capital to make necessary changes to their newly enclosed land. Costs of enclosure could be quite high; as well as the cost of surveyors and administrative expenses, the newly allotted land had to be fenced or hedges planted. When Stanford-in-the-Vale was enclosed in 1784, the costs to the Governors for their plot in Gentlemans Mead, which measured about 3¾ acres, was £18 18s 1d: the rent for land in Stanford before enclosure was £5 a year and afterwards it increased to £5 12s 6d a year. So although the land value did increase by enclosure there, it would have taken over thirty years for the higher rent to cover the enclosure costs. Wantage and Grove, East Challow and Letcombe Regis, and East Hanney were all enclosed by acts of parliament about the same time, between 1801 and 1804. Charlton and Steventon were not enclosed until much later, in 1868 and 1882 respectively. The enclosures of the early 1800s showed the Governors paying out over £180 for legal and administrative costs, which did not include the cost of hedging round the new allotments of land.

While the commissioners were working out how land would be divided up at the time of a parliamentary enclosure, owners were given the opportunity to exchange with one another if they and the commissioners agreed, to enable people to have land conveniently placed. So, for example, the Governors were allotted some land in The Ham enclosure in Wantage while Sarah Walcot was given a piece of arable and pasture ground in White Field in East Challow. It suited both of them to exchange these pieces of land which they did. In the case of the Steventon enclosure, the Governors were not happy with the lands they were allotted but the commissioners would not change them and as there cannot have been any other person agreeable to an exchange, the Governors had to accept the lands they had been given. The Steventon lands belonging to the Governors before enclosure (see page 98) consisted of a cottage with attached homestead buildings, a garden and a small close of land behind, along with twelve strips at various places in the open fields of the parish. After enclosure, they still possessed the cottage and homestead complex and their dispersed strips were replaced by two blocks of land, one two miles from the homestead and the other one mile away, so not a very convenient arrangement for letting all the properties to one person. A few years later, in 1886, there was a fire at the homestead and as the Governors reported that an old thatched cottage, a barn and a shed had burned down, it appeared that the whole group of buildings had been destroyed by the fire. Luckily the buildings were insured but because the fields belonging to the Governors were so far apart, they decided that the rent would be similar whether they had buildings or not, so the destroyed cottage was not rebuilt. Instead, the site was included with the paddock at the back to make a larger paddock.

There were occasions when the Governors had to organise the cultivation of some of their land, if the property was between tenants at an inconvenient time. Stephen Barr rented land at Grove in the first half of the eighteenth century, but by 1738 he was getting old and gave up his lease. The Governors must then have organised the farming of this land until Farmer

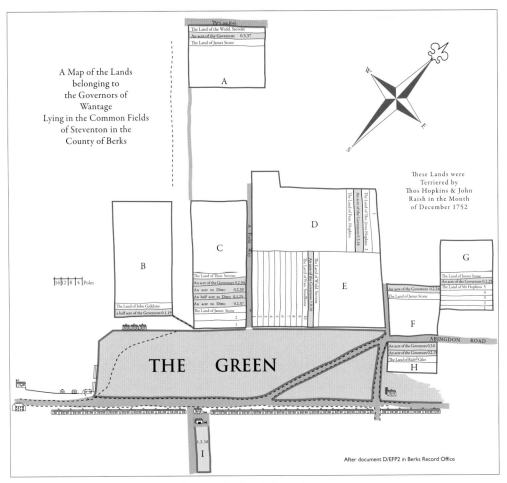

Steventon holdings before enclosure

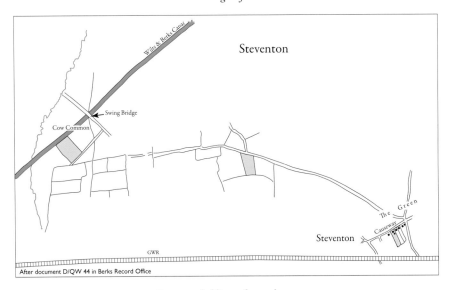

Steventon holdings after enclosure

Hobbs took over at the end of 1739. They paid Barr for "dunging and plowing", which he must have carried out prior to leaving so that the land was in good heart. The Governors then paid for more ploughing and for sowing, for mowing the grass, making the hay and weeding the wheat, so both arable and meadow land was involved. There was a long list of the produce sold during the year; wheat, barley, beans, straw and hay. At a different time, land in Grove was again between tenants and was planted with oats. Ten bushels of oats were bought to be sown, labourers were paid for ploughing and sowing the land, followed by weeding, cutting and cocking the crop, and finally for threshing and winnowing the grain. After the harvest, 28 bushels of oats were sold, along with some oat straw. The Governors may have used some of the harvested oats for feeding animals on the land they were farming. Two years later, the same land was planted with wheat and again labourers were paid for similar work.

Drainage of the land was carried out in some places from 1850. In that year, it was agreed that John Castle, who farmed at Grove, would be allowed 2,000 draining tiles, and in 1861 Mr Lay's farm at Grove was to be surveyed with a view to improvement of the land by draining. Land at Challow was drained a few years later. Ditches were always kept in good condition and when the Governors found that a Mr Fawler, not one of their tenants, had filled in a ditch belonging to them, he was ordered to re-instate it immediately. In 1737, a pond was dug at Grove and anyone who would benefit and who had land in the vicinity, was expected to contribute to the cost: the Governors paid 15s and the following year a further 19s towards this pond.

Gates, stiles and bridges were repaired or replaced by the Governors when necessary. In 1812, new gates were erected at the Governors' expense at the entrance to a close at the bottom of Chain Hill. Usually either the tenant was given the wood, so he could have new gates made, or a local person made the gates and the posts for the Governors. For some unexplained reason,

a pair of gates was brought from Leckhampstead, on the downs, when Mr Barr needed new ones on the land he rented at Grove in 1722, and the extra cost for carriage from Leckhampstead had to be paid. When Edward Freeman took a new lease on some land in 1686, it was agreed he would be given 5s to make a stile and bridge there, although for such a small amount, the bridge must have been rather small and basic, perhaps just planks. In 1770, a new stile at Grove cost 5s just for the stile. As mentioned in Chapter 3, a rather more sturdy bridge was built over the brook at a farm at Grove where Mr Belcher was the tenant, in 1856, to give him access to the meadow there.

Marking boundaries accurately was obviously important. In medieval times, the manor court presided over any arguments relating to land boundaries, and this continued into more modern times. In 1785, the Governors recorded that the jury of Letcombe Regis and East Challow, which would be the jury attached to the Letcombe manor court, had been asked to fix the markers, known as 'meer stones' at the boundary between a close belonging to the Governors in Challow and another plot of land there known as Painters Orchard, "to prevent disputes as to the boundaries". There appeared to have been some sort of trouble involving land of the Governors in Letcombe Regis earlier that century. In 1745, three of the Governors were deputed to go to Letcombe "with what convenient speed they can" to have a look at the arable strips belonging to the Governors, in a field called Eblands Field. A certain Mr Bance had land on each side of one of the Governors' strips and he had "encroached upon and plowed away" the edges of the Governors land. After viewing the damage, the tenant of the Governors' land was told to take the matter to the Letcombe manor court the next week, explain what had happened, and ask for the jury to go to the field to see for themselves with a view to fixing meer stones where the boundary was supposed to be.

Stones to mark a boundary were used in towns as well as in fields: in 1888, the treasurer was asked to fix a stone to mark the boundary between the Governors' land behind the Eagles Close almshouses and the garden of the Wantage Brewery Company. One wonders what sort of boundary stones were used in 1884 when the treasurer was asked "to fix the boundary stones which define the position of the site of the Chantry House, pulled down many years ago, in front of the Alfred's Head Inn". As this site was in the middle of the open space used as a road, with carts and people passing over it, the stones must surely have been set into the road surface rather than have been upstanding. They were still there in 1920, as Mr Gregory was paid 10s for "cutting letters on the boundary stones marking site of old Chantry Houses".

Stones served as markers between strips in the open-fields, where it was not possible to have a fence or a hedge, but land which existed as a close or small field would usually have a more permanent boundary. The Governors continually referred in their documents to 'mounds' as boundaries. A dictionary published in the eighteenth century defines a mound as: a hedge or bank, a rampart or fence, so the mounds could be various ways for marking out the edge of a property. Some were wooden fences; there was a rubble pit, where rubble was dug for mending roads and for use in building repairs, and this was fenced in 1752, with sixteen oak posts and five rails being bought "to mound the rubble pit". A few boundaries were stone or brick walls: in 1768, William Hazell agreed to "build a brick wall as a mound to the garden" in Wantage, which he rented from the Governors, to separate it from that of the next door neighbour. The majority of boundaries, though, were marked by hedges. Sometimes it sounded as though there was a mound of earth which had a hedge planted on the top of it, and old hedgerows around the fields at present can often be seen to have a raised earth foundation, as though the bushes had been planted on a long narrow mound of earth. Tenants were required to take great care of their mounds and to keep them in good repair, whatever they were made of, although it appeared that the Governors often paid for new hedges or fences and for the repair of old ones. In 1836, they reimbursed Henry Tripp £1 for the cost of repairing his mound, and the same year they paid Michael Crane 6s for the work he had done on the quick hedge at the mound of another tenant. In 1862, Mr Wheeler's bill of £21 12s 0d was paid "for repairing Garden Mound at the College School", in other words for the boundary of the garden at the grammar school.

After the enclosure of the open-fields, new hedges had to be planted to mark the new boundaries. Particularly after the parliamentary enclosures, most of these were of hawthorn, or quickthorn as it was called. In 1720, it was agreed with the lord of the manor at Grove to enclose Wick Green, where the Governors held some land. The following year, Stephen Barr was granted a new lease of land at Grove, including the land which had recently been allotted to the Governors at Wick Green. In March 1722, several loads of bushes were taken to Grove and Richard Hinge was paid for hedging a length of 104 poles at 1s 3d a pole: he was planting the bushes. A pole was equal to 5½ yards, so the total length of the hedge he planted was 572 yards, which gives the size of the field as probably just over four acres. Gates were put in the hedge round the new field. Then in November, 2s 6d was paid "for weeding the Grove setts", the setts being the newly planted bushes. This weeding was obviously important until the hedge became established, so that weeds did not smother the young plants, and took place every time a new hedge was planted. Five further payments for weeding this hedge at Grove were made over the next four years. When the Wick Green land was hedged, hawthorn bushes were used as the minutes record the agreement for a 'quickmound' to be planted, and a little later, when John Lamboll did some hedging work for the Governors, they refer to him 'quicksetting' eleven poles, so hawthorn bushes were also being used on that occasion. He provided three loads of bushes, and was paid for planting five hundred 'setts'. The parliamentary enclosures between 1801 and 1804 involved large areas

Hedge growing on a mound of earth as a field boundary

of the Governors' land and the cost of putting up new hedges of hawthorn was quite large. In 1803, Henry Tilling was paid £7 19s 9d for quicksetting, probably on the Challow and Letcombe lands, and a further 17s 6d the following year. As usual, these new hedges were weeded in the following years. Fences were also put up as £15 19s 6d was paid for posts and railings in 1804. Occasionally, other types of bushes were used for hedges, rather than hawthorn. When hedging was carried out at a close being rented by John Heath in 1716, possibly in Grove, a load of "black bushes" were taken to the site from Denchworth. These bushes may have been blackthorn, but in October 1717, more hedging material was paid for and this time it was "beach and hasle".

Fencing was necessary round some of the plots of land in the town. When Mr Willoughby took over the orchard at the bottom of Locks Lane in 1899, this was on condition that he planted new apple trees there, ten small trees being provided by the Governors. It was decided to erect an unclimbable iron fence round the orchard, no doubt to keep out the Wantage lads once the new trees began fruiting, or so the Governors hoped. When it was found that this would cost £25, a cheaper wire fence was erected.

Timber was a valuable resource which was carefully husbanded by the Governors. Many of the properties had trees growing on them but tenants were not allowed to cut these down without permission, which was usually granted when wood was needed for repairs. Two or three Governors would be delegated to inspect the trees, decide how many were needed for the repairs and then choose the ones best suited. In 1691, Richard Belcher was needing to carry out repairs to his house and the outhouses on the property he rented from the Governors at East Hanney. Trees were chosen by the Governors for this work, and at the same time they selected other trees on this land to be used to repair the Swan Inn in Wantage, which did not have suitable timber growing on the site. This system was used through the years; if timber was available on the property where repairs were needed, a tree or trees would be cut down for the purpose; if repairs were to be carried out where timber was not available, then some of the Governors would choose suitable trees on another of their properties. William Savory, who was a tenant of a house down Mill Street where The Shears now stands, bought some wood when he repaired his house and he was reimbursed 15s to cover the cost of this. Although tenants were expected to pay for most repairs, it seemed that the timber costs were the responsibility of the Trust. Timber could also be required if new buildings were to be erected, but the same process of checking and allotting trees by the Governors would be carefully followed. Richard Belcher, mentioned above, was to be allowed the necessary timber from the trees growing on his premises when, in 1710, he was about to build new stables, with at least two of four named Governors visiting him and deciding which trees he could cut down. Trees would be granted for repair or building of bridges, gates or stiles, and on one occasion for making a pump. If more than the allotted number of trees were cut down, the tenant had to pay. John Lockton took more than he had been allowed for repairs to his property, in 1715, and had to pay thirty shillings because of this. At a meeting in the summer of 1696, it was ordered that "such persons as stole a Tree for a May pole out John Tayler's Close be prosecuted". Whether or not the Governors managed to find out who the culprits were, we are not told, but there did not seem to be any mention of the cost of a prosecution in the accounts, so perhaps it was a case of no-one having seen anything! As people had enjoyed all the May festivities, including the maypole dancing,

it would probably have been considered best to keep one's mouth shut. John Tayler rented Barwell Close, which was on the edge of the present Grove airfield.

When, in the winter of 1761, it was decided to cut the timber on one side of Barwell Close, the records and accounts for the next few years showed some of the work which would be carried out when this happened. As the timber was to be "applied to such uses as the Governors think proper", some of it could have been used for various repairs without this being recorded. Some wood was sold: 106 feet of oak at one shilling a foot, and 56 feet of elm timber at nine pence a foot. As well as the large timber, there would have been plenty of smaller pieces, particularly as it sounds as though part of the hedge was also dug up, with Robert Jordan, Stephen Garlick and Joseph Aldworth being paid for at least twenty four days between them 'grubbing' up bushes and roots at the close, each being paid 1s 2d a day. The smaller timber was sold for firewood as cords and faggots: a cord of wood being a parcel of firewood 4ft broad, 4ft high and 8ft long; while a faggot was simply a bundle of sticks. When this work was done at Barwell, seven score and nine (149) faggots were sold for 18s 6d, and 7 cords of wood for £6 6s 0d, as well as "hardwood and chips" for £1 8s 0d. As work progressed, Thomas Whithorn was paid 2s 4d for whetting the saws which the labourers were using to cut down the timber, and beer was bought in for the workmen. After the cutting down had finished, new hedging was planted and hurdles and stakes were used to protect the young bushes until they had grown. Then, for the next few years, there were entries in the accounts for men paid for weeding the new bushes, replacing a few that had died and mending the mounds at Barwell. One little animal which could be a nuisance in the meadows was the mole, and when mole hills began to appear in too many places, the Governors considered it necessary to get rid of the culprits. In 1762, at the time the new hedging was planted at Barwell, William Griffin was paid 1s for killing the 'wants' (i.e. the moles) in Barwell Close, and more were killed the following year. The going rate seemed to be 3d per mole.

Firewood was often bought from the Governors when trees were cut down. A report published in 1809, explained that although the inhabitants of Wantage used coal, it was too expensive for the poor. In the Vale, bean stubble was one source of fuel, and in Wantage old tan (oak bark) from the Wantage tan yards was burnt. Hedges and coppices also supplied fuel for the poor, but one problem with this source was that hedges could be destroyed if too much firewood was taken. This could have been the reason that one of the Governors was paid his expenses in 1749 for "prosecuting and sending to Bridewell (i.e. prison) John Greenwood of Grove for breaking the Governors hedges". The report of 1809 suggested that to prevent damage to hedgerows, it would be an excellent plan for parish officers to buy coal when it was cheap and then sell it without profit in small quantities to the poor during the winter, which is what the Governors did, although in their case the coal was given free to the poor. Whether the people buying faggots and other firewood from the Governors when trees were felled was for their own use or to sell on at a profit, we can only guess. In 1831, Charles Holloway, who often did labouring work for the Trust, paid the Governors for faggots and short logs but we cannot tell what he did with this firewood. Elm roots were grubbed up by Robert Salt in 1757: he was paid for doing this work and for cording up the roots, and they were then sold to John Savory, who could have been John Savory the blacksmith at the bottom of Mill Street, as he would have needed fuel for his forge. When the elms were cut down at Wick Green at Grove in 1760, the Governors paid a labourer for eleven days work making 444 faggots which were then sold to William Stone. William cannot have used as many bundles of firewood as that himself, so he was no doubt selling on at least some of them, at a profit. It was William who bought the seven cords of wood from Barwell in 1761, so it sounded as though he had a little business buying and selling firewood. John Smart probably did the same, as he bought "29 score faggots" in 1775. A score is twenty, so this was a large number of bundles once again (580).

The number of trees on some of the estates was surprisingly large. Mostly they were elms, which disappeared from the English landscape in the 1970s, killed by Dutch elm disease, so the landscape would have looked vastly different to its appearance today. A list of the trees on the lands in Grove in the early 1750s is given below. To have over six hundred elms was a lot of timber. Mostly they would have been growing in the hedgerows, rather than in the middle of the fields.

TREES ON THE GOVERNORS LAND IN GROVE IN THE MID EIGHTEENTH CENTURY

	OAKES	ELMS	ASH'S
In Spicers Close are		187	3
In Chancery Close are		74	5
In the Little Orchard are		10	
In the Marsh Close & the Butts adjoyning		12	3
In the Close called Wick Green are		145	1
In the North Field at the Two Three Yeardens		18	
In Swinhill Field at the Three acres of Picks		26	2
In Town Close are	2	66	1
In Black Breach Field at the Nine Halfs		14	
In Norton Field at the Lands End		26	2
The Whole number of Trees	2	608	18

Also around this date, a large number of trees were growing in two small fields in Wantage: there were sixty elms and two ashes in Town Close, which is where King Alfred's School now stands; and on the opposite side of the road in Freemans Croft, there were thirteen elms and four ashes.

Over the years, timber would be cut down and sold, which occasionally raised substantial sums for the Governors. At the beginning of the nineteenth century, the price for oak, ash and elm had nearly doubled over the preceding twenty years. Four elm trees growing in Barrow Lane (also referred to as Barwell Lane, now Denchworth Road) were sold for £21 in 1804, so the Governors were profiting by the premium put on timber at the time. This was the period of history when the country was fighting the Napoleonic wars and when there was also a large increase in population. Timber would have been needed for building ships and houses. During the seventeenth and eighteenth centuries, it seemed that private sales were the norm, but when it was decided, in 1820, to make a survey of the trees on all the estates with a view to felling and selling some, it was agreed that "the most advantageous way of disposing" of them would be to hold an auction. The sale raised £84. From then on, throughout the nineteenth century, auctions were held at intervals for the sale of timber, although private sales were also made. Both private sales and auctions provided a boost to income. In 1832, an auction was held at the King Alfred's Head and from the accounts that year it appeared that five men had bought the timber being sold, at a total of over £220. Rental income at the time was around £460 a year. The Governors had to pay some costs out of this: the auction bill, the cost for transport of some of the timber and the payment to men for moving the smaller logs. Other auctions or private sales over the years, right through to the twentieth century, brought in substantial sums, but not quite as much as this.

We have seen that at the time of parliamentary enclosure, for the sake of convenience, land allotted to one person was sometimes exchanged for other land which had been allotted to a second person. If there were trees growing on these plots, an agreement would be reached as to the relative value of the timber on the land in question, and payment would be made to make matters fair. One exchange of land resulted in the Governors being paid £21 10s 0d "for exchange of timber at East Challow".

As trees were cut down, new ones were planted. In 1740, every tenant was told that if they were given permission to cut down a tree, then they were to plant another tree, worth a shilling, to replace it. They were

then to "cherish the same in a husbandlike manner": it was no good just planting new trees, they must be cared for to ensure that they had every opportunity to grow well. Some early leases stipulated that three or four trees of oak, ash or elm were to be planted by a tenant each year on the land he rented. These trees were planted at the expense of the tenants, but there were also times when the Governors organised and paid for tree planting. For example, in 1806, it was decided that some young elms would be planted on the Governors' lands. A lot of timber was sold around this time, so the new trees were probably replacing trees which had been felled. Mr Wells was paid £6 10s 6d for young elms, which could have come from Faringdon, as a couple of years later Charles Holloway was paid for "going twice to Faringdon to fetch the elms", as well as for planting them. Half a century earlier, the Governors had paid for fifty small willow saplings to be bought and planted on part of their estate, most likely by a stream at the edge of one of their meadows.

Occasionally, damage was done when timber was felled. Mr Lailey, the tenant at Hanney, had the fence alongside his meadow destroyed when timber was felled on the Governors' land there in 1866. A similar complaint came from John Heath, in 1716, when his land at Grove was damaged by moving timber which had been cut down. Both men were compensated by the Governors. Damage could be done to timber by the tenants. If tenants used the trees in the hedgerows as posts when nailing up a fence, this was obviously damaging to the timber. So in 1831, it was decided to prevent this happening by putting a covenant in future leases prohibiting tenants from driving nails into trees growing in the mounds or hedges. Sometimes the damage was not done by a tenant but by a neighbouring farmer. In 1871, Mr de Vitre, a gentleman of Letcombe Regis, had cut down trees and grubbed up a hedge along one side of a meadow which was Town Lands' property. The Governors and their tenant inspected the damage and "were of opinion that the act committed by Mr de Vitre was wrongful", so they suggested that he should put up a wooden fence, plant some trees and bushes and repair the drainage, which he had also damaged. A letter was read from Mr de Vitre at the next meeting, in which he expressed his regret and acknowledged that the hedge and trees were not his to cut down. He carried out the suggested work almost immediately, and the tenants reported back to the Governors that he had "done all in his power to repair the damage" and they were satisfied with the result.

It was obviously important to have good relations with neighbours, and on another occasion, after complaints from Mr Tame who worked a mill at Grove, two of the Governors inspected the trees growing alongside the brook in a cottage garden owned by the Town Lands, to check whether or not they obstructed the flow of the water. At the meeting, in 1805, where the matter was discussed, it was decided that if the trees were a problem, they were to be taken down.

We have looked at the land belonging to the Trust and following chapters will deal with some of the houses belonging to the Governors. During almost three hundred years after the setting up of the Town Lands charity in 1597, there was no indication of any of the land or properties being sold. During the mid nineteenth century, the Governors began to get requests to sell. In 1854, the vicar of Challow, the Rev George Purdue, wanted to buy a close in East Challow in order to build a parsonage on it. The Governors were agreeable and set the price at £210 but the Charity Commissioners would only agree to letting Purdue have the land if he bought a plot of similar value and exchanged it for the close he wanted. Nothing more was heard of the sale and in fact a vicarage was not built in East Challow until the twentieth century. A similar proposition was put, in 1847, when the vicar of Grove asked to purchase a small piece of land he rented from the Governors, behind his vicarage. He was also told that if he could buy a similar piece of land, the Governors would have no objection to an exchange, but they did not want to sell: the matter was still being discussed in 1876. Between 1868 and 1873, three properties *were*

sold: the site of the old almshouse in Newbury Street, a small meadow on Chain Hill, and a garden with a workshop in Grove Street.

From then to the turn of the century little changed in the Town Lands portfolio of properties, but at the end of the 1800s and into the early 1900s, the accounts show that for several years the Town Lands expenditure was greater than the income, partly due to large repair bills over those years, which was probably why a large arable field in East Challow was sold in 1901. In 1897, to help out with the finances, the Reverend Archer-Houblon, vicar of Wantage and one of the Governors, and his sisters, made a donation towards the allowance paid weekly to the almspeople, which would have provided about six weeks of these payments. The two previous years he had refunded his annual payment from the Town Lands for preaching the four sermons during the year. The Governors were reluctant to spend any money unnecessarily at this time, if they could possibly avoid it, and when Joseph Aldworth installed a new copper in the house he rented in Mill Street and asked to be reimbursed for the cost of it, he was told that the Governors would only pay when a valuation of improvements was made on his death, which hardly benefited the poor man himself for the money he had spent. He asked for the shutters to be varnished and the front of the house to be painted; both of these requests were also refused. He had recently been granted the use of his cottage in Mill Street rent free for the rest of his life, so possibly it was felt that as there was no income from the property, the Governors could not justify spending on its up-keep, even though Joseph had been told he would not be liable for any dilapidation.

In 1894, the Governors decided that as their income was insufficient to meet all their outgoing expenses, they would stop paying any of the voluntary subscriptions to good causes such as the Radcliffe Infirmary or the Reading Hospital, which they had been happy to donate to in the past. The following year ended with £150 owing to the Grammar School treasurer, and with no funds to meet this debt, it was decided to take out a bank loan to enable this to be paid, as well as other outstanding bills. It was also agreed that the weekly pay to the almspeople would be reduced by one shilling each week, and Morland and Co. were asked to increase their rent for the Alfred's Head from £40 a year to £50. In 1893, Mr Whiting, a Wantage builder who regularly worked for the Governors, was asked to do repairs to the Grammar School during the school holiday, on the understanding that he would have to wait for payment for the job until the Governors had sufficient money to pay him. In the early 1900s, several men who had done work were left with payment outstanding at the end of each year, particularly Mr Gregory who seemed to be owed money over quite some time, including the large sum of almost £60 at the end of 1906. By 1913, finances settled down with a small positive balance shown in the accounts each year from then on.

Whether or not the Governors began to think that managing their property was becoming more of a liability than it had previously been they do not say; certainly many of the Wantage houses were in constant need of repair and some were in a rather dilapidated state. The Governors may have felt that having most of their assets invested in stocks rather than land would be easier to manage. Whatever the Governors' reasoning, it was decided to ask the permission of the Charity Commissioners to hold an auction of some of the Town Lands, and this having been granted, the outlying lands at Stanford, East Challow, Charlton, Hanney, Steventon and Grove were put up for sale in 1920. This auction was so successful that it was immediately agreed that permission would be requested to sell some Wantage land — the orchard in Locks Lane and land in Manor Road, as well as the King Alfred's Head. These sales had taken place by the end of the year.

Just over a year later, the house and shop at the top of Grove Street was sold, with two small remaining plots of land at Grove and Challow going in 1921 and 1922 respectively. By the end of 1922, therefore, apart from Town Close in East Challow which was not sold until 1946, the Trust possessed property in Wantage town only, and even that was greatly reduced. A cottage and garden in Wallingford Street had been sold earlier to help fund the rebuilding of The Shears Inn in 1912. Now, in addition to the almshouses, the only property left was a terrace of four houses in Grove Street opposite the end of Garston Lane, a group of very dilapidated cottages on the opposite side of Mill Street to the almshouses, a house and orchard in Newbury Street, The Shears Inn and the Eagles Close land.

Farm land went through another depression in the 1920s and the Governors must have felt relieved that they had sold when they did. As land and houses were sold off, the proceeds were invested to provide an income for the charity. In 1936, the Town Lands 'Sale of Property' account, which was invested in Consols, was £24,115 so would have brought in a satisfactory income each year, in addition to the smaller investments of the various charities administered by the Governors. Between 1946, when The Shears was sold to Morrells Brewery, and 1989, when the small plot of land in Mill Street at the back of the Shears was sold to the owners of the mill, all the remaining Town Land property, which had previously been rented out, was sold. By the end of the twentieth century only the two sets of almshouses remained as the property of the Wantage Town Lands, and after 1980, the Eagles Close almshouses were legally a housing association, so not actually regarded as part of the Town Lands, although the Governors were still responsible for administering them.

7
Houses belonging to the Wantage Town Lands

We have seen how farm tenants were given rules as to how they should use the land they rented from the Governors. Similar instructions were set out as to how tenants should care for Governors' houses. Mostly the Governors were ensuring that houses were kept in good condition but one regulation, given in the minutes in 1786, stipulated that no poor person inhabiting any house belonging to the Governors would be permitted to keep a dog or a bitch in their house. If they did so, they would be turned out of the house and would not be allowed any charity or pension from the Governors; which seemed a bit harsh. This probably only applied to those paying a weekly rent for a 'poors house' in Mill Street or a room in the almshouse, not someone leasing a property for seven years or more.

Quite often, the Governors put a property in good order at the time a new lease was issued, and then the tenant was expected to keep everything in the same condition while it was in his occupation. William Savory took out a lease on a house in Mill Street in 1827 and signed a paper as follows: "The Governors having first put the said house in good tenantable repair, I covenant to keep the same in repair so long as I shall hold it and to leave it in as good a state and condition as it was in when I took to it ..." George Stone rented cottages and other buildings in Newbury Street, and in 1857 the Governors had to ask him to carry out repairs. He offered to pay £2 or £3 instead of having the repairs done himself, but the Governors felt this was an inadequate amount for the work that needed doing. When George Stone died ten years later, the buildings must still have been in a poor state as the Governors called the attention of his executors "to the present condition of the premises". Samuel Plumb was not only to keep his property in Mill Street in good repair, when he took the lease in 1778, but he had to agree to put on a new tiled roof "when the present covering is

worn out". It did not say what the roof was made of at the time, but it sounded likely to be a thatched one. An interesting clause in the lease taken out by Robert Stevens in 1735, stated that if Robert decided to build a house on the land being rented to him, at the end of the fourteen years of his lease he could take this house down and carry away the materials it was made from, which gives a whole new meaning to moving house. This cannot have been too unusual at the time, as the previous year Aaron Jones had had a similar clause in the new lease he was granted for the small piece of land he rented from the Governors behind the old almshouse in Newbury Street.

Tenants were responsible for most repairs, in which case there is no record of what was done, but when repairs were carried out by the Governors, it is sometimes possible to deduce what work was necessary. There are no records of any repairs in the first account book, so it is possible that the tenants carried out all repairs in the first half of the seventeenth century. In 1659, there was the first mention of the Governors having repairs done on one of their houses. Edward Cottrill had rented a house and shop in Wantage but he had died and his sons were taking over the lease for a fine of £5 and an annual rent of £4, with one son, George, a woollen draper, living on the premises. It was agreed at a meeting of the Governors that the brick chimney at the north end of the house or shop was to be taken down and a new chimney built in its place, with other unspecified repairs being carried out on the shop at the same time. At the time this decision was made, both the fine and the rent for that year were owing, and it appeared that over the years George was not very reliable with regard to paying his annual rent, because in 1663 the Governors consented to some of his goods being confiscated to make up for the rent he was owing to them. The Governors had paid for rebuilding this chimney but when John Symons took a new lease of a house in Grove Street in 1703 he was obliged to build a new chimney at his own expense as part of the agreement with the Governors. Work was done by the Governors on another chimney on a town property in 1699, possibly their house in Wallingford Street. This was at the house rented by William Harding and 1s 6d was paid "for stones for Harding's chimney", so a stone rather than a brick one. The cost was rather a small sum of money, so perhaps in this case it was for a repair rather than rebuilding the whole chimney. The following year, 1700, other more extensive and expensive repairs were done to this house, costing the Governors £20. Another chimney was referred to in 1702, when John Kimber had one built at the house he rented from the Governors: the accounts do not specify whether this was a brick or a stone chimney, but the Governors contributed £2 5s 0d and they also allowed John to put two years rent towards the cost of erecting it. His rent had been 10s a year, but after the chimney was built this increased to 14s.

As with the chimneys, it is possible to deduce what some of the houses in Wantage were made of, by the materials bought when the Governors carried out repairs; bricks, wooden boards, lime for plaster and hair to mix into it were often paid for when repairs were needed. The rebuilding of the cottages in Mill Street, as detailed in the chapter on the almshouses, shows that these cottages were being re-thatched. Four loads of straw were bought and the work necessary for thatching the houses was demonstrated by the jobs people were paid to do. Spratt Farmer was paid 2s 9d for five and a half days spent "elming" the straw (6 pence a day): this was the process of yelming, which aligned the stalks of the straw to make neat bundles ready for the thatcher to use on the roof. It appeared that the straw was sometimes wetted at this stage, and quite often it was a woman who did this job, although not this time. John Heath was the thatcher; he would have served an apprenticeship and would have been a skilled man, which showed in his rate of pay as he

earned 1s 7d, or 19 pence, a day. He worked on the roofs for almost two weeks, and a labourer was also paid as his assistant "serving thatcher and binding". The assistant was usually paid more than the person yelming the straw but less than the thatcher, so skilled but not a fully trained man.

Most houses belonging to the Town Lands appeared to be thatched in the seventeenth and eighteenth centuries, although the old almshouse in Newbury Street, the grammar school and the English school had slate roofs. The slates would have been stone slates, like the Stonesfield slates used in the Cotswolds. Like the Governors' houses, the majority of houses in Wantage at the time would have been thatched, but in 1828 the Wantage Improvement Act was passed by Parliament, one clause of which banned the use of thatch, which was a fire risk. From then on, no houses were to be newly thatched in the town and the act even forbade the repair of existing thatched roofs. How well this rule was enforced is a little dubious. Shortly after the act was passed, in 1835, the Governors' minutes recorded that "cottages late in the occupation of Joseph Blissett to be thatched". These cottages were in Newbury Street, so surely should not have been thatched at that date. After this, the Governors' accounts have several entries relating to thatching being carried out, but the locations of the properties in question were not given, so they could have been out of Wantage; as when in 1862 some cottages in Hanney were shown to have been re-thatched. However, in 1882, John Wheeler put in an application for the Governors "to repair the buildings in his occupation in Newbury Street", and they were re-thatched at a cost of £14 10s 7½d. Most likely these were the same cottages that were re-thatched in 1835, and again it appears that they should not have been repaired in this way. Two house fires in Wantage were reported in the newspaper towards the end of the century, where thatched roofs were involved: some cottages in Garston Lane in 1872 and four houses in Mill Street in 1893; this second fire being sixty five years after the 1828 Act which banned new or repaired thatched roofs in the town. Even into the twentieth century, some of the roofs must still have been thatched, as in 1905 straw and thatching work was paid for in Mill Street, while similar work was carried out in 1908 at the Newbury Street cottages. This thatched roof may have been on an outhouse, not the main cottages, as in 1915 Miss Liddiard, who lived next door to the Governors' property in Newbury Street, complained that the thatch on the Governors' outhouse had perished and was continually falling into her garden; at which point it was decided to replace the rotten thatch with tiles or slates. In 1916 a small part of the fire insurance premium was returned to the Trust "on account of thatch removed from buildings in Mill Street", which may have indicated that at least one roof there was no longer thatched.

Our ancestors would be shocked at how we waste materials these days. In the past, nothing was thrown away if it still had a use; and when buildings were pulled down, materials were re-used if at all possible. In 1724, John Hyde rented a house which needed repairing. As there were outbuildings attached which were in such a bad state that they were to be pulled down, it was decided that any materials from these outbuildings which could be used in repairing the house were to be utilised in this way, although an extra £10 was given to the tenant towards new materials as well. Two of the Mill Street houses, which are now the almshouses, were rebuilt in 1868, and the builders were told to use as much of the old materials as they could. And when some cottages in Cat Street, next to the Alfred's Head Inn were pulled down in 1871, the re-usable materials were sold for £22 10s 0d. Even old thatch was sold during the 1700s; for example, in 1787 when one of the Governors' properties was having some thatching work done on its roof, John Martin paid £1 1s 0d for the old thatch. Quite what the old thatch was used for is not explained; perhaps John Martin used it for animal bedding, or rotted it down and ploughed it into his fields.

Water supplies

People and animals needed a water supply and the Governors appeared to be responsible for some of the pumps in the town. At various times over the years, they had pumps at the schools, the almshouses, and at property they let to tenants, which required mending or new ones to be installed; but in addition to these pumps which would be expected to be the Governors' responsibility, reference is often made to a pump in the market square which was repaired at the Governors' expense. The first mention of any pump was in 1681, when the Governors paid just under 5s "for mending the Town pump". This pump was at the church end of the market place. It is not possible to know for certain when this town pump was set up. Before its existence, all water may have been obtained from the brook, or from wells. There were several entries regarding repairs to the pump during the 1680s, and during the 1690s it had to be mended five times and cleaned out once; but after all, it must have had to put up with constant hard usage.

In 1718 the Governors decided at a meeting that the rent gatherer should find out whether the people living next to the town pump would prefer to have it repaired or to have a new one made. These would be the townspeople who used the pump, and the Governors were prepared to carry out their wishes, with the rent gatherer given permission to cut down timber to make the pump serviceable once more. As John Oakley was paid £3 5s 5d for doing this work, it was probably decided to make a new pump, while at the same time John Stiles was paid to clean out the well at the pump and 'stean' it, which was to line it with stones. His bill was only for 9s 4d so more likely repairs to the stonework of the well shaft rather than a completely new well lining. In the 1730s, the almshouse well underwent similar repair work when eight bushels of stone were bought and a mason and his labourer were paid for their work on the well there. Repairs continued to be carried out at intervals: in 1787 the town pump, the almshouse pump and the workhouse

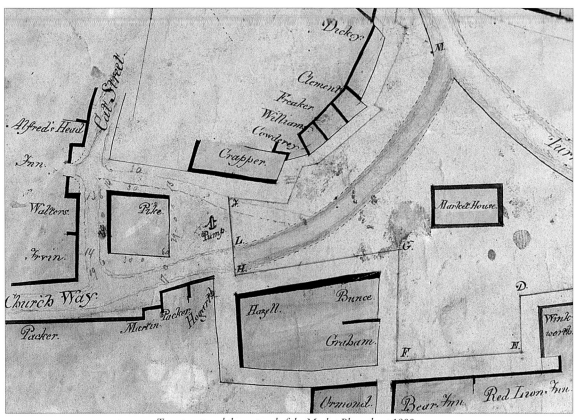

Town pump and the west end of the Market Place about 1800

pump all needed their pump handles mending, which was done by William Savory, the blacksmith.

Pumps and wells on property rented to tenants in the town by the Governors were sometimes repaired at the Town Lands' expense, as when in 1800 Mr Kent was paid £5 5s 2d for repairing the pump at Mrs Markwell's house at the top of Grove Street, which she rented from the Governors. The four new cottages in Grove Street needed repairs to the pump there in 1861, three years after they were built. Farm properties and land, on lease from the Governors, were also provided with pumps or had pumps repaired. In the early days of the Town Lands, tenants would be provided with wood towards making a pump: in 1686 Symon Arnell, on being granted a new lease of the land he rented from the Governors, was allowed a tree to make a pump; and in 1765, John Collins of Hanney was also given a tree to make a pump on the property that he leased there. In 1858, Mr Jackson, who leased Pound Close,

the meadow opposite the Grammar School where the Recreation Centre now is, sank a well and installed a pump there, which was most likely to enable him to water animals on this ground. In 1892, the Governors had a well dug in the garden of the Shears, even though by this date some Wantage houses had piped water.

So in the eighteenth and nineteenth centuries, at least some of the town properties had access to water from below ground and would not need to use the brook or the water running down Newbury Street, which were the water sources for some of the Wantage inhabitants. As well as obtaining water, it was necessary to be able to dispose of sewage, and in the early days much of this waste ended up in the brook. The later part of the nineteenth century saw Wantage townspeople becoming more aware of the problems with the water supply and sewage in the town and some of the surrounding villages. Grove's water supply was appalling as almost all the water for that village was obtained from the stream which had first run through Wantage, receiving the town's sewage; a situation made worse in 1874 when Wantage decided to improve its drains and run more sewage into the stream. The vicar of Denchworth, in 1877, reported that Grove had the filthiest water in the district and went on to describe the conditions suffered by Grove inhabitants: "They drink the contents of Wantage privies etc diluted with brook-water and flavoured with Charlton sewage, and the refuse of gas-works and farmyards". An inhabitant of Grove was reported as saying that it was not necessary to use tea to make the water brown in Grove. The Wantage Water Company was formed in 1877 and was given permission to supply pure water to Grove the following year, but not all the inhabitants could afford this. In 1881, the Governors paid for laying on water at Mrs Belcher's, one of their properties at Grove, so they were keeping their facilities up to date there. The connection of the Governors' town properties to the water supply mostly occurred in the early years of the twentieth century, between 1901 when water was laid on at one of the Mill Street cottages to 1927 when the Newbury Street property was linked to mains water. There was some disagreement regarding the payment of the water rates for the Shears in 1913: the Governors felt the outgoing tenants, Belcher and Hopgood, should pay but the tenants had other ideas. The entry in the accounts for that year shows that the rate for the water supply at the Shears was "paid under protest" by the Governors to prevent the water being cut off. Belcher and Hopgood finally settled for paying a proportion of the water rate and as Morrells took over the inn at that point, there were no more problems.

We know that a privy was installed at the old Grammar School in the late 1600s, but how other houses in the town coped with this aspect of life in Wantage is not mentioned until 1814, when Phillip Skeef was paid 15s "for emptying the privy in Mill Street". In 1820, the 'necessary' (i.e. privy) at the house at the top of Grove Street, where Thomas Chivers lived, was emptied at a cost of 7s 6d; and then over

the following twenty years there were four further accounts of privies being emptied; two in the cottages in Mill Street, two more with their location not given. In 1827, as well as paying Henry Herbert 5s for the usual emptying, an oil cask was supplied "for the privy", which one hopes had a seat fitted before use. In 1892, at the request of the tenant of the Shears Inn, the drain from the WC at the inn into the brook was lowered, to improve the drainage from the WC. Which sounds as though the WC discharged straight into the brook. As the Letcombe Brook eventually discharged into the Thames, the Thames Conservancy was responsible for trying to ensure polluted water did not flow into the brook. In 1909 the Governors had a complaint from this body, as the Shears was discharging waste washing water from the sink into the stream. It only seemed to be washing water, not waste from the WC at this stage, but even so the tenant of the inn was warned not to let this happen again.

Many of the original Wantage buildings, owned by the Town Lands, would have been medieval or Tudor. The records tell us of rebuilding work on the various houses and cottages as time passed, and most of the buildings on these sites are now modern, or at the earliest, Victorian; apart from the house at the bottom of Mill Street and King Alfred's Head, which are older. Along with houses and cottages in Mill Street, Grove Street, Newbury Street and Wallingford Street, there were several other interesting properties in Wantage owned by the Town Lands, including the almshouses, two inns, property used for a time as a workhouse and a building known as the Chantry House. Some of the history of the last four of these buildings will now be outlined.

The Chantry House

As has been mentioned earlier, in the fourteenth and fifteenth centuries, rich townspeople all over England left money for masses to be said for their souls in chantry chapels in their parish church. The chantry priests, who were paid to say these masses, would have needed somewhere to live, so it is possible that the Chantry House in Wantage was originally built for this purpose. When the reformation brought an end to chantry priests, and the king took chantry property into his own hands, the building could have passed to the Wantage Town Lands, to prevent it being confiscated by the Crown.

The first mention of this building in the Governors' records was in 1620 when John Snodham paid 40s rent "for the Channtry House that Winbolt dwelleth in". Before that date, rent for a property had been paid by both John and William Snodham, and sometimes Mathew Winbolt paid part. These payments must have related to the Chantry House. From 1620, John Snodham continued to pay the 40s for the Chantry House and it appeared that Winbolt continued to live there. John Snodham paid £5 to the Town Lands in 1631 for a licence to allow him to sell "his estate which he had in the Shoppe in the Chantery House adjoining to the highe Towne" while the following year the Governors paid out £5 "for the buying in of a lease of Mathewe Winbolt's howse". So perhaps the Governors were letting the Chantry House in two parts; a shop in one part of the building to John Snodham and the remainder of the building to Mathew Winbolt. By other indications over the years, it is possible to work out that the Chantry House was on the open triangle of road in front of the shops next to the Alfred's Head.

Mathew Winboult (or Wynbolt, Winbolt or Winball as his name was sometimes written) was a tailor who was employed by the Governors to make clothes for the poor. In 1624, he made a suit for Henry Pyper for which he was paid 2s, and "cloathes for John Marriott's mayd" (i.e. his daughter) for the sum of 4s 10d. Most years his bill for making clothes for the poor was between 6s 8d and 30s 6d. So even in a good year this work did not cover the cost of his rent and must have been only a small part of his total business. In 1644, the Governors paid out 40s to be shared by Mathew Winbolt and Widow Snodham, which indicates that

John Snodham had died and his widow and Winbolt were both needing financial help. Mathew had been making clothes for the poor for at least twenty years, so could have been getting old. John Snodham was one of the original Governors after the Act of Parliament. He was a draper so may have supplied the materials used by Winbolt in his work. He did occasionally supply cloth for the poor's clothes, along with other tradesmen. After John died, Hugh Snodham, possibly John's son, appeared in the accounts. He also made clothes; in 1644 he was paid for making hose, doublet and two shirts for Richard Wright, being paid 3s for this work. As seen in Chapter 2 he also worked for the Governors as their bailiff.

John Clement, a mercer (a person who sold silks and other high quality materials), was granted a lease in 1663 of the building in Wantage "called the Channtery house, except the shopp in the possession of Mr Robert Brooke", for an annual rent of £5 10s 0d. This confirms that the Chantry House was let in two parts, one part being a shop. John Clement was given permission to take down the chimney "in the chamber in the possession of John Gilman", so the part of the building being leased by John Clement had at least one sub-tenant. Several tenants came and went, including a barber, until 1711 when Mr John Lockton took it over, who may have been one of the local doctors. There were two people occupying it as separate under tenants, Joseph Pusey and the Widow Tarlton. John Lockton was given permission to pull down the old buildings, so the house must have been getting dilapidated. In its place he was to build two substantial houses, for which he could use any of the materials from the old buildings so long as he built in brick from the ground up to ten feet above ground. The roofs were to run east and west and he was also to have a cellar with walls of brick and stone. The two existing tenants were to have first refusal on the new properties, at rents which the Governors were to agree were reasonable. Lockton was to be allowed four trees towards his new building work, from the Governors'

The approximate position of the chantry house

land. Four trees did not prove to be enough and he had to use more wood than expected, for which he paid the Governors thirty shillings.

From then on information about the Chantry House is sparse. Nothing is recorded for nearly a hundred years, from 1711 when it was rebuilt, to 1804. At this point Mr John Pike was the tenant, paying a rent of £12 a year, and the Governors asked him to repair the building. By 1849, it seemed that the Governors were renting the two tenements out as separate entities, with the tenants of both houses letting them to sub-tenants for small weekly payments. Neither of the houses was in very good condition and the Governors were wanting to pull them down because, they said, "The Chantry Houses are such nuisances and the tenants so poor and those who would live there most probably would not be able to pay any rent". This comment was made at a meeting in January and by May it was agreed that they would accept the money offered by Mr James Walter to pull down the houses. Both tenants were in arrears with their rents and at the beginning of 1850 they were given notice to be out of their tenements by the end of March, or else they would have their

belongings confiscated. The materials from the houses were sold by auction later that year, raising the sum of £44 19s 4d and the piece of ground where the houses had previously stood was later rented to the tenant of the King Alfred's Head Inn for 2s 6d a year. Then in 1875 it was agreed to let it to the Commissioners of the Town of Wantage, still at a rent of 2s 6d a year. The Town Commissioners were the fore-runners of the Wantage Urban District Council which later took over the rental of the piece of ground and finally bought it for £25 in 1937. The site is now simply part of the road.

The Swan
… which turned into King Alfred's Head

The Swan was an inn in Wantage before 1671: not where the present Swan is, by the church, but on the site where the King Alfred's Head now stands. When, in 1671, Richard Webb took out a new lease on the Swan Inn, which belonged to the Governors and which he already rented under an old lease, it was in need of repair, so had already been in existence for some time. It seems almost certain that the Swan building had been acquired for the Town Lands in late

Elizabethan days, shortly before 1597. At that time, it was named Silverlocks and may not have been an inn. The Act of Parliament, which set up the Wantage Town Lands, referred to the property as having been "lately purchased with the profits of the Town Lands". Richard Gybbes (or Gibbs) was the first tenant, and over the next seventy years it had several tenants.

In 1667, the lease for Silverlocks had recently been given to the Richard Webb mentioned above, and this lease also named a Martha Cottrill. Later that same year, Martha married Richard Gregory. Then in 1671, when Richard Webb took out his new lease, this old lease on the building was recorded as having been granted to him for his life and for the life of "Martha the wife of Richard Gregory". The minutes record that the old lease was for 'the Swan', but this must surely be the same property which was previously called Silverlocks, particularly as the same rent was paid for the Swan as had been paid for Silverlocks. From then on there was no further mention of Silverlocks. As far as the Town Lands' records were concerned, the property was known as Silverlocks up to 1667 but had become the Swan by 1671. However, in the Wantage churchwardens' accounts the Swan appeared by name much earlier, in 1653, when Anthony Webb paid the church tax for it. He could have been Richard's father, as a Richard Webb, with a father Anthony, was baptised in 1637. The Governors' accounts are missing over the period when Anthony was mentioned. It is possible that Anthony was a tenant of Silverlocks but ran an ale house or inn there and called it the Swan, and by the time his son Richard had taken over the tenancy, the people of Wantage knew the property as the Swan.

Richard died in 1684, leaving a will and an inventory of his goods and chattels, which listed his belongings from bedsteads and pillows to a butter dish and four chamber pots. The most interesting entries, though, recorded the furniture in the part of the house being used as an inn. In the parlour at the Swan there was a table, a form, five stools and two chairs; while in the hall at the Swan were two tables, a form, four little stools, an old carpet and a dresser. These were the only two rooms given as being part of the Swan, and by the furnishings the place does not appear to be very large. The building would have been a typical medieval house, where the hall was the main room. Other chambers were given, which might have been used to sleep visitors to the Swan; there were fourteen sheets on the list which seems quite a large number for a household where Richard appeared to live without wife or family. The cellar was most probably part of the Swan as it contained eight and a half hogsheads (large barrels which would each contain over 50 gallons) of beer. The beer must have been brewed on the premises as there was a brewhouse containing a furnace and a brewing vessel. Richard left the majority of his belongings to his sister, Jane Williams, and her husband paid the rent for the next four years.

From 1689, the inn was being rented to Charles and John White and they were given timber for repairs, some of it to make a new loft. Every few years they were given more trees to carry out repairs; the condition of the building was a recurring problem for them. Although the Governors helped by supplying wood, the Whites would have paid most of the cost of repairs themselves. As they borrowed £50 from the Governors at the time, this sum was most probably to fund these repairs. One or both of them continued as tenant of the Swan until 1717, when John's executors paid the rent for about six years, so John must have died. Over the following years, the rent was paid and trees were supplied to provide wood for yet more repairs. As well as the Swan building itself, there were cottages and buildings which belonged to it and which were part of the premises rented from the Governors. These buildings had been there in 1684 as they were mentioned in Richard Webb's will.

By 1756, the inn was not in a good condition. The tenant, Mr Sedgely of Oxford, was warned that if he did not carry out the necessary repairs and pay his rent arrears, the Governors would sue him. So he gave up his tenancy, leaving Thomas Roser and Richard Attewell,

The King Alfred's Head in 2012. The original vehicle entrance was where the green doors are now

his sub-tenants at that time, in charge. These men were probably running the inn as the Governors paid Roser for beer supplied to workmen working on the Governors' land. The Governors appeared to carry out the repairs on the Swan, with timber being cut down to do this, as usual, and with five named Governors put in charge of deciding what repairs were needed and making sure these repairs were carried out properly. In 1759, bricks were brought in, the yard at the back was levelled, and George Miles was paid sixpence for digging up a vine at the Swan, probably some sort of creeper that was growing over the building. After what were fairly minor repairs, the building was still not in a good state and the Governors had it surveyed with the intention of valuing the materials it was made of. Once this was done, four of the Governors were to sell these materials and find a person willing to take on the lease

of the ground where it had stood. So it was about to be pulled down. A year later in December 1761, this had not been done, whether because of a change of plan or because the four Governors had not got round to it, or even because no-one wanted the materials in the building, we are not told; but it was then decided to advertise that the Governors would let the building instead of pulling it down.

John Stevens, who already rented some of the Governors' properties, including cottages in Mill Street and in Wallingford Street, took the lease of the Swan in February 1762 and it is probable that he then rebuilt at least part of it. From the accounts it is not possible to be sure which entries refer to rebuilding the Swan, but as a lot of work was paid for directly after Stevens took over the lease, and as William Stone and three labourers were paid for "sorting and telling out the bricks at the

Swan", it seems reasonable to assume that the 11,100 bricks sold by the Governors that year came from the old building, and that it had been, at least partly, taken down. John Stevens would have been responsible for the payment of much of the rebuilding work, so the full cost of this did not show in the Governors' accounts, apart from some timber from Barwell Close, one of their properties, which they agreed to give to John Stevens. One important indication that Stevens had carried out extensive restoration work came when he paid his rent in 1763, as he had changed the name of the Swan and the inn was now called the Alfred's Head Inn. We can be certain that the two names refer to the same place as it is minuted at a meeting at the time that "the Swan Inn (now Alfred's Head)" was leased to John Stevens. It would be interesting to know which part of the present King Alfred's Head is the building which was put up by Stevens in 1763: it has been suggested that it could possibly be the right hand wing but as the old building was possibly a medieval style of hall house, the likelihood is that he rebuilt the majority of the present building. John Stevens was in arrears with his rent in 1769, not only for the Alfred's Head but also for the other property he leased from the Governors, and Henry Stone had taken over the lease of the Inn. By the following year Henry must have died, as a new lease on the Alfred's Head was taken by Mrs Sarah Stone, his widow. It appeared that John Stevens had included other people in the cost of improving the inn. Mrs Stone's late husband had put large sums of money into the project and so because of this the Governors only charged her a small fine to take on the new lease, whereas she would normally have paid a much larger sum to do this. Mrs Stone continued to pay the annual rent for the Alfred's Head for fifteen years until 1785.

From the time the inn changed its name to the Alfred's Head it became one of the town's more important meeting places. Auctions were held there, the Governors' meetings took place in a room there and in 1782 the Alfred's Head, sometimes referred to as the King Alfred's Head, was appointed as the place

The room in the King Alfred's Head where the Governors most probably held their meetings

where tenants would bring their annual rents. As seen in Chapter 2, the rent receiver was allowed expenses at these rent meetings, possibly for drinks. No doubt the gathering of tenants was lucrative for the landlord of the Alfred's Head. When auctions were held there, bills were sometimes paid for drinks supplied during the auction; in 1802, 5s was paid for "liquor at the auction when Mr Belcher's land was let", and later the same year 3s 9d was the cost of "liquor at the time the Ham Land was let". In 1801, a local newspaper advertised that Assemblies were held at the Alfred's Head — shades of Jane Austin in Wantage.

From the records it seems likely that none of the tenants actually ran the inn, but either employed someone to do that for them, or sub-let. Various members of the Morland family were tenants from 1786 until 1854. The last Mr Morland owned land adjacent to the Alfred's Head; with buildings on this land, which were pulled down in 1854. The Governors offered to buy this land and the materials from the buildings that had stood on it, and Mr Morland agreed to a price of £100 provided he approved of the stables, sheds and harness room, which were to be erected there by Mr Hunt, the Wantage builder. This must have met with the Governors' approval as they cashed some of the Consols belonging to the Trust to raise the £100 to pay to Mr Morland. The cost to the Governors of those new outbuildings was £115, with an additional £5 when they asked Mr Hunt to cover the dung pit with a roof. Several tenants followed Mr Morland, until in 1870 a lease was agreed with Messrs Field and Company of Shillingford, near Wallingford. Mr Field was to spend not less than £200 on repairs, with some of the cost deducted from his rent each year.

The street which ran past the front of the Alfred's Head, down to Mill Street, was called Cat Street at the time that the inn was taken over by Mr Field but later became Alfred Street, as it is now. At that time, there was a collection of very old and dilapidated cottages in Cat Street, next to the inn, and the Governors decided that it would be a good idea to buy them and pull them down. They did not say why, but it could have been to improve the surroundings of the Alfred's Head, as the cottages were described as being a nuisance, which at that time could mean a health hazard. The cottages belonged to John Collins Belcher and Edward Panza Belcher, the Wantage auctioneers and they offered

to sell them for £205. The Charity Commissioners were consulted and they agreed to this purchase and suggested that the £120 which the Governors had just received from the sale of a building and garden in Grove Street, to George Dixon, should be put towards purchasing the Cat Street cottages. The cottages were bought and almost immediately pulled down, with the re-usable building materials in them being sold. The land where the cottages had stood was now used as the site for some more new stables for the Alfred's Head, which were built by George and John Kent for £148. Once built the new stables were offered to Mr Field for an annual rent of £20: he agreed to rent them for £15.

Next door to the Alfred's Head, at the opposite side to the new stables, was the shop and premises of Alfred Kent. In 1876 he built a new extension at the back, which blocked the light from the WC at the Alfred's Head. He was told that he must pay for a new

King Alfred's Head stables

WC in a different part of the inn, or else the Governors would sue him for damages. The matter came up at the next meeting without anything being resolved and finally the Governors decided not to take any further measures, so everyone must have learnt to live with the lack of light, and Alfred Kent did not have to pay up.

By 1879 the Alfred's Head was once more "falling into decay for want of proper repair". The negotiations between the Governors and Mr Field, as to who should pay, dragged on for several years and finally he paid for the repairs but was charged a reduced rent. Morlands, now Morland and Company, were once more the tenants by 1890; but in 1896, the lease was offered to Messrs. Hanley and Company of Oxford. This firm then amalgamated with Hall's Oxford Brewery, who were the tenants until December 1920 when the King Alfred's Head was put up for sale by the Governors. In 1915, a request was made by the Wantage Urban District Council, to rent a piece of ground which was part of the stable at the King Alfred's Head, so they could construct a public urinal on it. But "after careful consideration" the Governors "came to the conclusion that they could not regard the request favourably". A small building, which the Governors probably considered a necessity, but didn't want in their back yard.

In the 1920 sale catalogue the building was described as a seventeenth century coaching hotel. There may have been parts remaining from the seventeenth century; or even parts that were earlier, as some anonymous notes at the Vale and Downland Museum in Wantage refer to a large open cellar when Arthur Merritt kept the inn (1916-1935), where there were carved stone corbels: on one occasion when plaster fell off the cellar wall it revealed not wattle and daub, but rushes. There were also said to be several passages towards the Market Place and the church, which were filled with water and fallen brickwork. As this cellar is now supposedly bricked up, all this can no longer be seen, although there are extensive cellars still in use. The sale catalogue informed prospective

Problem with light - the narrow gap between the buildings after Alfred Kent built his extension

buyers that the inn was in "the old historic Market Town of Wantage, famed for its salubrity, and situate in a fine position at the foot of the Berkshire Downs". The advert went on to give a glowing description of Wantage: "Its Market Square, with noble statue of King Alfred, is one of the finest in the Kingdom, and now that Motor Traffic is bringing more and more custom, the Town is beginning to be appreciated, and to regain its former favour." The King Alfred's Head was described as having "a large room suitable for a Coffee and Dining Room, a spacious Billiard Room, and considerable Bedroom accommodation." There was also "a spacious Bar with Parlour attached" as well as a market room and a commercial room. The billiard room was on the first floor, with three circular headed windows, so was the room looking out onto the street, as the windows are still there. It was suggested that the billiard room could be joined with the next room which had two similar windows, to form a "grand ballroom or club room"; which has now been done, the room being used for wedding receptions and other functions. The two rooms had been one large one before 1899, when a partition had been put in. There were eight bedrooms in all, nine if the room next to the billiard room was used as a bedroom, some on the first floor and some on the second; with stabling for twenty five horses outside. The billiard room had had two old oil paintings hanging on the wall there, which were noticed by an Abingdon photographer in 1918. He pointed out that they were in bad condition but said he was prepared to buy them. Mr Jotcham, the clerk, took them to an expert for advice and they were sold later that year to the Oxford High Street firm of Ryman and Co. for ten guineas (£10 10s 0d). It would have been interesting to know what they were and where they came from originally.

Part of the cellars at the King Alfred's Head

The King Alfred's Head Hotel was sold by auction in December 1920, being bought for £1,900 by Halls Brewery. And so it passed out of the hands of the Governors of the Wantage Town Lands, after over three hundred years in which it had provided the charity with an income in all its different guises.

The Shears Public House

Another Wantage public house owned by the Governors of the Wantage Town Lands was the Shears in Mill Street. The first mention of this pub by name in the records was in 1811, when William Savory "at the Shears" paid £25 to alter his lease there. The Savory family had rented the building from the Governors for over a hundred years by then, with various William and John Savorys paying the same annual rent of £2 10s 0d as far back as the late 1600s. In 1755, a John Savory was in arrears with his rent. His son, John, paid half and the Governors decided that because the father was "poor and infirm" the remainder of the arrears would be "forgiven him". Often the lease passed from father to son. The son John, mentioned above, took over his father's lease, and after he died as an old man in 1799, the lease was granted to his two sons Thomas and William.

This William was the William Savory "at the Shears" when the pub was first mentioned. He was a blacksmith and for many years after this there was a blacksmith's forge at the Shears. Whether the Savory family also ran the pub is not clear, but we know that William's father, John, had also been a blacksmith. After William died in 1828, the lease passed to his nephew, another John Savory and also a blacksmith. From various wills, the Savorys in Mill Street all seemed to be blacksmiths. William, who died in 1716, left all his stock of coal and iron to his son John, as well as his tools and implements of his trade, and articles he had made which were in the blacksmith's shop a the time of his death.

Finally the long line of Savorys came to an end, and in 1881 the Governors decided to advertise the

Mill Street in the late 19th or early 20th century.
The Shears is in the right foreground and cottages belonging to the Governors are in the left foreground

public house and blacksmith's shop to be let, once they had improved the building. A plan and estimates were obtained and it was agreed to let Mr Whiting, of Wantage, carry out the work for £85. Because the tenancy had stated that the building was to be left in good condition, the Governors had an estimate made of the dilapidation and the cost of putting this in order, and Mr Savory's executors were asked to pay this cost, which came to between £50 and £60. The executors thought this was too much and employed their own valuer to assess the dilapidation. There was a certain amount of argument between the valuer appointed by the Governors and the solicitor appointed by the executors. Finally an arbitrator between the two parties set a sum of £75 as a fair amount, plus half the costs. It would have been cheaper for Savory's executors if they

The bottom of Mill Street circa 1900 with The Shears on the left

The Shears in 2011

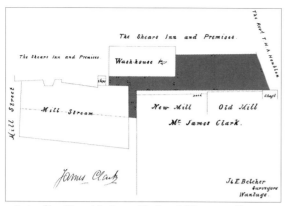

Strip of land leased by James Clark and following mill owners

had paid up in the first place. The Governors then had part of The Shears pulled down and alterations were carried out by Mr Whiting.

At this point the tenancy of the Shears passed to Ryland James Walford who was given permission to sub-let the Shears and the blacksmiths shop. At the same time the Governors agreed to let a small strip of land between the back of the Shears and the mill, and part of the mill stream, to Mr James Clark who owned the mill, for £5 a year. Successive mill owners rented this land until it was bought by the then mill owner, just over a hundred years later in 1989, for £5,000.

At the beginning of the twentieth century, the Shears was "out of repair both internally and externally". It was rebuilt in its present form in 1912. The Governors had considered selling the old building but were worried that the sale money invested would not bring in as much income as the rent and they decided to rebuild the inn instead. To help pay for this work, which cost just over £700, the Governors sold their property in Wallingford Street, raising £222, as well as taking out a loan for £250. There was still the blacksmith's shop attached to the inn, with a shoeing house and other buildings belonging to the blacksmith, and these were rebuilt at the same time as the inn, along with a stable there. Once the Shears had been rebuilt, the lease was taken by Morrells, the Oxford brewers, who remained tenants until the company bought the Shears from the Governors for £5,000 in 1946.

The Old Workhouse

In the next chapter, we will find out that the original almshouse in Wantage was used as a workhouse for two years, between 1668-1670, to keep the poor of the town employed. After that there was no further reference to a workhouse until 1732, when the Governors mentioned that they might decide to build a workhouse for the poor. The idea of finding work for the poor to do was strongly embedded in the poor law. There were no entries in the minutes or the accounts in the following years from which it could be deduced that a workhouse was built, but then in 1742 two small amounts (15s 5d and 14s 2d) were paid to people for doing work and providing materials "at the workhouse". Not enough, by any stretch of imagination, for building a new building, so an old building or buildings must have been taken over, as from that time onwards the overseers of the workhouse paid rent each year to the Governors of between £8 and £12. The overseers were the Overseers of the Poor for Wantage town, so although the building belonged to the Wantage Town Lands charity, the workhouse was not actually run by the Governors. Later references to the workhouse make clear it was in Grove Street, on the opposite side of the street to Garston Lane and a little nearer the town centre.

The history of the Town Lands properties in Grove Street is not completely straightforward: sorting it out is like doing a jig-saw with many of the pieces missing and no picture to guide you. However, the most likely scenario for the building which became part of the workhouse was that it belonged to the Town Lands in late Elizabethan days and in 1597 was rented by a shoemaker, Thomas Aldworth (or Alder). The lease remained with the Aldworth family until about 1720, when Thomas Whitehorn took it over for a few years.

The property was probably first used as the workhouse in 1741, as in that year it was agreed at a Vestry meeting at the church that a Mr Gilbert was to employ the poor and "set them to work in the best manner he can", as well as keep them at the cost of the parish. He was to be paid £30 a year and the churchwardens and overseers bought fuel, malt for brewing and various utensils, including two coppers, to fit out the workhouse. They also rented land adjoining the workhouse known as High Garden from John Martin. This was the land at the back of the buildings on Grove Street and one assumes the overseers were using this land in connection with the workhouse. Three years after Mr Gilbert was appointed to run the workhouse, James Allen, a sailcloth weaver, installed a loom there so the people could be employed in spinning and sack weaving. John Noke took over the running of the workhouse in 1747 and John Farmer of Wantage in 1750. Farmer was told he must provide all the inmates with "good clean lodgings and sufficient, wholesome, meat and drink"; and make sure there was adequate provision for washing themselves, and their clothes which he would also provide. The overseers paid him 1s weekly for each person in the workhouse and £10 a year towards their clothing. He could take any profit which was made from the work done by the inmates but he was to pay the rent to the Governors of the Town Lands. No doubt he would have tried to make a little extra by keeping the poor for less than the sum paid to him by the overseers, but food and living conditions had to be reasonable as the overseers told him that they would make random checks on how the poor were being treated.

Next to the building in Grove Street, which was being used as a workhouse, was an outhouse or hovel which, in 1745, the Governors rented from the owner for 10s a year, and which was also used as part of the workhouse. The workhouse was insured each year with the Sun Fire Office at a cost of 6s, but details of how many inhabitants there were and what work the poor did there, apart from the mention of James Allen's spinning and sackcloth weaving, were not given. Wantage was known for the making of sacking, so this type of work may have been the main occupation. When the buildings were advertised for sale in the

newspaper in 1802, the advert stated that the premises were "well adapted for carrying on an extensive Hemp Manufactury", so hemp spinning or sackcloth weaving sounds a reasonable possibility for the work given to the paupers when it was the workhouse.

Small amounts of work were carried out on the building in the first few years it was in use, but at the end of the 1750s major work was undertaken. William Stone the bricklayer worked there and provided materials; two thousand tiles and fourteen ridge tiles were bought, so re-roofing must have been carried out. Three hundred and thirty three feet of timber were sawed up for use there and Samuel Field the glazier repaired the windows. After all this had been done, the building was in much better condition and the rent the Overseers of Wantage were now to pay was increased. Improvements continued to be carried out. A thousand paving bricks were put down in 1769: the floor could previously have been of beaten earth and the brick floor would have been a great improvement.

Also in 1769, the Governors agreed to buy a house belonging to Nicholas Clement, most probably next to the workhouse, and in 1771 they paid him £32 10s 0d for it. This was the building later referred to as the Little Workhouse. In 1797, the Governors decided to buy another property next to the workhouse, which at the time belonged to Thomas Beck, paying him £60 for it. This could have been to extend the workhouse premises, but shortly afterwards it seemed that the workhouse buildings were no longer needed as such. The last payment of rent by the overseers was in March 1801. As a map of 1803 shows that by then the Wantage workhouse was situated a mile and a half from the town, on what is now the Hungerford road, it had probably been decided by the town inhabitants to build a new workhouse to replace the one in Grove Street. This was a time of increasing population and worsening poverty in many areas, including Berkshire. The extending of the old workhouse and then replacing it with a larger new one was most likely because it was proving necessary to provide more accommodation for paupers. The new workhouse had room for one hundred and twenty inmates, which must have been more than a few old cottages in Grove Street could squeeze in.

As the buildings owned by the Governors were not now needed as a workhouse, in 1802 it was decided to sell them. Seven shillings was paid out to cover the cost of having hand bills printed to advertise the sale and for the town crier to announce it in the town. In

buildings, renting them out to a number of under-tenants until 1854 when John Whitehorn gave up the lease. The Governors allowed the lease to be cancelled even though it had not come to the end of its term as they realised that the tenants were too poor to pay any rent or to carry out repairs. All the people living in the cottages were told to pay their rents to the Governors in future, although the Governors were not expecting this to be necessary for very long as they immediately asked

New cottages on old workhouse site

the end, the buildings were not sold, but were let the following year, 1803, to Thomas Whitehorn who was a carpenter. In 1837, the property was described as fifteen cottages in a range of buildings with a yard and garden, lately occupied by the parish as a workhouse and known by the name of the Old Workhouse; with a building next door now used as several cottages and known as the Little Workhouse; and next door to that a cottage commonly called 'Becks'. The Whitehorn family remained the tenants of all the old workhouse

a builder, Mr Kent, to give them a quote for pulling down the fifteen dilapidated old cottages and building ten new ones in their place, using as much of the old materials as possible. A couple of months later, Mr Kent's plan for rebuilding at a cost of £280 was shown to the Governors. The Governors would have liked to sell Town Close in East Challow to raise money to pay for building the ten new cottages in Grove Street, but the Charity Commissioners would not agree to this. Also for some reason, the commissioners were reluctant to allow new cottages to be built where the old workhouse buildings had been, and said they would prefer the old cottages to be sold rather than have new ones built. By then the Governors had reduced the number of cottages they wanted to build from the original ten to four, and they thought it would be better to have an income from four new cottages rather than the sale money for a lot of dilapidated old ones. However, to comply with the Commissioners' request, the Governors had the old buildings valued, and arranged to sell them at auction. At which point the Commissioners changed their minds and so "the Governors were driven to erect the proposed cottages in as much as the repairing of the present buildings would be a waste of money." Which, judging by comments earlier, was what they wanted to do anyway. John Kent signed a contract for taking down the old cottages and building four new ones, facing the street. He was to use the decent old materials and to have an additional payment of £240; so only a little less than when he was expecting to build ten rather than four houses. His contract was agreed in October 1857 and the cottages were finished by May 1858 when they were each let for three shillings and sixpence a week.

After renting out the houses for nearly a hundred years, the Governors decided to sell them in 1952. The Charity Commissioners gave their agreement and the Wantage Engineering Company bought all four houses, possibly to rent out to their employees. The selling price was £1,850 for the four; a big increase on the £240 cost of building them but nothing like what they would fetch today, sixty years later. At the time they were sold, number 63 was empty but the three others had Mrs Herring, Mrs Talboys and Mr King living there as tenants. The four cottages had gardens, they were brick built with tiled roofs, each containing a sitting room, a living room and a wash house. Two of the houses had three bedrooms while the other two had two bedrooms and a bathroom; the weekly rent being six shillings for each cottage, with the rates paid by the owner (the Governors before the sale).

Having looked at the stories of the more unusual buildings belonging to the Wantage Town Lands, the history of the other houses the Governors owned is briefly covered in Appendix 4, while the almshouses are dealt with in the next chapter. All have played a part in the lives of the people of Wantage and nearby villages.

8

The Governors' Almshouses in Wantage

Almshouses have existed since medieval times, often being paid for by wealthy inhabitants of a town to house the poor, usually the elderly. There had been an almshouse in Wantage for some years when the act of parliament regulating the Town Lands was passed in 1597, but we shall most likely never know who originally gave the money to have it built. In 1598, and again in subsequent years, the Governors' accounts showed a payment of a quit rent of 7½d on account of "the Almse Howse", so we know there was an almshouse under the care of the Town Lands at that time. An earlier reference to the almshouse was made in 1526, at the time that Henry VIII was on the throne, when William Fettiplace of Childrey founded a chantry at Childrey and also directed that twenty shillings was to be given to the Wantage churchwardens each year for ever, on the anniversary of his death, for the almshouse in Wantage; the money to be used for repairs, renewing bedding and relief for the poor men in the almshouse. These payments had stopped by the time the act of parliament was passed regarding the Town Lands. Another reference appeared in a will of 1541, when Stephen Fordeham bequeathed "to every person and persoones of the Almys howse in Newbery strete ... ijd (2 pence) apece." The Wantage parish registers also give evidence that there was an almshouse in the town before 1597. The burial register records thirteen almspeople who died between 1550 and 1595. In 1552, Father Tanner, an almsman, was buried; in 1591, there was the burial of Sara Shepherd "out of the almeshouse", and in 1559, "a poore childe of the almeshouse" had died, so children lived there as well as both men and women. There must have been an epidemic in 1557: between the end of April and the middle of June, five deaths occurred in the almshouse; two married couples and another man. Three of these people, Margret Kitchin, and Richard and Agnes Maidman, were buried on the same day.

In 1623, extensive repairs were carried out on the almshouse by the Governors. Judging by the long list of items paid for at this time, it appeared that the building was being re-roofed: John Barnes supplied over fourteen hundred slates, while other men were paid for extra slates. Laths, ridge tiles, nails and pins were used, with eight quarters of moss to stop the gaps and prevent the wind and rain getting under the slates. It was interesting that the building was roofed with slates, most probably Stonesfield type slates, at a time when the majority of the houses in Wantage would have been thatched. William Gammon was paid 4s 6d

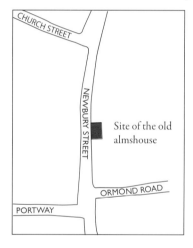

for "casting the spought" so some sort of removal of rain water from the roof was being attended to. Over the 1630s various other building work and repairs took place at the almshouse. In 1631 a fence (or 'pale' as the Governors called it) was put up, which must have been quite a substantial one judging by the timber and nails used, and the fact that it took Robert Symons and William Warner about twenty nine days between them to saw the timber. There was probably other work done at the same time, as payment for laths and for lime and hair to mix into the lime plaster probably indicated work on lath and plaster walls. Robert Barber supplied

The old almshouse site in 2011

the lime and was also paid for two and a half days work, while Robbins the smith made two locks for the doors. More work needed to be done on the roof in 1636 and 1637: four men supplied over two hundred slates, six bushels of lime were used as well as laths, nails and pins. Surprisingly, the seven quarters and a half of moss used cost 6s 3d; about a third of the cost of the tiles. A later description of the almshouse refers to it as being built of stone, so it was originally a good solid building and had probably been given to the town by a reasonably wealthy benefactor.

From comments in the Governors' records, it was obvious that the almshouse remained in Newbury Street, which agreed with the earliest references we have for it. Quite where in Newbury Street was a bit of a problem, as remaining maps of the Governors' town properties were mostly late nineteenth century in date, made after the old almshouse site had been sold and no longer belonged to the Governors. Then an earlier map drawn up in 1753 was found (page 176), which showed that the almshouse was on the site shown above, where part of St Mary's School was formerly situated.

By 1668, the almshouse was empty but the Governors did not give any details as to why this had happened. They decided that it would be a good idea to turn the empty almshouse into a workhouse, where the poor people of Wantage could be given employment, to enable them to support themselves, if they had

no work in the community. To bring this about, the Governors wanted to appoint Robert Burchell, a clothworker of Wantage, to be in charge; so it appeared that the intention was for the poor to be involved in the making of cloth. The rent collector was to bring a hundred pounds to the next meeting of the Governors, which would be given to Robert Burchall to fund the setting up of the workhouse scheme, on his giving the Governors adequate security for this money. As well as using the old almshouse for a workhouse, there would also be a house of correction in part of the building "to punish obstinate poor". Robert Burchall had to be appointed under an order granted by the Justices of the Peace made at the Berkshire quarter sessions, to make everything legal. A few months later, he recommended that John Burchall the elder, who must have been a relative of his, be made the master of the house of correction which was "for the punishing of such poor people who refuse to work and of such who do work and spoil the work trusted with them."

Using the almshouse as a workhouse did not last long; in 1670, two years after the Governors first decided to set it up, Robert Burchall had left, there was no mention of poor people working there, and the Governors agreed to let it to Peter Tubb at an annual rent of £2 10s 0d on a twenty one year lease. Peter probably let out rooms to the poor, as over the years people were occasionally recorded as living in the almshouse. When, in 1691, his lease came to an end, he was ordered to give up the possession of the almshouse and the land belonging to it, as it had been decided to make it habitable for poor people once more. Several of the Governors were put in charge of carrying this out and it was agreed that trees would be cut down on the Town Lands' property, to provide any timber needed for the necessary repairs. Once the work was done, the Governors who lived in Wantage would appoint suitable people to move into the rooms there. Five loads of timber were needed; the main repairs cost over £40, with extra small amounts for brickwork, for work done to the pump and the well, and the house of office (the privy). Repairs were almost constantly needed at the almshouse, even if these were small, such as 1s 4d to mend the windows in the room belonging to a man named Giles, or 4d to mend a door. The pump and the well there often required work done on them.

It was not clear from the early records how many people were living in the almshouse at the time; a few names were given over the next few years as people were moved in, but there must have been more not mentioned. Peter Wilkins was ordered to leave the house he was living in and go into the almshouse in 1694; Moses Rivers moved in in 1697, at which point he lost the pension he was being paid by the Governors; and at the same time Leonard Willis was admitted into an empty room at the almshouse. These three were men but women could be given places there too; in 1701 the Governors ordered that Anne Giles should be admitted into a room in the almshouse. A report of 1837 explained that there were six large rooms and two small ones, with an open court behind. At that time and later there were seven inmates, so probably each person occupied either one large room or the two smaller ones. Living in one room sounds rather cramped to us, but for a poor person that would most likely be what they were used to before they moved in. Their rooms were their private property; a lock was provided for Mary Clement's room in 1701, and on other occasions locks were repaired on the doors of individuals living at the almshouse, or new locks made.

It was noted above that Moses Rivers lost his pension when he went into the almshouse in 1697, and this happened quite regularly in the early days. The pension was probably being paid to cover the cost of accommodation for that person, and would therefore not be required when they moved into the almshouse. Some payments were made, though, to almspeople. In 1658, Richard Tubb was paid 10s a year to help him cope with his living expenses as he was old and infirm and so would not be able to work to support himself very easily; and Widow Allen who lost her pension when she moved in, was paid 1s shortly afterwards as she was not well. By 1837, all the almspeople were paid pensions of £4 a year.

Some of the Governors' properties in Wantage town were let to tenants who then sub-let, and in a few cases where properties were old, these inhabitants were poor. A few small properties were also let directly to poor people by the Governors; rents paid in 1698 by John Smart (1s a year), Thomas Tull (5s a year), William Lay, Edith Fisher and Isabell Jones (all 10s a year) were more than likely for tiny cottages or parts of houses, with the people living there not very well off. Leaving the Newbury Street almshouse and moving to Mill Street; the Governors referred to five cottages needing repairs in 1719 and 1720, which could have been the cottages rented directly to the poor by the Governors, mentioned above. An order was made for timber to be cut down "for the repair of that house and others of the Governors on the south side of the hollow way in Mill Street", which puts them where the present almshouses stand in Mill Street. For the next two years, large amounts of building materials were bought, such as eighty rafter poles which were brought by barge from London, most probably up the Thames, and then over land to Wantage. (In 1716, Rev J. Aldworth, vicar of Lockinge, got a supply of coal from Streatley Wharf: the rafters could have been landed at the same place.) The rafters cost £2 15s 0d, the barge carriage and 'wharfidge' was £1 and the land carriage a further 7s. In 1722, four thousand, nine hundred bricks were obtained at 24s per thousand; stone, wood, lime and earth were also brought to Wantage. A large building operation was under way, with the houses being rebuilt rather than repaired. John Oakley was paid £18 for the workmanship on the five houses, while John Smart did mason's work on them and was paid £9 1s 6d. The Governors began referring to the Newbury Street almshouses about this time as "the old almshouses" and as they also referred to "the new erected houses in Mill Street" these five new houses were probably the earliest form of the Mill Street almshouses, which we know were again rebuilt over a hundred years later. These original houses on this site were thatched, as loads of straw arrived and the thatcher and his men were paid for at least two weeks work. Work carried on over the following years; more bricks were bought, forty pairs of rafters and twelve 'joystes' were carted in, more thatching took place, elm and deal boards were used and Silvanus Wiggins and his partner were paid for sawing up four hundred and ninety feet of elm boards as well as some deal boards. John Mackrell, a glazier, put in the new windows. Although it appeared that these houses were thatched, sixty years later in 1780 it was decided that their roofs would be tiled "as soon as it is thought necessary". Perhaps it was not thought necessary for some time, as there was no obvious tiling work carried out over the following years.

When the Mill Street houses were ready for occupation, the Governors agreed that they would be let to people who the in-town Governors thought suitable and these Governors were to decide on fair yearly rents. Although people who lost their pensions when they had moved into the old almshouses probably were housed for free, the records show that other poor people there paid rent. At the time the new houses were being built, Thomas Stiles paid 40s a year for "that part of the old Almshouse in Newbury Street which is now in his occupation"; although his rent was later reduced to 30s a year. Richard Didcock moved into a room there and when it was then found that he was not an inhabitant of Wantage he was moved out again and was to be prosecuted for his rent arrears. So it seemed reasonable that rents were to be paid for the new houses in Mill Street too.

Although the almshouse in Newbury Street was usually referred to as the 'old' almshouse after the houses were built in Mill Street, the Mill Street houses were not called almshouses at this stage, just "the Governors houses in Mill Street" or "the poors houses in Mill Street". In the early 1790s there was a reference to "the Upper and Lower Almshouses"; the Newbury Street building would have been the Upper Almshouse and the houses in Mill Street the Lower Almshouses, at

this stage still only five houses. In 1837, the Governors were recorded as owning "an almshouse on the south side of Mill Street consisting of five tenements with two rooms below, and one above extending over the two lower ones; each tenement has an equal portion of one common piece of garden ground." At that time, the Governors also rented out a tenement on the south side of Mill Street with a small garden behind, to William Birch at £5 a year, so this was possibly next to the almshouses and could have later been incorporated into them. In 1842, William was no longer renting this cottage and it was divided into two cottages and two old people took up residence in them. Two years later, the tenants of these two cottages were to be "placed on the same footing as the inmates of the almshouses" and given pensions of 20s a quarter, which sounds very much as though these two dwellings were now being regarded as part of the almshouses in Mill Street. In 1848, the Governors refer to eight almshouses in Mill Street, so another tenement had been incorporated at some point after 1837, in addition to the cottage made into two dwellings; or one of the almshouses may have had the larger upper room divided in order to form two houses each with one room up and one room down, it is just not possible to tell where the eighth house came from. A Charity Commission report made in 1908 refers back to early references to the Mill Street buildings and comes to the conclusion that "the so-called almshouses were never more than cottages belonging to the charity in which the Governors placed poor persons of the town, either at no rent or at reduced rents."

Nineteenth Century Improvements

By the beginning of the 1860s, the Governors were considering the future of the Newbury Street almshouse which was reaching the end of its life. A few years earlier it had been described as "built of stone but repaired with brick." Although it had had regular repairs carried out on it over the years, there did not seem to have been any rebuilding programme on that site and it is likely that the almshouse standing there in 1860 was the one that had been there since Elizabethan days or earlier, so probably around three hundred years old or more. With completely new almshouses being considered, the Governors began putting money aside to fund these. In 1861, the Town Lands were given a small legacy when Robert Pumphrey died. The Governors wanted to ear-mark this for the building project, but the Charity Commissioners would not agree.

At the beginning of the 1800s there was a meadow on Ormond Road (known at that time as Pigeon Lane), on the site where there is now the fire station, Eagles Close almshouses, and the land between. This meadow was bought in October 1832 by a man named Thomas Fewson Eagles who lived on the outskirts of London. He paid £290 for the field and had obviously bought it with the intention of giving it to the Wantage Town Lands because two months later he did just that. He made one condition, that the Governors should build almshouses on part of the land, which was one of the reasons that Eagles Close was chosen as the site for the new almshouses rather than rebuilding in Newbury Street where the old almshouses had been. Thomas Fewson Eagles wanted nine "respectable and substantial" almshouses to be erected. In the event, ten houses were finally built there. He gave directions that each almshouse was to have at least three rooms, with some of the remaining land being used as gardens. He also laid down rules regarding the poor people who would live in the almshouses: they were to be natives of Wantage or people who had lived there for at least twenty years, and were to be over fifty years of age. It appeared that these poor people were to be 'respectable' poor, not persons of the lowest level in society but to be people who had owned their own homes, or to be widows of former house-owners. There were also regulations as to their income; perhaps not surprisingly they must never have received poor relief. The inhabitants were not to be too respectable, however, as a person was also not to be eligible if they had an income over £20 a year. So most probably the

people chosen to live in the almshouses would have been tradesmen or craftsmen of Wantage who because of old-age were no longer able to earn a living and support themselves comfortably. Once a resident, an almsperson would be able to stay to the end of their life, unless they were guilty of gross immorality, annoyed or molested other almspeople or misbehaved in any other way. Thomas Fewson Eagles lived in Brixton, which in those days was a small rural settlement just beginning to experience new development. His link to Wantage was through his late wife who came from Wantage. When the almshouses were built, he wanted them to be called Eagles Alms Houses, with an inscription put up at the front of them reading, "Founded by Mr Thomas Fewson Eagles out of respect to the memory of his late beloved and affectionate Wife, a Native of Wantage, as an Asylum for decayed Housekeepers, on Christmas Day 1832"; the document giving the land having been signed on that date. (A house-keeper was a person who owned their house.)

Until the almshouses were built, the income from the meadow, which was £7 per annum in 1862, was to be put aside towards the expense of building them, and afterwards the income of any land not built on was to be used to cover the costs of repairs and a small weekly allowance to the almspeople. It appeared later that the Governors had been under the impression that Thomas Eagles would leave money on his death towards the cost of building the almshouses, but this did not happen; although an investment of £1,000 was left to the Wantage churchwardens to use the dividends for the benefit of the inmates of Stiles almshouses. The bulk of his property was left to a young lady who was one of his distant relatives, on condition that she did not marry any of the individuals he named in his will! If she had disobeyed his wishes by making an undesirable marriage, his money would still not have come to the Wantage Town Lands but would have benefited various London charities.

In 1863 the Charity Commissioners were asked for their permission for the old almshouses

Eagles Close almshouses

in Newbury Street to be sold and for new ones to be built in Eagles Close; but as usual, time passed before everything was sorted out and it was not until three years later, in February 1866, that an architect, Edwin Dolby, was commissioned to draw up plans. Matters moved quickly from then on, with the plans discussed and alterations made to lower the cost. It was hoped to erect the new houses for under a thousand pounds. At the end of May 1866, James Thomas of Abingdon was chosen as the builder and the following week the contract was signed to build ten almshouses for £1,093; to be completed by the December of that year. The Eagles Close almshouses were not finished by the December as planned but were completed by April 1867 "except for the pointings", which costing only £5 was a small job. A boundary wall had then to be built and a pump installed, but this work was carried out by Kent of Wantage, not by James Thomas. In 1908, a

description of the almshouses was that each contained a living room, a scullery and a passage with a wooden staircase to the upper floor, where there were two bedrooms. The present houses only have one bedroom and this also appeared to be the case in 1980 when they were renovated. It is possible that a mistake was made in the 1908 report as there is no record of the two bedrooms being converted to one and the space is really much too small to have been two rooms. The description continued that at the back of each house was a small enclosed yard with a 'closet' and a wood shed: the almshouses were connected to the town drainage by the turn of the century, but water was still obtained from the well in the garden.

The Charity Commissioners, having been asked again, in June 1866, for permission to sell the old Newbury Street almshouses, replied that they thought it necessary to hold an enquiry into "the circumstances and condition of the Charity." An inspector from the Charity Commission met with some of the Governors at Wantage Town Hall in December 1866 when the treasurer produced the books for inspection. By this time three quarters of the cost of the new buildings had been paid to James Thomas, the builder, and the Governors were anxious to sell the Newbury Street site to give them more funds. The Governors put the old almshouse materials on the market but had only one offer, for £27, which they felt was too low. George Haines was given the task of pulling down the almshouses and stacking the materials. However, it was not until September 1868, that the land in Newbury Street, cleared of the old almshouses, was sold to a Mrs Burd for £100. Mrs Burd died in 1871 and left £2,000 for the use of the inmates of the almshouses in Wantage; the ones belonging to the Wantage Town Lands and Stiles Almshouses.

When Eagles Close was completed, a nurse was appointed to live in one of the new almshouses, to care for the elderly people who would be living there: she was paid seven shillings a week. In 1874, the nurse was Mary Francis. However, in 1878 the Governors decided that she was not to be employed any longer as she had not "discharged her duties as nurse of the almshouses to the satisfaction of the Governors". Other nurses were appointed over the following years until, in 1895, Mrs Salisbury resigned as nurse and as the Governors were experiencing financial difficulties at the time, it was decided not to replace her, although the treasurer was to make arrangements for someone to attend to Thomas Carter, an old and feeble inmate of one of the almshouses, who needed some nursing. It was possible that both Eagles Close and Mill Street almshouses had a nurse for the inmates, as the year after Mrs Salisbury resigned, it was reported that one of the Mill Street almshouses was vacant because Nurse Mason had died. She also was not replaced on a permanent basis, and when shortly afterwards one of the Mill Street inmates needed nursing, the Governors paid 2s 6d a week for a nurse to attend him. From then

on, the Governors paid for nursing only when it was necessary: for example in 1935, Mrs Belcher in one of the Mill Street almshouses was practically an invalid and a female attendant was paid 10s a week to look after her; while in 1937, the same amount was paid for a nurse who would sleep in the almshouse at night, to care for Mrs Blunsden. In 1937, it was also decided to give an annual donation of £5 5s 0d to the Wantage and District Nursing Association, as their district nurse visited the inmates of the almshouses every week. A report in 1908 had explained that as there was no longer a permanent nurse at the almshouses, some of the inhabitants were allowed to have a daughter or other caring relative to live with them, which would normally have been against the rules.

The successful building of the new Eagles Close almshouses, to replace the old almshouses in Newbury Street, had decided the Governors that the almshouses in Mill Street were also needing replacement. Mr Spencer, of North Shields, was chosen as architect (not the same person who had drawn up the design for Eagles Close) and his plans for eight new almshouses in Mill Street were approved shortly after the Eagles Close houses were finished. Different builders were also chosen for this second building project: a Wantage firm this time of John Wheeler and William Gregory. The Governors accepted their tender in December 1867, adding, "provided the Charity Commissioners agree". Which probably showed foresight! The main problem seemed to be that the Governors would need to borrow money for the building work, but after various meetings and correspondence with the commissioners, permission was not given for the Governors to borrow the £700 they needed. The Governors had set out for the Charity Commissioners what they hoped to achieve in Mill Street, giving details of the state of the old almshouses there. They explained that two of the eight houses had become positively dangerous and they had had to be taken down, with their inmates removed to temporary lodgings in the town. The remaining six would cost too much to repair, which was why it was proposed to pull them down too and rebuild all eight of the cottages. The ten almshouses completed in Eagles Close had been built with the savings of the charity, but to rebuild the Mill Street houses would necessitate borrowing money, as the Governors wished to start the building work immediately. Using the good materials from the old Newbury Street buildings and also any sound materials from the Mill Street houses when they were demolished, it was estimated that the extra cost would only be about £740, particularly as there was great competition in the building trade at that time, which would ensure the work could be carried out for a moderate amount. As the annual income of the Town Lands was then about £100 more than the annual expenditure, it was thought that if £700 was borrowed, this could easily be paid back over fifteen years. The poor in the almshouses at that time were paid weekly maintenance allowances. The Governors pointed out that they thought that it was better to put almspeople into houses belonging to the charity, rather than to allow them an increased weekly sum so they could provide themselves with lodgings, which possibly had been suggested as an alternative by the commissioners. A meeting was held in February 1868 between a representative of the Charity Commissioners and the treasurer and chairman of the Governors, after which the refusal to allow the £700 to be borrowed was made clear. So in May 1868, the Governors came to the decision to rebuild the two almshouses in Mill Street that had been in a state of ruin, and Gregory and Wheeler offered to do this for £189. The £100 from the sale of the old Newbury Street site was probably put towards this. Then in 1870 it was agreed to build two more houses, with four others added later that year. All were built by Gregory and Wheeler, and without the Governors borrowing any money, being partly funded by a bequest of £200 from Robert Cowper, a former Governor who had resigned in 1860. The final payments were made in 1872, so the building work must have been finished by then: the Governors did not indicate when the Mill Street almshouses were

ready for people to move in. A pump was installed at the back of the almshouses when the first two were built, in October 1868, and the yard at the back was finished in 1873. Each of the eight cottages had a living room, scullery and larder, with one bedroom upstairs. The yard at the back had an earth closet and a shed for each house.

Only rarely did the Governors make any comment on individuals living in the almshouses. In 1874, Henry Tylee (or Tiley) was causing trouble to his neighbours as he was often drunk. The Governors warned him that if he gave any further cause for complaint he would have to leave his almshouse. He must have behaved himself and stayed on, as he was still living there when he died in 1878. A few years later, the Governors were worried about one of the Mill Street inmates, a Mrs Stroud, whom they said was incapable of taking care of herself and was in danger of burning down her house. It sounded as though she had become senile and her behaviour had become unpredictable. They agreed to pay her weekly allowance to her daughter, Mrs Webb, if she would take charge of her mother; one assumes they meant by moving her mother out of the almshouse into her own home. Another possible move they suggested would be to the Moulsford Asylum, the Berkshire lunatic asylum. At first they felt that satisfactory arrangements had been made, although they did not say what these arrangements were, but the following year things had come to a head again and the Governors recorded in their minutes, "In consequence of the disorderly and weak-minded conduct of Mrs Stroud, an inmate of one of the Mill Street almshouses, and her inability to take proper care of herself, she is to be removed from the house." A carriage was hired to take her to the workhouse, so at least to begin with she was not moved to Moulsford Asylum, but the matron would keep an eye on her in the workhouse. The workhouse could be used as a threat if an inmate did not behave in a satisfactory manner. In 1893, the friends of one inmate were told that her almshouse was being kept in "such a filthy condition as to be a nuisance to herself and the neighbouring inmates." The friends were asked to remove her and if they would not do so, her weekly money would be stopped and she would have to go into the workhouse. They would have been long suffering friends indeed if they had taken her into one of their own houses and although there is no record of what happened next, it was most likely a move to the workhouse.

Over the years, before a new person moved into one of the almshouses, minor repairs and redecoration would be carried out, either as an opportunity to ensure the house was in good condition for the incomer or because the property had not been well cared for by the previous inmate, as when in 1892 a work man was paid for papering, whitewashing and repairing the almshouse in Mill Street "which Mrs Postlethwaite left in a filthy condition".

There were some rules and regulations that anyone taking an almshouse was supposed to obey. Almspeople were not to allow friends and relatives to live with them at their almshouse and this rule was occasionally broken. In 1915, a complaint was made that a relative of Mrs Clemson was continually in the almshouse in disobedience of the rules; and in 1917, George Cue was found to have a permanent lodger and was told that if this continued he would have to be deprived of his almshouse. It was then found that he was ill and in a helpless condition, so no action was taken as the other person living in his house was taking care of him. Requests to share an almshouse, except by married couples, were always refused. In 1899, a new inmate of one of the houses in Eagles Close asked if she could share it with a friend but this was not allowed by the Governors.

Inmates were also expected to be in regular occupation of their almshouse and not to stay away. Sometimes illness could be the reason a person was no longer living in their almshouse. When Mrs Collins had her leg amputated, in 1933, she was absent from her Mill Street house for over twelve months, being paid her almsperson's allowance of 7s a week all that time. She was told that after that length of time, she must vacate her house if she was not intending to return, at which point she came back. Mrs Evans, absent from an Eagles Close almshouse for a long time in 1912 was similarly warned but when she had not returned two months later, her furniture was removed from the almshouse and another person moved in.

In 1891, the accounts showed a healthy balance of over £300 for the year and a suggestion was made to use some of this money to build one or more extra almshouses. At the next meeting, Mr Llewellyn Jotcham, a solicitor of Wantage who was one of the

REGULATIONS
FOR THE
ALMSHOUSES.

I. No person, except the proper occupants of these Houses, will be permitted to sleep or regularly to take meals in them, without special permission given in writing by the Treasurer of the Governors for the time being.

II. No Tenant will be permitted to remain in any of these Houses, who causes scandal or annoyance to others by disorderly or immoral conduct.

III. No Tenant absent from these Almshouses for more than a month will receive the weekly allowance.

IV. It is expected that the Houses and Gardens will be kept in good order, and that the Tenants will look upon them as God's Gift to enable them to pass their declining days in freedom from anxiety and earthly cares, and to prepare to meet Him in Eternity.

BY ORDER OF THE GOVERNORS OF THE
WANTAGE TOWN LANDS.

June, 1867.

J. LEWIS, PRINTER, WANTAGE.

Governors, proposed that instead of building additional almshouses, it would be better to ask the Wantage churchwardens if the Governors could rent three of the Stiles almshouses from them. Although, if there was a need for more almshouses because the Governors had a waiting list of prospective customers, renting Stiles almshouses would not increase the total number of premises in the town. Also the suggestion made at a later meeting did not indicate that the Governors wanted to house more people: if the churchwardens agreed to rent three Stiles houses to them, the Governors wanted to take over the almspeople already living in the those houses and charge them a weekly rent of 1s 6d, which they suggested would enable the churchwardens to pay the remaining nine inmates an additional allowance. The Governors would pay their three inmates the same amount as the churchwardens' inmates were given. As the three houses rented by the Governors became empty, the new inmates would be nominated by the Governors not the churchwardens. Having sorted everything out in their own minds, the Governors put the proposal to the churchwardens but did not receive approval for the idea. The churchwardens replied that although they would be very happy to dispose of any monies the Governors were able to give them, they would not part with any houses entrusted to them. A meeting of Governors and churchwardens was suggested and after that meeting the churchwardens decided they were willing for the Governors to become tenants of three of the Stiles almshouses provided the Charity Commissioners and the church Vestry gave their consent. The Governors did not appear to take this any further, possibly because finances took a turn for the worse the following year and there was not the surplus money needed to extend the number of almspeople.

Twentieth Century Improvements

Gradually, the utilities we take for granted were installed. A water supply was put in at the Mill Street almshouses in 1905, ending the need to use the well there. The well water had been analysed by the Inspector of Nuisances (the fore-runner of the public health inspector) in 1902 and found to be "impure and unfit for drinking purposes". Although the well had been dealt with after this report, it was decided to connect the almshouses to the town supply to ensure clean water in the future. It was not until nearly twenty years later that the Wantage Water Company was asked to lay on water for drinking and sanitation at Eagles Close almshouses and the use of the well and pump ended there. The almspeople were offered gas and electricity in 1935, but at that stage they all said they preferred the status quo, which was cooking on a range and, one assumes, oil lamps and candles. Later that year a gas main was laid at Eagles Close and a few of the inhabitants decided to use it. Three of the Eagles Close inmates asked to have electric lighting in 1939 and Wessex Electricity installed it for them at no charge. The drains at Eagles Close must have been a problem for many years. From 1912, it appeared from the accounts that a man was paid to flush the drains out every week. This continued until 1933, when a suggestion was made, at a meeting of the Governors, to have a proper drain and "sanitary apparatus" (whatever that was — WCs?) at each of the Eagles Close houses "which would do away with the present system of flushing and its cost". That year Mr Payne was paid £95 12s 0d for drainage and repairs at Eagles Close and there were no more bills for 'flushing', so the problem had been solved.

At the beginning of the twentieth century, a report stated that both sets of almshouses belonging to the Town Lands were well built and in good condition, with accommodation equal to that of a good type of cottage. There was considerable demand for them and when a vacancy occurred there was no lack of applications to fill them. However, as the years passed, the almshouses grew older and people began to expect higher standards of living. The time came when both the Mill Street houses and the row in Eagles Close needed more than regular maintenance. In the early 1950s, the

Mill Street almshouses after further refurbishment, November 2011

Governors began discussing the possibility of making improvements and it was intended to upgrade both sets of almshouses. The Mill Street almshouses needed serious attention first and as it became clear that the cost of renovation was going to be a large sum, it was this row of houses that were dealt with in the 1950s and early 1960s: Eagles Close had to wait for several more years.

The Mill Street houses at the time had outdoor toilets, no bathrooms, and coal-fired cooking ranges in the living rooms, apart from one or two where the range had been replaced with an open fire. One of the Governors, Mr Loyd of Lockinge, produced drawings of the Mill Street almshouses in 1955, commenting that "I have looked at the properties and cannot see any way of improving the properties without halving their number and making one house where at present there are two." The stairs were too steep to come up to the standard of new regulations and there was no room to build extensions to increase the size of the living space as this would prevent access through the back yards. The Trustees of Stiles almshouses carried out extensive renovations on their almshouses at the end of the 1950s, during which the existing twelve houses became eight, to make room in each house for modern improvements such as bathrooms and indoor sanitation. The Governors of Wantage Town Lands were most probably aware of the planned renovations at the Stiles almshouses at the time that Mr Loyd made his comments about reducing the number of Mill Street houses. The architects, Kathleen Cornelius and Roy Pennison, who worked on the Stiles almshouses were

Rear of Mill St almshouses, October 2009

asked to draw up plans for the Mill Street ones. They had been recommended by the National Association of Almshouses, a body with much experience in all aspects of running old almshouses. It was found possible to renovate and keep all eight of the almshouses in Mill Street, installing indoor toilets, baths with hot water and sinks with hot water in the kitchen areas; replacing the cooking ranges with open fires in the living rooms and fitting small electric cookers. The outside WCs were to be removed and the area where they had been was to be turned into raised flower beds. It was also decided to remove the gas supply to the houses.

The discussions and arrangements dragged on for some time. The architects' plans had been given to the Governors by October 1957, builders had tendered for the work involved by August 1958 but the chosen builder was not offered the contract until April 1960, by which time he was committed to other work for

some time ahead. He told the Governors that it was almost impossible to recruit labour for building work in the Wantage area at the time as "Atomic projects" (in other words, building works on the Harwell research site) as well as the Oxford car works were absorbing most of the manpower. There seemed to be two main reasons for the delays. One was financial: it had originally been agreed that the Governors would sell some of their stocks, but there had been a sudden fall in the stock market prices and it was not a good time to do this. Not all the Governors were in agreement about taking out a bank loan to cover the buildings costs. The second disagreement was over whether to renovate at all. Some of the Urban District Councillors, who would be involved in agreeing the work and applying for any government loans, as well as a small group of Governors, were of the opinion that it would be better to demolish the almshouses and build new. The clerk at the time, Mr Hedges, made some quite scathing comments as he was very much in favour of renovation. He said that he knew that the Town Surveyor and the Town Clerk's staff "seem to be of the opinion that these almshouses should be swept away and replaced with their own new brick creations"; and referring to one of the Governors, he said this Governor, who lived in a modern house, was not in favour of restoring old buildings; "I gained the impression he would have preferred to have seen the houses razed to the ground and replaced with hard looking little red imitations of council houses."

A letter from the architects in January 1959 tried to inject a feeling of urgency, pointing out that the plans were still to be passed by the local council who would submit the application for an exchequer grant from the government, and that a new housing bill before parliament was likely to cut any grant by half, so there was no time to lose. Throughout the summer of 1959, both the architects and the National Association of Almshouses were questioning why the

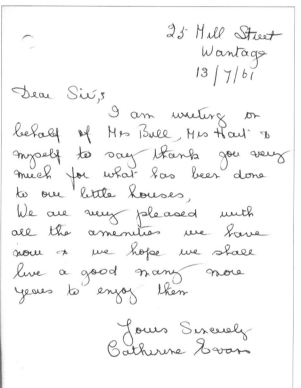

Letter from one of the almshouse occupants after the renovations

work had not started. There were long gaps between meetings of the Governors, which meant discussions occurred over a long period before any decisions were made. In February 1960, the architects, who had understood that work would start in early January, were worried that now this would be impossible before May even if a contract was signed "as in most places there are extensive delays in delivery of bricks." When the

chosen building firm had to turn down the contract in the April, a new builder had to be agreed upon, but it was nearly a year later, in March 1961, after considering several quotes, that A.J. Froud of Harwell was offered and accepted the contract. By April 1961 progress was beginning to be made, just in time to qualify for the larger exchequer grant. The inmates of four of the houses were moved out, the contents of their homes stored and work began on those houses. Once they were finished, the occupants moved back in June and the process was repeated on the remaining four houses. The work was finished, apart from small details, by November 1961.

There were problems over the layout of one house where an inmate needed to use a wheelchair, with the Governors having to explain to a hospital almoner dealing with the old lady in question that although the outer door was wide enough, a right angled turn and a narrower door inside meant it would be impossible to get a wheelchair into the bathroom. They pointed out that the almshouses were meant for people who were able to move about on their own. Another house was felt to be more suitable and the person who would be moving back into that one was asked, as an act of kindness, to exchange. This was felt to be a reasonable request, as by the time a resident moved back, the house would be quite different from the one they had moved out of. The old lady, who had been asked to move, refused point blank: "I shall keep to my own house. I am a cripple myself and have to get about the best I can with two sticks. I will remain yours truly ..."

The final bill was settled with the builders in May 1962. As the work had been done with a saving of £165 on the original quotation of £3,850 it was decided to fit an immersion heater in each of the houses. The architect wrote to the clerk, commenting on the new-look almshouses "I think they have made very good little dwellings and are so much improved". The people who lived there obviously felt the same judging by a letter of thanks, shown on page 137, sent to the Governors by the almspeople in the first group of houses to be upgraded. Before the rebuilding took place, the inmates of all the charity's almshouses received weekly pensions of 7/- and paid no rent. This continued after the renovations, although it would have been permissible to charge each person a weekly amount known as a 'maintenance contributions', not rent as the inmates were 'licensees' not tenants. In 1984, when further work was suggested on the houses, it was decided that maintenance contributions would have to be charged and the small pensions were stopped at the same time. Housing benefit would cover the maintenance contributions of those whose income was too small to pay this weekly sum. Almshouses did not have to pay rates, as charities were exempt, but when the payment of rates ended and the community charge was brought in instead, the people living in the almshouses became responsible for this payment.

Shortly after the renovations had been finished, in 1966, it was found that the retaining wall, fronting onto Mill Street, was in a poor condition. Snow and frost had caused it to give way and at the bottom corner it was saturated with water seeping through the brick work. The Governors hoped that as it was against the road, the district council might take responsibility for it, but to no avail. Mr Knapp was called upon to repair it and he had to rebuild it completely in brick on new footings at road level; the cost being almost £1,073.

When discussions first began in the 1950s, the Governors had hoped to renovate Eagles Close as well as the Mill Street houses, but had concentrated on the Mill Street houses and had postponed work on Eagles Close for the time being. Now Mill Street was finished, it was expected that plans could begin for work on Eagles Close. However, a new layout of the Wantage roads was being considered, which if it went ahead would have resulted in three of the Eagles Close houses being demolished and until these plans were either finalised or scrapped it was decided that Eagles Close building work would have to wait. There were some tentative moves made to find another site where almshouses could be built, to replace the Eagles Close buildings, but nothing materialised. It was not until the late 1970s, after plans for a new inner ring road in Wantage were dropped, that moves were made to improve the Eagles Close houses. The Charity Commission made a scheme to set up a new charity called Thomas Fewson Eagles Charity, which was registered as a housing association and this enabled grants and loans to be made for the renovation work. So prior to the beginning of 1980, Eagles Close almshouses were part of the Wantage Town Lands trust but after that time they were registered as the new Thomas Fewson Eagles Charity, although the Governors of the Town Lands were to be the trustees and were to carry out the day to day organisation. The Governors had applied to the Vale of White Horse District Council in October 1978, for planning permission to start renovations by demolishing the existing sub-standard outside toilets and coal sheds and to erect extensions in their place, which would accommodate new kitchens. Mr Talbot was chosen as the architect. The cost of the work was expected to be much more than the cost of renovating the Mill Street buildings twenty years earlier, being a little over £90,000. The new kitchens in the extensions were to have fitted units and plumbed in washing machines, with gas cookers and fridges supplied as well. Bathrooms would be installed with indoor WCs, and baths with bath and shower mix taps. Instead of the open fires in the living rooms, gas would be fitted to the houses so there could be a gas-fired boiler in each house to give central heating, with radiators in every room and plentiful hot water. Re-roofing, rewiring and decorating throughout completed the list of work to be done, a very major refurbishment which explained the high costs. As the work drew to a close, it was found that the water main was badly rusted and laying a new one to Ormond Road meant that six inch concrete had to be broken up across council land to the fire station in Ormond Road, at an estimated cost of £1,275. As well as a new water main, a new main sewer and gas main were also put in.

The building firm appointed to carry out the renovations in Eagles Close was K. H. Woodward Ltd of Grove, who had experience of renovating old houses and had done similar work for the Vale council. As with the Mill Street houses, the work was done in two phases, with the residents being moved from the houses while the work was carried out. Four of the houses were empty at the time the work started, due to deaths or moves away, which meant most residents could stay on the site even if they had to move into a different house temporarily. Two empty houses in Mill Street were used to house two of the residents from the Eagles Close site. The final cost of the renovations came to just over £100,000. Before the renovations, the almshouses were rent-free, but afterwards it was necessary to charge maintenance contributions to recuperate some of the costs of renovation. One resident, over ninety years old, had never cooked by gas and was not happy at the thought of having a gas cooker, so the Governors allowed her to keep her electric cooker and one gas cooker was kept in reserve until there was a change of tenant in that house. If possible, allowances were always made to accommodate the wishes of the elderly people living in the almshouses. Once the work was finished and the old Eagles Close tenants moved back, the vacant houses were filled. The re-opening ceremony was held in October 1981.

By 1984, the Mill Street almshouses were once again needing up-dating, although since their renovation they had been fitted with night storage heaters. The National Association of Almshouses felt that it would be necessary to put in full central heating and that the suggestion to put in showers instead of baths to make the bathrooms smaller and the kitchens larger would be acceptable, and that this work should qualify for a housing association grant. Secondary double glazing for the windows at the front of the buildings would also be an improvement. In 1988, Mr Akers who carried out maintenance work on the almshouses for many years, was trying to find the cause of flooding in one of the Mill Street houses, It appeared to be a problem in the bathroom but on removing the panel at the side of the bath, he found the reason was an underground spring!

Twenty first century Improvements

Repairs and renovations to the almshouses make continuing inroads into the funds of the Town Lands. In recent years, Eagles Close has had re-roofing carried out at a total cost of over £70,000; as well as refurbishment of two of the houses. The almshouses in Mill Street underwent a major renovation costing £256,000. The houses were gutted and given completely new interiors without altering the exterior of these Grade II listed buildings: damp proofing and insulation was attended to; complete re-wiring and re-plumbing took place; new floors, bathrooms and kitchen fittings were put in; as well as re-plastering and re-decoration throughout. The yard at the back was also improved and re-paved and new raised flower beds and wooden sheds were built there. These houses are now very much fit for purpose for many years to come. It would be amusing if it were possible to see the reaction of earlier Governors to the cost of present day work on the properties. The Governors of 1703, who spent just over one pound re-thatching the roofs of the Mill Street poors houses would be amazed that a re-roofing job could ever cost £70,000. And what would be the reaction of the Governors in the mid 1800s, who struggled to raise under £900 to completely rebuild the Mill Street almshouses, if they had been told that

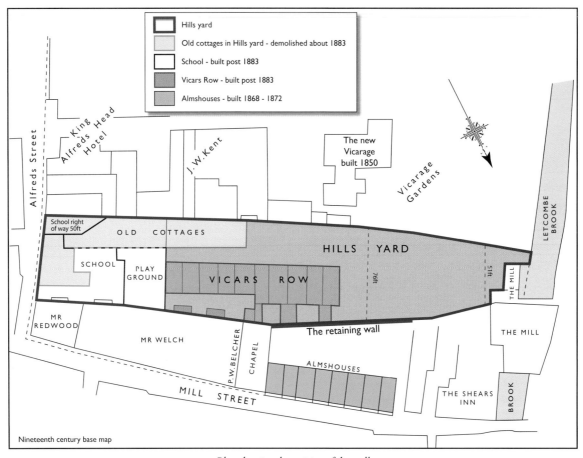

Plan showing the position of the wall

twenty first century costs for simply renovating those houses would be over a quarter of a million pounds? They would have found it impossible to believe.

The Saga of the Wall

In 1848, Thomas Haines, a Wantage builder, was paid £22 1s 11d, quite a large sum of money, for "rebuilding wall and repairs at almshouses". Unfortunately the entry in the accounts does not distinguish how much was spent on each item, nor does it show where the wall was. If it was the wall behind the almshouses in Mill Street, it would be the first mention of a wall that was going to cause many problems in the future. In 1891, the almshouses in Mill Street were in need of some repair and repainting, and the wall at the back was again in need of rebuilding. At this time the vicar of Wantage, the Reverend Archer-

Houblon, owned the land which ran behind the Mill Street almshouses and behind the Shears public house next to the almshouses. He offered to pay half the cost of building a wall between his property and the Shears and the Governors minuted that it had been agreed that this wall should be considered a party wall.

The almshouses in Mill Street are built on a terrace cut into the side of a steep slope, which is probably why the site was referred to in 1721 as the hollow way in Mill Street. Digging out the hillside to make a flat space on which to erect the buildings, some time in the past, had resulted in a 'cliff' fifteen feet high at the back of the almshouses. Similarly, The Shears next to the almshouses was on a flat site with a high wall at the back, but as this building was on a lower level than the almshouses there was also a retaining wall between the two properties. The wall built against

Scaffolding shoring up the old wall

doing nothing about the wall were minimal, as long as the wall did not collapse. If this happened, the result would be potentially catastrophic: the collapsing wall could bury the almshouses and destroy the foundations of the Vicars Row houses: both the Governors and the owners of the houses could be sued. It was suggested that the local council should be informed about the state of the wall immediately. At this early stage, the suggested budget for putting both the wall at the back of the almshouses and the wall between the almshouses and The Shears into good repair was in the region of £100,000 so a very large outlay for whoever owned the walls.

By March 1987, the Vale of White Horse District Council had decided that the wall was dangerous, and using its powers under a building act of 1984, the council hired scaffolding and shored the wall up, as a temporary measure until it could be decided who

The newly anchored wall before rendering

the side of the 'cliff', either to hold it up or to prevent it from weathering and slipping, had been repaired in 1891 which implied that the wall had been built some time before this date. It was part stone, part brick, with rendering on some areas of it, and at an unknown date, after 1877, small outhouses belonging to the almshouses had been built against it. By the early 1980s, mortar had been washed out of the wall by rain water flowing from the soil behind; the rendering had 'blown' and cracked due to frost damage and weathering; the stonework was decomposing; and in a nutshell, the wall was in a bad state of repair. There was however, one great problem: it was not known whether the wall legally belonged to the Town Lands or to the owners of five of the cottages in Vicars Row, built on the land behind and above the almshouses, and therefore it was not known who should repair the wall. Legal advice, given in 1986, pointed out that the consequences of

owned the wall and would therefore be responsible for making it safe. The land on the top side of the wall, behind the almshouses, had originally been a piece of garden ground, called Hills Yard, attached to cottages clustered by what was then called Cat Street but is now Alfred Street. In 1883 this land was sold to the Vicar of Wantage, the Reverend Archer-Houblon, who built a schoolroom for the boys as part of the church school, at the Alfred Street end of his newly acquired land, and then a row of ten cottages some time afterwards, in Vicars Row, to be let to tenants. Later, in 1920,

The restored wall and yard, Mill Street almshouses, 2011

Archer-Houblon sold the cottages and although they were still rented out at this date, they were later sold off to individual owners. The original cottages were built several yards away from the 'cliff' but at some later date, before 1920, they had extensions added at the back and these extensions were built right up to the edge of the 'cliff' with the wall being extended upwards so that the end of the extensions were resting on this wall and became part of it.

Meetings between the Governors of the Town Lands, the five owners of the cottages in Vicars Row which backed onto the almshouse site, various solicitors and the officials of the Vale of White Horse District Council took place over the years that followed, with first one set of facts being put forward to prove that the wall must belong to the cottages and then another explanation to prove that it was the Governors who were responsible. For example, the legal presumption that "an owner uses his land to the furthest extent" was quoted to show that the wall belonged to the Vicars Row cottages, which had their extension walls built on top of the wall in question; and the fact that the cottages were not there when the wall was built was used to suggest that the wall belonged to the Governors. All this time, the hire of the scaffolding which supported the wall was costing a regularly increasing amount, and by February 1992, the total bill owing for the scaffolding, consultations with structural engineers, builders charges and other expenses came to £9,372. Meanwhile, a separate but similar discussion was taking place between the Governors and the owners of The Shears on Mill Street, next to the almshouses. An agreement finally took place with Morrells, the brewery owning The Shears, that Morrells would take responsibility for the retaining wall between the pub and the almshouses and would rebuild it to the ground level of the almshouses, allowing the Governors to build it higher if they wished, which was done.

Discussions continued concerning the wall at the back of the almshouses. The insurance companies for both Governors and the cottage owners turned down requests to pay for the repairs, as it was felt that the damage was due to general deterioration over the years and so they were not liable. Legal aid was requested by some of the people involved but was refused. Counsel in London was consulted; the Vale Council threatened to file a summons; but no consensus was reached and no documents were found to prove who the owners were, and it seemed that the two sides were not prepared to treat the boundary as a party wall and share the costs. Readers of Dickens will remember how the High Court of Chancery case between Jarndyce and Jarndyce, in the book Bleak House, dragged on for more than one generation. The legal wrangling over the wall between Mill Street and Vicars Row began to take on the same long life. The case was listed for trial at the Oxford County Court in January 1995, but an adjournment was requested and by May of the following year, the Vale of White Horse District Council was suggesting a meeting of all the parties "with a view to finding a way forward on this difficult question, if possible without expensive County Court Action." No solution was found though and more than ten years later the matter was still unresolved. Finally, however, after much exchange of correspondence, it was agreed to share the costs between all the parties involved and in 2010, nearly thirty years after it first appeared on the agenda, the wall was repaired and will hopefully be good for many years to come.

The Land at Eagles Close

To return to the mid 1860s and the other almshouse site. After the almshouses had been erected, a large part of Eagles Close still remained as meadow land and was let out by the Governors to different tenants over the following years. In the early 1900s, there were various schemes considered, relating to the future of the close, none of which came to fruition. In 1901, the Governors were considering dividing the meadow into building lots and selling it off, but by the end of the year they had let it out as a meadow once more. A few years later, they were approached to see if they would consider renting Eagles Close as a playing field for the children of the town, but they decided against this. Later, in 1911, the Wantage Urban District Council asked if they would be willing to let any of their property in the town to be made into a recreation ground and the orchard in Locks Lane was suggested as a possibility, but nothing came of that either. There was a scheme to build an elementary school for boys on Eagles Close in 1907, but by the following year the school managers had abandoned that idea. By 1910, the main part of the land at Eagles Close was let to Messrs. Adkin and Belcher for £12 pa, while the small piece of garden ground next to the almshouses was let separately for 5s a year. People living near Eagles Close complained at one point as the tenants of the meadow had allowed a musical roundabout to be used there and the noise from it was becoming a nuisance. The clerk had a word with the tenants and the matter was felt to have been sorted out. It is possible that Belcher and Bowen, later to become Adkin, Belcher and Bowen, were sub-letting to the roundabout man, as they were part of a firm of auctioneers and would hardly be running a children's playground. Between the wars, they erected a long open shed along one side of the property and used the grass paddock as an auction sale yard for cattle. When, in 1940, the site began to be used as a cattle grading station, there were complaints from the neighbouring St Mary's School, not happy at the unsightly state of the field and the comings and goings of the cattle. The Governors replied to the school that, although they also did not like the field being used as a grading station, it had to be accepted "considering the present state of emergency". In other words, the fact that there was a war on.

During the later part of World War II, this paddock, with the shed, was taken over by the Ministry of Agriculture. The whole surface of the paddock was covered with concrete and several other buildings were erected on it. It was then used as a machinery

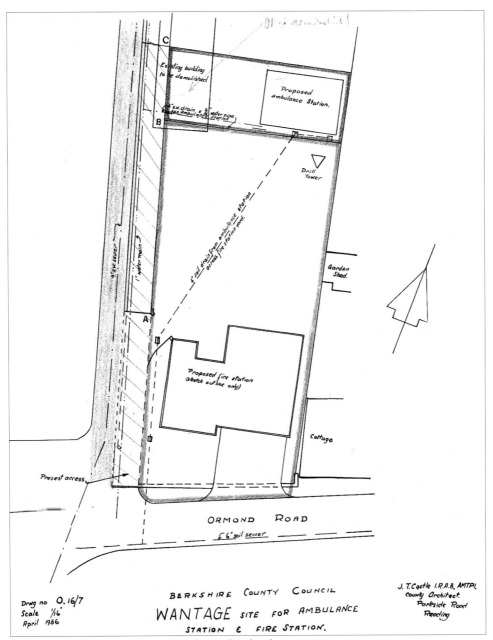

South part of Eagles Close in 1956

and repair depot, under the control of the Berkshire War Agricultural Executive Committee. When the time came after the war to de-requisition the site, the Ministry wanted to take a ten year lease on it. There was a meeting between the Governors, who felt Eagles Close had been ruined by having a depot there, and the Government Land Commissioners, who pointed out that there had been a large public outlay when the workshops, stores, petrol pump and tank had been built on the site, as well as the cost of concreting it and laying on electricity. In the end, the Governors agreed to a compromise five year lease, as they were worried that if they refused a lease completely, the site would be compulsory purchased anyway.

The Berkshire and Reading Fire Authority were the next body to show an interest in Eagles Close, and after some discussion they bought the part of the site nearest to Ormond Road in 1951, for £490. The following year the Ministry of Agriculture and Fisheries de-requisitioned the site and handed it back to the Governors, who had to pay £50 for the sheds on it. The fire authority then agreed to take a lease on this other part of the site for £70 a year, including the sheds. A fire station was built next to Ormond Road, and in 1956 the fire authority decided to give up the lease on the back part of the land. The iron building was sold to Smith Brothers of Elms Farm Dairies for £230 and the piece of land next to the fire station was sold in 1960 to Berkshire County Council for £100, so that an ambulance station could be built there. Finally, in 1976, the remaining plot of land at Eagles Close, nearest to the almshouses, was sold for £6,000 to the Vale of White Horse District Council as they wanted it as part of their new development of old people's bungalows on the land next to this.

The story of the Wantage Town Lands started with the charity in possession of a school, houses and land. As time passed, the assets increased and remained like this for around three hundred years. But times change: the nineteenth century saw road repair and education taken over by specialist authorities; the care of the poor became more organised and by the twentieth century much of the work of the Governors of the Town Lands had been taken over by the state or local authorities. Gradually, property was sold off until by the end of the twentieth century the Governors of the Wantage Town Lands were only responsible for two groups of the town's almshouses. The Mill Street and the Eagles Close almshouses provide comfortable homes, even now in the twenty first century. Although these are not the same buildings used in Elizabethan days, there is still the continuity of the Trust providing homes through the years since then. And as the Berkshire County Archivist commented in 1962: "The surviving archives of the Governors of the Wantage Town Lands ... are extremely valuable for the history of Wantage in general, since the Governors, in so many ways, played an important part in the town's social and economic life over the centuries and are a body unique in Berkshire."

9

Stiles Almshouses

The Stiles Almshouses in Newbury Street have never been part of the Wantage Town Lands but as the Wantage almshouses belonging to the Town Lands have been dealt with in this book, it seemed appropriate to look at the other group of almshouses in Wantage, the Stiles Almshouses, administered for many years by the Wantage churchwardens but now the responsibility of the Trustees of a charity named 'Almshouse of Robert Stiles' and known as Stiles Court.

It was relatively common after the reformation for rich people to give money to build almshouses, among other charitable donations, as a way of helping the poor but without the reason common in the medieval times of doing it to save one's soul, which by now was considered to be a popish practice. The earliest almshouse belonging the Wantage Town Lands had been in existence for at least a hundred and sixty years, and possibly much longer, when Robert Stiles donated money at his death to establish another group of almshouses in Wantage for the elderly poor.

Robert, born in 1625, was the sixth of seven children born to Henry and Eleanor Stiles, although one brother had died as a child before Robert was born. The children were all baptised in Wantage but that is all that is known of the family, while Robert was growing up. In his teens, Robert was apprenticed to Richard Cooke, a draper of

London. In January 1646 (by our present day calendar), Robert, aged twenty, was most probably coming to the end of his apprenticeship and he decided to travel to the continent. Before leaving England, he made his will, leaving everything to his brother-in-law, John Haskins, who had married Robert's elder sister Alice in 1637. He left John the goods that he had been given by his father, goods he had inherited from one of his brothers when he had died, and his personal belongings: a table at his lodgings, his clothing (three suits and cloaks, a hat and a pair of boots), and thirty shillings which was owed to him by his master. He then gave this will for safe keeping to Isabel Jones, who at that time lived in Smithfield in London but later moved to Wantage, so probably came from Wantage originally, which would be how Robert knew her. He told her that he was about to go overseas and sailed the following month to Holland.

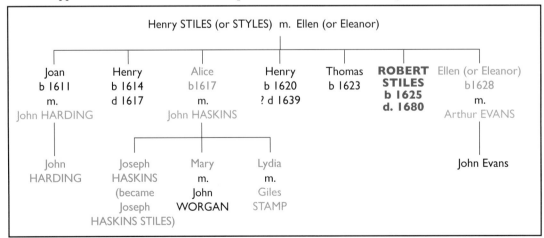

A simplified STILES family tree, with modern spelling of Christian names. The people shown in green were those named by John Evans as beneficiaries from Robert Stiles fortune, those coloured blue were Governors of the Wantage Town Lands

The Singel, Amsterdam, in the 20th century

Settling in Amsterdam, he became a successful merchant there and by the time of his death, in 1680, he was reputed to have a fortune of £150,000, a very large sum in those days and now worth nearly thirteen million pounds. He never married but took one of his nephews into his household in 1655 and employed him in his business. This nephew was Joseph Haskins, the son of Alice and John Haskins, and Robert got on with him so well that he finally made him a partner in his firm, asking him to add Stiles to his name, which he did. Perhaps surprisingly, Robert did not make a later will, so that when he died the only will in existence was the one he had made as a young man before leaving England, which was now very much out of date. On his deathbed, however, he told his nephew, now Joseph Haskins Stiles, how he wished to leave his estate and gave him details of the amounts he wanted to pass on to family and friends, as well as leaving money to build

and endow almshouses for the relief of the poor. Joseph was to be his heir and was to have everything remaining after the legacies had been distributed. He trusted Joseph to carry out his wishes, which it appeared Joseph did. Robert most probably died in his house in the Singel, bought in 1664 for 38,000 florins, and he was buried on 10th October 1680 in the Nieuwe Kerk in Amsterdam.

It is probable that nothing would have been known about Robert Stiles after he made his will as a twenty year old, if it had not been for the fact that another of his nephews, John Evans, the son of Robert's youngest sister Ellen (or Eleanor), felt aggrieved that he had not been left the legacy he felt he was entitled to and so took his case to the Court of Chancery. In the document relating to this, all the details of who benefited from Robert's estate, and by how much, were set out, as well as comments about the family and

Robert's relationship to some of them over the years. From this court case, it emerged that after Robert's death, his nephew Joseph came back to England to carry out his uncle's wishes regarding the distribution of his estate, with the agreement of Robert's remaining sisters and brothers-in-law. Robert's two living sisters, Ellen Evans and Alice Haskins, received £14,000 each; John Harding, the son of Robert's eldest sister Joan, who had died, got £9,000; and £9,000 was shared between his two nieces, Mary Worgan and Lydia Stamp, daughters of Alice and John Haskins and therefore Joseph's sisters; as well as smaller legacies to other family and friends of Robert, and 'large sums' to charities. John Evans did not say how much was left towards building almshouses, but he commented that they had been erected.

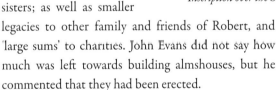

Inscription over the Stiles almshouses entrance

Evans was suspicious that he had been told by everyone, including his mother, that there was no will. He said that his uncle had promised to leave him a legacy of £10,000 to £12,000 and he was upset that he had received nothing; obviously suspecting his cousin of withholding the rightful payment and referring to him and two London gentlemen as "the pretended executors". Why his uncle treated him less generously than several of his other cousins became clear when Joseph Haskins Stiles gave his version of events. He explained that Robert Stiles had taken John Evans, as well as himself, into his employment in

Amsterdam, but that John Evans' demeanour "was so undutiful and displeasing to him that he hurried him off." It was only through the mediation of friends that Robert was persuaded to send John to London and to employ him in his business there. John, however, "being negligent and running into debt" in London, did the business no good and Robert Stiles decided to have no more to do with him. Not surprising therefore that nothing was left to John when Robert died. The Chancery proceedings were not brought until 1697, seventeen years after Robert's death: why John Evans decided to sue his cousin at that point is a mystery, but it would not have come cheaply and he probably lost yet more of his money by doing so, as it is very doubtful that he would have been successful. Joseph Haskins Stiles prospered, buying estates in Hampshire and Wiltshire and marrying the daughter of a Lord Mayor of London.

The almshouses in Wantage had been built by the time that John Evans took his cousin to court. Over the front of the almshouses is the following inscription: "The gift of Mr Robert Stiles of Amsterdam Merchant who died October ye 5th 1680. Deo et pauperibus" (For God and the poor). It is possible that Robert Stiles' three brothers in law were involved with the building of the almshouses, as they were elected as Governors of Wantage Town Lands, one after the other, between 1682 and 1692: being involved with new Wantage almshouses would have made them suitable to serve as Town Lands Governors. Another member of the family, Giles Stamp, became a Governor a little later.

As well as providing the funds to build the almshouses, it was Robert Stiles' wish that property would be bought with the money he left, to provide an income for the upkeep of the almshouses and a small weekly contribution to the almspeople living there. It was most probably Joseph Haskins Stiles who bought Dowles (or Doles) Farm at Tangley near Andover in Hampshire, about 240 acres in size, to fulfil this purpose. For nearly three hundred years, the rent of Doles Farm supplied the main income to the churchwardens for the upkeep of Stiles almshouses. Little is known of this farm between its initial purchase after the death of Robert Stiles and the end of the nineteenth century, apart from the fact that in 1733 the rent was £60 a year, when Abraham Park took over the tenancy from Matthew Gamball; and that it was leased for many years to the Holdway family: at the time of a charity commission report in 1837, the tenant was S. Holdway and he was paying £100 a year in rent. Whatever the extent of the property in early days, by 1893 there did not seem to be a farmhouse, as a tenancy agreement of that date referred to "two cottages, farm buildings and land called Doles Farm". The churchwardens at the time, Henry Denis de Vitre Esquire of Charlton and William Jackson, a Wantage butcher, signed the agreement on behalf of the Stiles almshouses, while Llewellyn Foster Loyd Esquire of Dole House near Andover was to rent the farm. As he was obviously a man of some means, it is reasonable to assume that he was intending to sublet to someone who would actually farm the land. In 1909, another tenancy agreement was signed which let the farm to William Vernon Judd Esquire of Eastanton Farm, Hampshire; with the two churchwardens, now given as Edward Brooks Ormond, a Wantage solicitor, and John William Kent, a Wantage ironmonger. The rent in 1909 was to be £125 a year, with the landlords (i.e. the churchwardens) paying the tithes, various taxes and the insurance.

Between the dates of signing these two leases, there had been a serious fire at Doles Farm. A letter, dated 10th July 1904, was sent to the churchwardens, which told them, "I am sorry to inform you a fire occurred early this morning and totally destroyed the cottages and out buildings. The occupants had a narrow escape. Happily there was plenty of water in the pond and the Farm Buildings were not damaged." The two cottages had to be rebuilt and letters from the builder, Sydney Bell, gave details of the cottages before the fire, when he asked the churchwardens about various possible plans for the rebuild. The old cottages had thatched roofs, and each had an attached woodhouse and bread oven. The new cottages, built of brick from a local brickyard, had tiled roofs; with outdoor WCs at the end of the gardens. The farm granary and a fence had been damaged in the fire, and these were repaired by Mr Bell. Many of his letters requested instalments of money to pay his workers and to pay for the materials. He had originally offered to carry out the work for around £350 and in the October he told Mr Ormond, the churchwarden, that he had started the building work and he asked for £50: when this did not arrive, he increased the request to £100 later that month. By mid November he had received £75 but had all the timbers and slates on site, the windows had been made and building work had been progressing, so he urgently needed more cash. On November 16th he wrote, "The job could be pushed on if you send £50 for wages this week"; and the following day a further letter told the churchwardens that he had had to lay off one bricklayer, and that it was impossible to pay the men unless he got the cheques when due. By the end of November, the roofs were going on and he asked for another £100, which it appeared was not sent as he wrote at the beginning of January 1905, "I note your suggestion that I should finish the cottages before you advance any more cash. This is very inconvenient just now. I am having fires kept up and am pushing on with plastering. All grates are fixed except the range." It appeared that he had problems with his cash flow and was relying on the churchwardens to supply this, while on their part it was perhaps understandable that they wanted to see the building work completed before they paid over more money. The cottages were finished and ready to be inspected by the beginning of March, although the wood-houses were built after that, of timber framing, weatherboarded and roofed with corrugated iron. The cost of the wood-houses and the repairs to the granary was £10: the granary being given two coats of tar like the wood-houses.

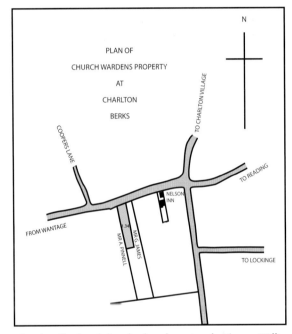

Land at Charlton believed to have been given by Thomas Willis

In 1930, the tenant at that time, a Mr Colebrook, asked for the pond to be remade as there was no water supply, and in 1933 cow pens for milking were built at a cost of £55 14s 0d. That year the Andover Rural District Council registered the farm as suitable to run a dairy. A document issued in November 1940 by the Hampshire War Agricultural Executive Committee referred to the farm being occupied by the Sterling Poultry Products Ltd and listed in detail how some of the fields on the farm should be cultivated the following year. One field was to be planted with barley undersown with sainfoin, another field was to

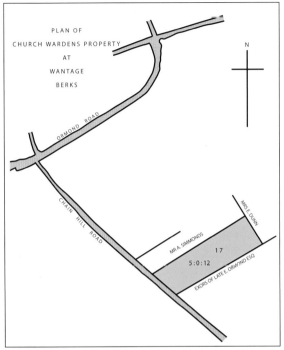

Land on Chain Hill in Wantage believed to have been part of Thomas Willis's bequest

grow potatoes, a third field was to produce winter oats, while the two fields down to pasture were to be grazed and cut for hay. The document, which was to be used with an earlier document which is missing, only gave orders for land covering 73 acres, out of the total 239 acres of the farm; so whether the remaining part of the land was used for dairying or for raising poultry, or for growing crops, it is not possible to tell. Doles Farm was sold in November 1943 for £3,820 and this money was invested in Savings Bonds, so that the interest could be used for the upkeep of the almshouses in the same way that the rent from the farm had been used in the past. At the time of this sale by the Wantage churchwardens, there were still only two small cottages at Doles Farm — one with three bedrooms, a living room and scullery and the other with only one bedroom. There were also farm buildings, stables, a barn, a bull pen, calf sheds, cow sheds and a granary. The farm changed hands again in 1951 and by then a modern four bedroom farmhouse had been built there.

Income from other charities, which had started as bequests to the churchwardens for the use of the almshouses, also helped to maintain the buildings and give subsistence money to the almspeople there. Most had been founded in the nineteenth century but the oldest was the charity of Thomas Willis, who had given land to provide income from the rents to support Stiles almshouses, as well as land in East Challow given in 1714 to the Governors of the Wantage Town Lands. Although no documents of title remain for the land given by Willis to benefit Stiles, most probably also in 1714, which would initially have been strips in the Wantage and Charlton fields, it was believed by the mid 1800s to have become three plots of land in the parish of Wantage: (1) a small piece of freehold arable land, measuring just under half an acre, by the main road to Reading in Charlton: (2) five acres of freehold arable land on Chain Hill: and (3) a building on the west side of the Market Place (the end of the Market

The probable Market Place property, next to The Bell, currently The Jade Palace

Place towards the church). Notes made by one of the churchwardens in 1923 refer to the building in the Market Place being sold, in 1860, to Robert Sansum for £130. The piece of land in Charlton was sold in 1921 for £30 and the land on Chain Hill was sold in 1923 for £125; the purchase money in all three cases being invested in Consols in the care of the Charity Commissioners. There are no remaining plans showing exactly where the building in the Market Place was

situated, but it was referred to as having The Bell on its north side, so it was probably the small shop next to the Bell. After obtaining the Commissioners' permission to sell the land at Charlton, a notice had to be put on the doors at both Charlton church and at Wantage church; and an advert had to be put in two local newspapers: in this case the churchwardens advertised in The Faringdon Advertiser and Vale of White Horse Gazette and in North Wilts Herald and Cirencester Times in October 1921.

A letter of 1843, written to the Reverend Button of Wantage parish church, after the death of Thomas Fewson Eagles who left Eagles Close to the Wantage Town Lands for almshouses, mentioned a legacy of £1,000 in 3% Consols which had been left by Mr Eagles to the minister and churchwardens of Wantage. The dividends were to be used for the benefit of the twelve inmates of Stiles almshouses; suggesting the money was to be used to purchase bread or other provisions, fuel and blankets; to be distributed during winter. However, there was no later reference to this bequest, so what happened to it is not known. Other people provided income for the almshouses and their inmates by making bequests in their wills over the years. Joseph Belcher left money in 1808, Harriet Floyd in 1856, Caroline Smart in 1876 and Jemima Caudwell in 1894. The churchwardens also referred to Thomas May's charity, which was invested in Consols, as a source of income for the almshouses but, like Thomas Fewson Eagles, his name was not listed with the names of other benefactors when the trust passed from the supervision of the churchwardens to a group of Trustees in 1958. Charlotte May, who could have been related to Thomas, was named at that time as someone who left money for the benefit of Stiles. She had been schoolmistress at Charlton for many years and had lived at Fern Cottage at Belmont. When she died in 1914, she left the residue of her estate to be shared between three charities: half was to be for the maintenance and general benefit of Stiles almshouses, a quarter for Wantage Cottage Hospital and a quarter to the Society for the Propagation of the Gospel in Foreign Parts. Originally, the churchwardens received £711 when her estate was distributed: part of this was used to repair the almshouses and the remainder was invested. However, in 1942, it was discovered that she had, unbeknown to her executors, had Stocks now worth £356 and these were then shared out between the three charities. Mary Burd, who died in 1871, had left £2,000 to be invested by the Governors of the Wantage Town Lands and for the proceeds to be distributed to the inmates of Eagles Close and Stiles almshouses: each year two fifths of the income from these investments was used for the almspeople living in Stiles almshouses.

Mary Viel had left money on her death in 1824, mainly for the preservation of a monument to her mother in the church but with any surplus income to be given to the poor of Wantage. When church restoration was carried out in the late nineteenth century, Mary's mother's monument was buried under the floor and about thirty years later the Charity Commissioners were asked to approve of all the income from the Viel charity, which had not been touched for all those years, to go to the poor. In 1922, an agreement was reached whereby the vicar and churchwardens would apply the income from this charity "in supplying to poor persons, members of the Church of England and not in receipt of Poor-Law relief, with clothes, boots, linen, bedding, fuel, tools, medical or other aid in sickness, food or other articles in kind." Later it appeared that the income was used, at least partly, for the upkeep of the Stiles almshouses.

One other charity supplied annual payments to support Stiles almshouses in later years. This was known as the Newbury Money and £2 was paid each year to the churchwardens by the clerk of Newbury Church and Almshouse Charities. The origin of the payments from this charity have disappeared, and why money was paid by Newbury to Wantage is a mystery. It was sometimes called the Newbury Bread Money and it appeared that thirty shillings was given

annually to the Vicar of Wantage and ten shillings to Charlton for distribution, and originally was not connected to the support of Stiles. In 1764, the Wantage churchwardens' accounts show that £12 had been received from the churchwardens of Newbury as six years' payments due "from houses in Newbury" and the entry states that this money was given out to the poor, which seems to mean the poor of Wantage generally, not necessarily those living in Stiles almshouses. Later, in 1908, this Newbury money was still paid each year: on Good Fridays the vicar of Wantage distributed one or more 4lb loaves to about 32 people, depending on the size of their families. He selected which people were to receive the bread and most of them were members of the Church of England. In Charlton, at that time, Mr Castle shared out the ten shillings in bread in a similar way. When this Newbury money was diverted to the use of Stiles almshouses is not known but it was certainly part of the Stiles income by 1958.

The almshouses were originally set up for twelve men but women seemed to be admitted to the houses from quite early on. In January 1732, an entry in the vestry minutes recorded that Widow Kimber and the other women in the almshouses must take it in turns to help Old Green out of his bed and wash his clothes. If they refused to help in this way they would be turned out of their almshouse. In the early 1800s, an elderly lady of Wantage confirmed that both women and men had lived in Stiles almshouses throughout her life time. As we have seen above, part of the income of the charity was used to give a small sum of money to the almspeople each week: in 1837 this was 3s 6d in summer and 5s 6d in winter, with an extra Christmas gift of 5s each; coals were given out if and when the funds permitted, although the extra amount in winter must have been to pay for heating. By 1908, the allowances came to a similar total each year, with each person getting 4s a week plus the 5s extra at Christmas: the inmates were also given £1 each at Christmas towards warm clothing. The churchwardens noted in 1923 that each almshouse was given 5cwt of coal in March and again in November, as well as orders to Wantage tradesmen for warm clothing costing £1 for each house. So although the almspeople were able to choose their clothing, it seemed these items were ordered for them by the churchwardens rather than the inhabitants of the almshouses being given money to spend on their new clothes.

There was a time when the Wantage Town Lands also gave allowances to the inhabitants of the Stiles almshouses, as well as their own. In 1806 it was minuted that pensions of £1 a year were to be paid to the twelve poor persons in the Amsterdam Almshouses, which would have meant Stiles; the following year this was increased by an extra 5s. In 1836, the annual amount was reduced and it was decided that no new inmates of Stiles would be paid a pension by the Town Lands,

Sheep knucklebones used in a footpath at Stiles almshouse

although three of the Governors signed a paragraph at the end of the minutes of that meeting saying they totally disagreed with both these decisions. No more pensions were paid to Stiles inmates from the Town Lands income after the middle of 1848.

In 1908, water was obtained from a pump in the middle of the courtyard, although a report at this time mentioned that the outside 'offices' (toilets) had recently been connected to the town water supply. There was evidently a steady demand at this time for admission to the Stiles almshouses, with similar criteria operating for admission as to the Eagles Close almshouses; preference being given to people long resident in Wantage who had never received poor law relief. The churchwardens tried to choose both members of the Church of England and nonconformists, in a similar proportion to the members of the different denominations in the town.

The almshouses were insured, but during the first world war extra insurance was taken out to cover the buildings against damage by "Aerial craft (hostile or otherwise), or Shots Shells Bombs or Missiles from or used against Aerial Craft". Fortunately Wantage survived the war years unscathed by any of these.

The Wantage churchwardens ran the Stiles Almshouses until 1958. It was then decided by the Charity Commissioners that a Scheme would be set up to administer the almshouses and the other charities given over the years for their support, under the name 'Almshouse of Robert Stiles' and under the control of nine Trustees, instead of the churchwardens. The list of the amalgamated charities was as follows:

1. The Charity known as Stiles' Almshouses
2. The Charity of Joseph Belcher, founded by will dated the 15th July 1808
3. The Charity of Mary Viel, founded by will dated the 22nd May 1821
4. The Charity of Harriet Floyd, founded by will dated the 10th April 1850
5. The Charity of Thomas Willis, (blank)
6. The Charity of Caroline Smart, founded by will

proved at Oxford on the 2nd December 1876

7. The Charity of Jemima Caudwell, founded by will proved at Oxford on the 20th March 1894

8. The Charity of Charlotte May, founded by will proved at Oxford on the 16th June 1914

9. The Charity known as the Newbury Money

Of the nine Trustees, two were the churchwardens (who were ex-officio trustees); two were Governors of the Wantage Town Lands; two were appointed by Wantage Urban District Council, later Wantage Town Council; one was appointed by Grove Parish Council; and two were 'co-optative' trustees, who were to be people living or carrying on business in or near Wantage. The almspeople were to be "poor persons of good character" who lived in Wantage parish; they were not to let or share their rooms; and they were not to be absent from the almshouse for longer than three days at a time without getting the consent of the Trustees. It appeared that one of the earlier regulations had been droppped: this ordered that the tenants would look upon the almshouses "as God's Gift to enable them to pass their declining days in freedom from anxiety and earthly cares, and to prepare to meet Him in Eternity." Each of the charities, which had originally left money or land to Stiles Almshouses, existed as various sums in Consolidated Stock, with the interest providing the annual income; and in addition there was nearly £4,000 in Savings Bonds which came from the sale of Doles Farm, in October 1943.

The above Scheme, which was sealed in June 1958, appeared to have missed out Mary Burd's charity. This charity had not been included with the ones above, even though Stiles almshouse benefited from it annually, perhaps because it had been left for the Town Land Governors to distribute, not the churchwardens. In April 1960, the Charity Commission dealt with this, making a legal division with two fifths of the invested stock endowing the Almshouse of Robert Stiles, which would be administered by the Trustees; and with three fifths being administered by the Governors of the Town Lands for their almshouses. None of the charities brought in much income, the individual amounts varying year by year depending on the stock market, but ranging from less than £5 to about £25.

When the Trustees took over, there were twelve almshouses, each with one room downstairs and one up, but with no bathrooms and no indoor sanitation. One of the first things discussed by the Trustees was the need for renovation of the houses. At the time, the almspeople were given an allowance of 3s 6d per week and they did not pay any rent, but it was realised that as the renovation was going to be costly, the allowance would have to be discontinued and the tenants might have to pay rent in the future. So that bathrooms could be installed, it was agreed to turn the twelve houses into eight, which would allow a small bathroom with indoor WC to be added to each house downstairs, with four of the eight houses having an extra bedroom upstairs. There was to be a lobby in each corner of the building with an outer front door, the lobby and door to be shared between two houses; each house having its bathroom off the lobby. The cost of the renovations was originally expected to be around £10,000 which was a very large sum to be found by a charity with only relatively limited finance. Various suggestions were discussed, including demolishing the old almshouses and building new ones in their place. Mr Hackett, from the National Association of Almshouses, attended some of the meetings to advise the Trustees and he explained that this would not be practical, as grants to build new were much smaller than those given for renovation of old buildings. He also pointed out to the Trustees that somehow they would have to find the money to improve the almshouses, as they could not continue in the condition they were in. The local council would make a closing order and rehouse the inmates, at which the Charity Commission would order the site to be sold. Although there was land at the back of the houses, it was not practical to sell this off for building as there was no means of access. The fact that the almshouses were listed added to the problem. Finally it was decided that the only way forward was to preserve the buildings and carry out restoration, by means of appeals and whatever grants could be raised.

Two years after the new Scheme had been set up, with investments of around half the sum needed for the restoration, the plans had been drawn up by the architects, Mr Pennison and Miss Cornelius, and the Wantage Urban District Council had reacted favourably towards giving planning permission, a grant and a mortgage. A year later and three firms had tendered for the rebuilding work, at prices ranging from £8,600 to £11,400. The contract was given to A.J. Froud and Sons who had put in the lowest tender. As some of the almshouses had been allowed to become empty, the almspeople were able to move into empty houses to allow the builders to carry out work and only one lady had to move somewhere else while the work was done: she went to St Katharine's. Work began in March 1962 and was completed by the beginning of 1963. The re-opening ceremony was held in May

1963, with everyone who had been involved being invited and John Betjeman doing the honours as the special guest. The vicar, who was one of the Trustees, was there and the ministers of all the other Wantage denominations had been invited. Between speeches, Mr Betjeman was handed the key to one of the vacant houses and by opening the door he declared the renovated almshouses open.

To repay the mortgage of £2,500 over thirty years at an interest of 6%, it was realised that it would be necessary to charge the almspeople rents, or 'maintenance contributions' as they were officially called because, as seen in Chapter 8, the occupancy of an almshouse was legally by way of a licence, not a tenancy and so rents could not be charged: this also meant there was no security of tenure. The Trustees had to ask the Charity Commissioners to allow them to charge up to 15s a week for the maintenance contributions as the original Scheme had stated that

Reopening of Stiles Almshouses, May 1963.
From left to right: Mr Penney (a trustee); Mrs Leach; Martin Collard (clerk); Mrs Buckland; Rev Schaufelberger (vicar);
John Betjeman; Mr Johns (Baptist minister); Mrs Betjeman; Mr Hackett (National Association of Almshouses); Mrs Hackett;
Miss Watson & Mrs Sentence (almshouse residents); Councillor Conway; Mrs Collard

not more than 5s could be charged. The people in the two-bedroomed houses were to pay the full 15s, with the occupants of the one-bedroomed houses paying 12s 6d. The Trustees were not completely happy at having to charge the weekly sums, particularly as the occupants of the other almshouses in Wantage, belonging to the Town Lands, did not at this time pay anything. Any almspeople who found the new 'rents' beyond their means would, however, be able to ask for a contribution from the National Assistance Board. As it had been realised that the prospect of selling off any of the surplus land at the back of Stiles for building was not possible without access, it was decided to offer it to the houses along Portway which were between this land and the street. Three residents took up the offer to increase their gardens, bringing in a total of £600 for the land. The garden ground nearest to the almshouses remained as part of Stiles and the almspeople were able to cultivate their own plot if they wished.

After the upheaval of the renovations, the people living in Stiles Almshouses settled down once more to daily life. Decorations and repairs were an ongoing expense for the Trustees, with the replacing of a dormer window, treatment to damp walls, repainting and other general maintenance taking place. Gradually small modern improvements were introduced into the almshouses. In 1965, the occupants were asked if they would like to have an 'Osokool' refrigeration box and six of them requested these. In 1969, one of the almspeople had a telephone installed for her own use, the first at the almshouses. One tenant was found to be using a paraffin cooker and the Trustees decided that in the interests of safety, the use of paraffin stoves and heaters would be banned as the fire risk was too great. New electric cookers for the houses had been suggested at a meeting shortly before this incident. By 1970, central heating in homes was becoming more common, and the Trustees investigated the costs of having night storage heaters in the almshouses. On asking the opinion of the tenants, it was found that the lady who had installed a phone had also put in

night storage heaters, but the other people were not interested. Having agreed that it would anyway be difficult to find room for the heaters in some of the houses, the Trustees decided to forget the idea, but only two years later made the decision that as houses fell vacant, an electric night storage heater would be fitted. The following year the houses were wired to take the heaters and it was decided to supply them to any of the almspeople who wished to have one, at a cost of £50 each to the Trust. By 1983, washing machines and fridges were normal household appliances and extra power points were put in the lobbies so that the almspeople could also have these modern aids.

A frightening experience for the people living in the almshouses took place in May 1989, when during a thunderstorm one of the chimneys was struck by lightning, causing high voltage damage to much of the electrical equipment in two of the almshouses. Mr Akers, the builder who acted as the clerk of works, did emergency repairs which included clearing debris from inside one of the houses and washing off the soot from the living room area. The chimney which had been struck had to be taken down and rebuilt, which involved using old hand-made bricks because of Stiles being a listed building: damage to the roof also meant finding old hand-made tiles for that repair. The cooker and immersion heater in one of the houses were damaged, and M&A the electricians had to do a complete rewire of the other affected house where there were signs of excessive high voltage in most electrical appliances there. In their report, M&A commented that the switch boxes were completely shattered and "parts of bakelite were found embedded within wooden framework on the other side of the passage". The insurance paid out £4,029 for the storm damage.

Each Christmas the Wantage Nursing Amenities Fund made a donation to Stiles, usually £24, and this would be distributed to the almspeople in the form of coal and cash. By 1975, the amount had increased to £40 and each almshouse tenant received £5 at Christmas. When the TV licences went up from 5p per house to £5 each, the Trustees, who had previously paid this, asked the occupants if they would agree for the donations from the Amenities Fund to be used for the TV licences, which they did for a few years. Then from 1993, this Christmas money was given in the form of Waitrose vouchers.

In the early 1970s, the garden next door on the south side, at the house called Woodlands, had become very overgrown causing light and air to be cut off from the almshouses on that side. The house had been let and the landlord thought it should be the duty of his tenant to clear the garden. The tenant agreed to do this but then assigned his lease to another person and went to Australia! Shortly afterwards, the landlord had died, the new tenant had gone and nothing had changed in the overgrown garden. New owners agreed to pay a small sum for work on the garden, which slightly improved the view from the almshouse windows but cannot have completely solved the problem, as four years later the tenant was asked to reduce the height of the trees in the garden and to clear the bushes. By now this nuisance had been occupying the Trustees at fairly regular intervals for seven years, and was obviously still not sorted. In fact, the trees in this next door garden had created a problem for even longer: in 1916 a letter was sent to Mr J.N. Arbery, the owner of Woodlands who lived on the far side of this property, at Brooklands. The churchwardens were trying to sort out the problem of the right to light, and they suggested that the trees in the garden were too tall. After consulting a surveyor, a document was drawn up for Mr Arbery to sign, agreeing to the churchwardens' suggestions, but he did not appear to comply with the request. On the envelope containing the unsigned agreement is a handwritten note in pencil, possibly in Mr Arbery's hand, which states, "Re Ancient light which was not signed by me. No thank you." More problems surfaced in 1985, when the brick wall between Stiles and Woodlands collapsed and the owner had to be asked to rebuild it. 1988 came and the wall had still not been repaired: the responsibility had been handed to the tenant and as he had done nothing, the owner was about to take him to court. What happened subsequently was not recorded, but a minute of August 1991 reports "Wall adjoining Woodlands repaired by owner". It had only taken six years to sort out. Finally, in the summer of 1994, the owner of Woodlands had to be asked once again to cut back the trees as they were obstructing the light in breach of a light agreement entered into in the 1940s. This was very much an on-going problem.

Stiles Almshouses had gone under this name for nearly three hundred years, when in 1973 it was decided to change the name to Stiles Court. A panel of Derbyshire stone inscribed with the name was fixed by the entrance door at the front of the building. The lettering must have been done in lead, as someone damaged the plaque a few years later by removing the lead from one of the letters, repeating the damage later the same year. When more vandalism to the stone plaque occurred in 1989, it was replaced with a metal nameplate instead.

As costs of maintaining the houses increased over the years, the subject of a fair 'rent' for the inhabitants to pay came up at meetings on a regular basis. Each time it was felt necessary to make an increase, the Charity Commissioners had to give their approval and the Trustees usually sought the advice of the local Housing Officer, who would suggest an appropriate rent. The 15s and 12s 6d charged from 1962, when the renovations were carried out, had not changed by 1975 but due to decimalisation was now 75p and 62p a week. As an indication as to how low this was, the cost of redecorating one of the houses and carrying out some small repairs came to £368, which when compared to the rent received shows that an increase in rent was desperately needed. The Charity Commissioners, however, only agreed to a maximum rent of £3, not the £5 the Trustees had requested.

There were not always tenants willing or able to work on the garden ground at the back of the almshouses. People could have their own little plot if they wished and at times there would be people prepared to keep the communal parts in good order. In 1976, even after some of the land had been sold to the houses alongside, there was enough unused land to make two allotments and the landlady from the Royal Oak across Portway asked to have one of these, with the owner of one of the houses in Portway taking the other. Both paid a nominal rent of 25p a year, but it was better to have the ground tidy and cultivated than unused and overgrown. Later, a third plot was let to a householder in Portway.

Suggestions were made in 1976, to amalgamate three Wantage charities; Stiles, the Wantage Town Lands and the Wantage Coronation Amenities Fund. The idea was discussed with the Charity Commissioners who were agreeable for the two almshouse charities to join, with certain conditions. For whatever reason, this did not take place. It may have been because the Stiles Trustees would have been replaced by the Town Lands Governors, as that was a corporate body; or because the Governors could not prove when the Town Lands had acquired the site of the Mill Street almshouses.

Around this time, the Trustees were finding it difficult to fill their almshouses. In February 1977, four of the eight houses was unoccupied, due to two deaths and two people moving away over the preceding months. After advertising in the local paper and contacting the area housing officer, only two possible replacements had applied. The Vale of White Horse District Council had recently built new sheltered accommodation complexes: The Chestnuts at Charlton and St Johns Court at Grove; as well as housing being provided by the Downland Housing Association. The council and the housing association also had vacancies, so it appeared that the area had more than enough housing suitable for elderly people. With this decreasing demand for almshouses, the Trustees once again raised the suggestion of demolition of the Stiles buildings to enable new building to take place on the garden ground at the rear, but by that autumn, all the houses were occupied and the idea was dropped. Over the following years, all the houses were generally occupied, but there were times when there were no names on the waiting list and in 1992, it was decided

to change the regulation whereby people applying to live at Stiles had to be Wantage residents, replacing this with the qualification that they had to be "a person of limited means now or formerly resident in Wantage or having some association with Wantage". This allowed people to move in who had come from away but wished to live in Wantage because they had close family members there.

There was a time, in the 1970s and earlier, when Wantage had no traffic lights. When the lights were installed at the cross roads by Stiles Court in 1981, the noise and vibration of the traffic became a real nuisance to the people whose almshouses were on the Newbury Street side of the building, so much so that one lady told the Trustees it was affecting her health. This led to double glazing of the windows on that side being considered, although it took until 1986 before this was completed, at a cost of £1,042. The two houses which now had the double glazed windows paid 75p more each week in the rent.

The Clerk to the Trustees was paid a small salary for his services but in 1970 he became a churchwarden, so also a Trustee of Stiles, and could not then be paid, apart from expenses. When his term of office as churchwarden ended, he was again paid a salary, which increased gradually over the years and was an indication of the amount of day to day work carried out by the clerk in the smooth running of Stiles. When the original clerk, Martin Collard, retired in July 1993 he had been clerk for thirty four years. The position was taken over by Mrs Caldwell-Nichols, who was a member of the same firm of solicitors as Mr Collard. The clerk of works, Mr Akers, also gave many years service to Stiles Almshouse; often giving his time out of hours to help the almspeople, as shown in a letter to the clerk, in December 1991, from one of the old ladies living at Stiles, which tells that Mr Akers had to be called out one Sunday afternoon when a water tank burst over the arch. She writes that the water would not stop, so one of the old men who lived there had gone to the pub to phone Mr Akers, who came out that afternoon and was still working after seven o'clock that evening, "leaving his comfy chair and wife" in the words of the letter-writer.

Fire safety regulations meant that the almshouses had to be inspected by a fire officer, but because of the historical nature of the building it was not always possible to bring the houses up to the expected standard with regard to fire precautions. The living rooms were directly connected to the upstairs bedrooms by means of a staircase, which was against regulations. However, the Trustees carried out what precautions they could, and in 1986 each lobby had a fire extinguisher and each house a fire blanket, with the common roof space having fire-proof partitions put in. By 1998, doors had been fitted to the top and bottom of the stairs in each almshouse, which meant they now complied with fire regulations. At this time, six of the eight houses had telephones and the Trustees were keen to put phone lines into the remaining two so that each of the almspeople could be issued with a personal alarm. Smoke detectors were bought for each house in 1995 and carbon monoxide detectors in 2001.

In the early 1980s, the Trustees would have liked to remove the old privies in the gardens, dating back to the time before the alterations in 1963, which would have made room for garden sheds instead. However, the money to do this was not available at the time and the idea was put on hold. An opportunity for getting rid of the old privies came about a few years later, when a derelict old building in Portway, previously motor workshops, was replaced by a block of flats called Lloyd Court. At the time, the usual discussion took place as to whether it would be a good idea to pull down Stiles and build at the back, behind this new development. But the Trustees were told that as the Stiles buildings were listed and of considerable architectural interest, this would not be allowed, and the matter was dropped once more. The developers, however, agreed to remove the old outside toilets belonging to the almshouses at the same time as they removed the old boundary wall, and the Trustees paid £300 toward a new fence at the boundary. All of which must have been quite an improvement at the back of the almshouses.

In 1963, when the twelve almshouses were converted to eight, and bathrooms were installed in the lobbies shared by two houses, these lobbies also provided room for cupboards and coalhouses for each house. By 1992, the coalhouses were mainly no longer used. The bathrooms, each containing only a WC and a bath, had poor insulation and inadequate heating. The hot water was provided by Fortic tanks, some in the roof space where they froze in cold weather. The bathrooms and indoor toilets had been a big improvement when they were provided in 1963, but thirty years later the Trustees felt they were not really suitable any more. Suggestions were made for changes in the bathrooms, such as showers instead of baths and low level WCs. With heating installed this would have cost around £2,100 for each bathroom and the Trustees decided that instead of carrying out piecemeal renovations, it would be better to draw up plans for complete renovations on a larger scale, which would improve the almshouses by bringing them up to date. Mr Andrew Talbot, a chartered surveyor, who had been involved with improving other Wantage almshouses, was asked to draw up some plans. Finances were discussed, grants were investigated, and Mr Haddrell of the National Almshouses Association was asked to give advice. By November 1992, the plans were well forward and three tenders from builders had been received, ranging from just under £150,000 to £220,000 (not including VAT). The lowest tender was accepted, from Terry and Green, and the work was expected to start in February 1993. By now, the plans included gas central heating. The shared lobbies were to be done away with, there were to be bathrooms inside the houses, showers with seats and a new water supply. Steel ties were to be put in the roof to stop the bowing of the walls which the structural engineer had noticed. It was thought that the original building, erected at the end of the seventeenth century, was single storey and that a second storey had probably been added during the next century; the walls not originally being designed for the added weight.

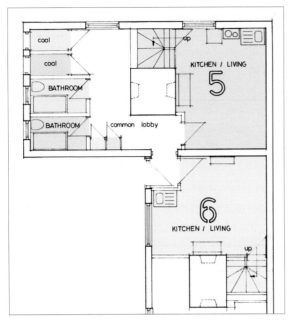

After the 1963 refurbishment (top)

...and the 1994 redesign of the layout

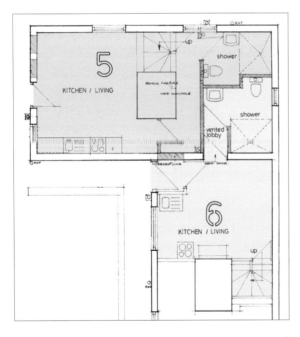

Whereas when the 1963 alterations were carried out, the people living in the almshouses were mainly able to stay on the site, moving into empty houses while their houses were altered, this time it was decided that the safest and most convenient solution would be for

all the occupants to move out completely until the work was finished, probably for about six months. The Trustees kept everyone informed as to what the plans were and held a meeting for the almspeople to ask questions about the move and the alterations. For two pet lovers, the main worry was what would happen to their cats, but the Trustees went to a lot of trouble to put their minds at rest and to find alternative accommodation for the animals while their owners were in temporary housing.

Once the houses were empty, the work progressed well, apart from slight problems with two new windows in the plans on the north (Portway) side. These were to light the new bathrooms in the houses on that side of the building, and were to be small with frosted glass. Listed building consent had been given for them, subject to the consent of the two adjoining owners, which unfortunately was not forthcoming. One would only agree to giving their consent if they received compensation of more than £1,000 and the other would only agree if various legal documents and agreements were entered into, which would have been slow and costly to acquire. So in the end these windows were not installed, leaving one house rather dark and the other getting light through an internal glazed door. The original cost had increased by between £12,000 and £15,000 due to additional unexpected items, such as replacement of rotten windows and fractured purlins in the roof, and the laying of a new electricity main.

It became clear that a rise in the 'rents' was going to be necessary, and the almspeople were informed that a rent of £12 a week would soon have to be charged for the one bedroomed houses, with £18 for the larger ones. In future, the almspeople would only be allowed one domestic pet and a cage of birds, although they could keep any they already had. It was hoped that everything would be finished by September 1993. After everyone had moved back and the houses were once more occupied, there was a repeated problem with the main drain which ran across the courtyard. It had blocked and backed up into the almshouse several times. The Trustees then found that there had been problems with it before the renovation, but one of the men living in the almshouses had 'rodded' it when it blocked without anyone reporting that there was a problem. Sorting it out while other work was in progress would have been easier than dealing with it once all the houses were re-occupied. The drain, with a shallow run, had originally been there to carry away the waste water from the sinks, but by this time it was having to deal with the waste from the showers and toilets as well. In the end a new drain was installed and was re-routed at a cost of almost £3,000; an expense the Trustees could have well done without at that time. Perhaps because of this, the rents had to rise once more in September 1994, to £14 and £21.

As far as the garden was concerned, it was felt that the almspeople showed less interest in gardening than in the past, so the garden was redesigned with a smaller area for individual plots. It had three sections, the one nearest the building being partially a lawn with rotary clothes lines and partially a paved patio surrounded by shrubs: this area was divided from the next part by a hedge of shrub roses. One old lady who wished to keep her own little garden, wrote to the Trustees to tell them this, and added, "The man up the road has given me some Donkeys to put in my garden." Hopefully they were garden ornaments and not the real things! In another letter from the same old lady, in which she was very complimentary about the new lay-out of the garden, she says, "Some of us round here are proud of our little gardens", and refers to hers as being "the one with the dogs and chamber pot etc", so the donkeys were not the only ornaments there. From 1997, Charlton Adult Centre took on the upkeep of the garden, sometimes with the help of individual almspeople.

The Prince of Wales was approached to re-open the almshouses after the renovation but the reply was that unfortunately it was not possible to fit this into his schedule. It was then decided to ask the MP for Wantage, Mr Robert Jackson, to officially open the renovated building, in recognition of the large contribution made by Government funds via the District Council grant. A descendant of one of Robert Stiles' sisters, Mr Hughes, who had given the Trustees details of the Stiles' history, was also invited to the opening ceremony, which took place on October 7th 1994. Robert Jackson planted a tree at the ceremony, met the residents and then shared refreshments with the residents and other guests, the tea party being laid on by the Grove Women's Institute.

After everyone had settled back into life at Stiles, there was a comment from one of the Trustees that there was "now a spirit of friendliness and co-operation not seen among the almspeople before". It appeared that everyone in the community was helping one another, whether by carrying out handy-man jobs, sewing curtains or generally being there for one another. Perhaps not surprisingly, the inhabitants did not always get on together. At one time prior to the renovations, the shared lobbies had caused friction between two old ladies, when frequently one of them would not let the other get to her fuel store. One of the men who lived at Stiles behaved in a way which upset and frightened some of the other inhabitants, quite often being drunk, and it was finally decided that he was not really suitable for almshouse life. After he went, the Trustees agreed that, in future, before a person was accepted they should have a medical examination, give two character references and should have an interview with the clerk and at least three Trustees.

The Trustees could have other problems with tenants. Occasionally almspeople were behind with their rent or houses were left in a mess when a person moved out. There was one time when an old man died and the district council had to clear out the rubbish from his house, charging the Trustees over £200 for doing so, which probably meant it was in a very bad state. Very often when there was a change of tenant, the Trustees took the opportunity to redecorate and enable the new tenant to move into a freshly painted house. On this occasion, some rewiring was also done, but the total bill for the rewiring, repairs and redecoration came to £3,337. The rules now stated that tenants were not to decorate their houses themselves. The clerk wrote on one occasion, "There have been some remarkable schemes in the past when the residents were allowed to decorate." However, one lady was given permission to do some decorating as long as Mr Akers, the clerk of works, checked and approved of what she intended to do. When another tenant moved out, Mr Akers was asked to redecorate the house and was told that the previous tenant "unfortunately disregarded the terms of agreement and painted the interior walls, so the sitting room is a heavy pink. Please could you restore the magnolia colour." Probably more serious than pink walls, it was found on one occasion that one of the almspeople had a lodger, which was definitely against the rules. One morning another resident got up early to put out the rubbish and was very shocked to find this lodger lying on the floor of the shared lobby, wrapped in rugs he had found there, trying to sleep. He was advised to move into the toilet as it would be warmer! And later the kind neighbour took him into his own house to get warm.

A problem with a neighbour in one of the almshouses was reported by one of the old ladies at Stiles, in a letter to the clerk: it appeared that the neighbour in question was probably showing signs of dementia, as she had been putting the rubbish out at rather unusual times. The letter explained that the almspeople helped one another with putting out the rubbish but then continued, "but maybe you can tell her she must not get up and go out at one o'clock in the morning." The old lady in question, who was nearly ninety, was moved from her almshouse to Stirlings later that year, as she had started wandering round the town late at night. The almspeople had to be able to take care of themselves, as without a resident warden or other means of support, vulnerable people could be a danger to themselves as well as their neighbours.

Residents were expected to report any problems so that repairs could be done or the matter put right in other ways. When the same old lady wrote again to the clerk to explain that she and her neighbour had opened a window and could not shut it, she told the clerk that they had tied it up for the time being. She then went on, "Its only right to report it and my toilet seat is Broken again, Mr Akers will be <u>cross</u>. But I was not Guilty this time, It was a Big Person, needed to <u>GO</u>." This old lady wrote many letters to the clerk, and must have been well known in the clerk's office. However, at one time, she caused problems by feeding the pigeons in the almshouse garden. The Portway residents, whose houses backed onto Stiles complained. Originally there had only been perhaps half a dozen birds but because bread and seed was regularly put out for them, there were now often more than thirty birds, messing up the residents cars and their washing. The Trustees knew at once who was to blame and a very kind letter was sent to the culprit by the clerk, explaining that "your kindness to the birds is causing a nuisance to your neighbours" and asking that no more food was put out. The clerk then softened the blow by making a suggestion that a peanut feeder could be put in a tree for the greenfinches and bluetits. "Much better than feeding the greedy pigeons."

Stiles Court, in the same way as the Mill Street and Eagles Close almshouses, will continue to need ongoing repairs and refurbishment over time, but after three hundred years is still providing pleasant little homes for the elderly in the Wantage area. No doubt Robert Stiles would be pleased to know that his gift continues to provide shelter and that he is remembered so many years after he gave the almshouses to the town.

Appendices

Appendix 1

Governors

From 1598 to 1643/4, where only the accounts exist, the dates shown are the years that the Governor in question signed the accounts. He may have been a Governor over a longer period. Where records are not in existence between 1643/4 and 1656, dates for Governors are not accurate.

After 1656, in a few cases where the minutes do not record the date a person ended his Governorship, the date given is the date of the last meeting where he signed the records.

		REASON ENDED
1597-1613	Edmund Fettiplace, Esq of Childrey	died.
	(The church bellringers were paid 2 shillings at his funeral)	
1597-1600	John Dolman, Esq of Frethornes Manor, Childrey	
1597-1618	Francis Moore, Esq of Fawley	
1597	Thomas Aldworth Merchant of City of Bristol	died 1598
1597-1613	Robert Wirdnam (or Wyrdnam) Esq of Charlton	
1597-1606	William Talbott	
1597-1635	William Anger	
1597-1625	William Tubb	
1597-1613	Richard Webb	
1597-1634	Thomas Aldworth the younger, a relative of Thomas Aldworth above, but not a son	
1597-1618	Thomas Clement of Wantage	
1597-1637	John Snodham, draper	
1597-1617	William Wilmot *(Not one of original names in Act of Parliament, may have replaced Thomas Aldworth)*	
1606	Robert Webb *(only mentioned 1606)*	
1607-1618	Thomas Grove	
1611-1627	Robert Hyde	
1613-1629	Thomas Winterburne	
1616-1625	George Wyrdnam, Esq	
1616-1637	Thomas Webb, Gent	
1619-1643	Sir George Willmott	
1619-1630	William Grove	
1619-1643	John Daniells	
1619-1631	Richard Talbott	
1624-1638	John Marriott	
1624-1629	Edward Galland	
1628-1643	Edward Cottrill the elder	
1630-1641	William Talbott of Wantage	
1632-1641	William Wyckens	
1634-1642	Francis Slade, Wantage vicar	

1638	John Fettiplace	
1638-1641	Robert Aldworth	
1638-1640	Edward Cottrill junr.	
1639-1643	Edward Blagrove	
1641-1644	Lawrence Castle (or Castell), Gent	
1643	Francis Keat	
1643	John Jennings (or Jenens) of Charlton	none attendance

At this point there is a gap in the accounts and the first minutes start 1656 - some of the men below (*) may be the same men appointed above

? -1656	*Edward Cottrill	died
? -1671	*Sir George Willmott	died
? -1667	*William Talbot of Wantage, woollen-draper	replaced - moved away
? -1700	*Edward Blagrove	died
? -1676	*Lawrence Castle	died
? -1667	*John Jennings (or Jenens)	none attendance
? -1656	Edward Samuell	died
? -1663	Richard Brooke of Wantage	died
? -1667	Thomas Clement of Wantage, tanner	died
? -1680	Edward Keate, Esq of Lockinge	died
? -1682	Thomas Aldworth	died
1656-1690	William Masemore, the younger, of Wantage	
1656-1670	Richard Winterbourne of Grove	died
1658-1665	John Fettiplace, Esq of Childrey, 'heir & kinsman to John Fettiplace deceased'	resigned, lived too far
1663	Richard Lyssett of Wantage	refused to be Governor
1665-1675	George Champion, Esq of Wantage	died
1665-1690	Sir Henry Moore, Esq of Fawley	died
1667-1697	Robert Brooke of Wantage	resigned
1667-1685	John Collins, Esq of Betterton	died
1667-1685	Jasper Scholes or Scoles, Esq. Gentleman	moved away
1669-1672	Richard Brooke	died
1671-1680	Dr Elias Clarke of Wantage	resigned
1672-1686	William Hardwicke	died
1675-1684	Joel Pocock of Wantage	died
1676-1677	Thomas Brooke of Wantage	died
1676-1712	Alexander Fettiplace of Letcombe Regis, Gentleman	died
1680-1694	Edmund Wiseman, Esq of East Lockinge	died
1680-1691	Adam Blandy, Esq of Letcombe Regis	died
1682-1684	John Haskins	resigned
1684-1691	Arthur Evans	died

1684-1729	Henry Knapp of East Hanney	died
1685-1696	Geoffry or Jeffery Masemore of Wantage	
1686-1688	Daniel Aldworth, Wantage	died
1686-1734	Charles Collins, Esq., Betterton - in place of father deceased	died
1688-1730	Thomas Butler, father of Joseph Butler, Bishop of Durham	died
1690-1701	William Moore, Fawley - succeeds father Sir Henry Moore	resigned
1690-1698	Robert Grove	died
1691-1692	John Harding, Charlton	died
1691-1699	Dr Elias Clarke *(may have been the Dr Elias Clarke who resigned in 1680)*	died
1692-1718	Richard Lissett (or Lissitts), Wantage	resigned - indisposed
1694-1702	John Loder, Esq., Hinton	died
1696-1704	Charles Ambrose, Wantage	moved away
1697-1721	Giles Stamp, Wantage	died
1698- ?	John Wightwicke, Charlton	
1699-1722	Gregory Geering, Denchworth	resigned
1700-1701	Thomas Pynner, Wantage	
1701-1709	William Masemore, Gent., of Symonds Inn, Middlesex	died
1701-1738	Sir Richard Moore, Bart., Fawley	died
1702-1721	Charles Loder, Esq. Hinton, son of John above	resigned
1704-1723	Petley Price, Esq. Gentleman, Wantage	died
1709-1728	Rev. John Birch, Vicar of Wantage	died
1711-1740	Alexander Boote, Lyford	died
1712-1730	George Fettiplace, Childrey, son of Alexander	died
1718-1732	John Price	died
1721-1743	Thomas Pinnor (or Pynner), Wantage	died
1721-1723	John Loder, son of Charles, above	died
1722-1742	Richard Aston	died
1723-1725	Francis Loder, Hinton, brother of John	died
1723	Bartholomew Tipping, Esq., Woolley Park	declined
1725-1738	Francis White, Esq., Fifield	died
1725-1743	Robert Pinnock, junior (or Pynnock), Wantage	died
1728-1755	Thomas Brewer, Vicar of Wantage	died
1729-1768	Henry Knapp, son of Henry Knapp above	died
1730-1755	John Bance, East Challow	died
1730-1750	Robert Butler, RN son of Thomas Butler above	died
1732-1758	William Stanley	died
1734-1751	Capt. William Birch, Wantage	died
1738-1756	Bartholomew Tipping, Esq., Woolley Park	resigned due to ill health
1738-1768	Sir John Moore, Baronet, Fawley, son of Sir Richard above	was asked to resign
	(was asked to resign 1766 for non attendance & 1768 as had moved away)	
1740-1750	Charles Malet (or Mallett), Wantage	died

1742-1746	Charles Price, Esq	died
1743-1775	Thomas Goodlake, Esq., Letcombe Regis	died
1743-1750	Thomas Mills, Esq.	died
1746-1778	Edward Towsey	died
1750-1790	William Stirling, Wantage, solicitor	died
1750-1775	Thomas Garrard (1)	resigned
1750-1785	Robert Butler, son of Robert above?	died
1751-1766	Thomas Garrard (2)	died
1755-1756	Rev. Dr. Saunders, Curate in charge of parish?	left vicarage
1755-1769	John Hippisley, Esq., Lambourne	died
1756-1799	Bartholomew Tipping, Esq., the younger, Woolley Park, son of Bartholomew above	died
1756-1762	John Tyrrell, Esq., Hatford	died
1758-1790	John Price, Esq	died
1762-1768	Thomas Giles, Esq	died
1766-1768	William Wiseman Clarke, Esq., Ardington	died
1768-1800	Thomas Justice, Esq., Sutton Courtney	resigned
1768-1775	John Giles, son of Thomas above?	resigned
1768-1789	Thomas Barnes	died
1769-1795	William Towsey, Wantage, son of Edward above	resigned
1775-1789	Thomas Goodlake, Esq., Letcombe Regis, son of Thomas Goodlake above	died
1775-1784	John Elderidge	died
1775-1790	Robert Garrard, son of Thomas Garrard above	died
1778-1795	Robert Graham, Wantage	resigned
1784-1809	Thomas Ansell, Wantage, tanner	died
1785-1802	John Butler, Wantage, brother of Robert	died
1789-1814	Edward Thornhill, Esq., Kingston Lisle	died
1789-1828	Rev Edward Shaw, Vicar of Wantage	died
1790-1814	Hon William Craven, of Benham Place	replaced, non-attendance
1790-1793	Ferdinando Collins, Esq., Betterton	died
1790-1805	Samuel Worthington, Esq., Lord of the Manor of Wantage	died
1790-1793	William Price, Esq., Charlton	died
1793-1826	William Wiseman Clarke, Esq., Ardington	died
1793-1806	Richard Taylor, Wantage	died
1795-1846	William Beckett, Wantage, solicitor, *(1840 changed name to Beckett-Turner)*	died
1795-1823	William Wise, Wantage, autioneer	died
1799-1820	William Henry Price, Esq., Charlton	resigned
1800-1812	Rev Philip Wroughton, Woolley Park	died
1802-1822	Thomas Warman, Wantage	died
1805-1854	Thomas Goodlake, Esq., Letcombe Regis	died
1806-1828	Joseph Belcher, Wantage	resigned

1809-1820	William Ansell, Wantage, tanner - nephew of Thomas Ansell	dismissed - bankrupt
1812-1826	Rev John Collins, Betterton	died
1813	Edward Ansell *(signs minutes once)*	
1814-1827	Atkins Edward Martin Atkins, Esq., Kingstone Lisle	died
1814-1859	Bartholomew Wroughton, Esq., Woolley Park	died
1820-1821	Robert Thomas, Wantage, Gentleman	died
1820-1831	Rev Henry Hippisley, Esq., Lambourn	resigned
1821-1826	Thomas Jennings, The Priory, Wantage, schoolmaster	resigned
1822-1871	George Butler, Wantage and later Woolstone	died
	(In 1826 moved from Wantage & was replaced as an in-town governor :	
	in 1827 was re-elected as an out-town governor)	
1823-1853	John Wise, Wantage, son of William above	died
1826-1830	Rev Charles Jennings, Wantage	died
1826-1833	Carew Packer, Wantage, gentleman	died
1827-1843	Sir Henry William Martin, Baronet, West Lockinge	died
1827-1831	William Nelson Clarke, Esq., Ardington	moved away
1828-1832	Charles Hammond, Esq., Wantage	died
1828-1851	Charles Liddiard, Wantage, grocer	died
1830-1832	Rev William Birkett, Wantage	resigned
1831-1857	Charles Eyston, Esq, High Sheriff of Berks, Hendred	died
1831-1839	William Shippery, Childrey	resigned
1832-1849	William Trinder, Wantage	died
1832-1847	Rev John Viney Button, Wantage, curate	resigned
1833-1850	Henry Hayward, Wantage, schoolmaster	died
1839-1859	Edwin Martin Atkins, Esq., Kingstone Lisle	died
1843-1890	Rev John Ferdinando Collins, Betterton	died
1846-1860	William Ormond, Esq., Wantage, solicitor	died
1847-1881	Rev William John Butler, MA. Vicar of Wantage	resigned
1849-1854	Henry James Palmer, Wantage	died
1850-1855	Rev William Hayward, Charlton House	resigned
1851-1879	William Dowell Wasbrough, Esq., Stockham, Wantage, solicitor	died
1853-1860	George Robert Cowper, Wantage	moved away
1854-1856	Rev Dr Nelson	died
1854-1863	Bernard Pumfrey, Wantage	resigned
1856-1885	John Samuel Bowles, Esq., Milton Hill	died
1856	George Stone, The Ham, Wantage	declined to act as Gov.
1856-1860	John Plumbe, The Wharf, Wantage, coal merchant	resigned
1857-1866	Charles John Eyston, Esq., Hendred, son of Charles above	resigned
? -1883	Charles John Eyston, Esq *(he was probably re-appointed after 1866)*	died in 1883 aged 65
1859-1860	Captain Leicester Viney Vernon	died
1859-1862	Philip Wroughton, Woolley Park, brother of Bartholomew	died

1860-1901	Col. Sir Robert James Loyd-Lindsay, Baron Wantage VC, KCB. Lockinge	died
1860-1920	Edward Ormond, Wantage, solicitor, son of William	died aged 92
1860-1889	Walter Rice Howell Barker, FRCS. Wantage, surgeon	died
1860-1867	Thomas Brown	resigned
1863-1876	Rev Thomas Vincent, Curate of Wantage	resigned
1867-1910	Philip Wroughton, Esq., Woolley Park, son of Philip above	died
1867-1905	Llewellyn Jotcham, Wantage, solicitor	died
1871-1885	Samuel Jones-Loyd, Baron Overstone	died
1877-1896	Philip Gibbons, Wantage	died
1879-1906	Henry Denis de Vitre, Esq., Charlton House	died
1881-1903	Rev Thomas Henry Archer-Houblon, MA. Vicar of Wantage	resigned
1885-1903	Thomas Sargent, Esq., Grove	resigned - extreme old age
1885-1944	William Butler Wasbrough, Esq., Stockham, Wantage	died
1887-1905	Stephen William Silver, Esq., Benhams, Letcombe Regis	died
1890-1899	Thomas Nalder, East Challow, engineer	died
1890-1903	William Brooks Reynolds, Esq., Challow Park	resigned
1896-1907	Thomas Gilbert Emerson, MD., Wantage, doctor	resigned
1899-1900	Arthur Samuel Francis Robinson, Wantage, engineer	resigned
1900-1907	James Clarke, Esq., Emerald Hill, Wantage	resigned
1901-1923	Archie Kirkman Loyd, Esq KC, MP., Downs House. East Hendred	died
1903-1917	John Joseph Eyston, JP., East Hendred Manor	died
1903-1920	Col. James Colebrooke Carter, JP., Ardington	resigned; died shortly after
1904-1918	Rev. Canon the Hon. Maurice Ponsonby, Vicar of Wantage	
1905-1926	Edward Thomas William Dunn, JP., Childrey	died
1905-1923	William Clarke Jotcham, Wantage, solicitor	resigned; died shortly after
1907-1926	John William Gilbert Candy, Wantage, retired chemist	died
1907-1932	Ernest Thomas William Nalder, Wantage, engineer	died
1907-1931	John William Kent, Wantage, ironmonger	resigned due to ill health
1911-1917	Philip Musgrave Nield Wroughton, son of Philip Wroughton who died 1910	killed in action 1917
1917-1922	Edward Stevens, Kingston Lisle Park	resigned - moved away
1918-1942	Albert Stone Castle, Charlton, farmer	died
1918-1919	Rev. Canon Lord de Mauley	resigned
1919-1932	Rev. Augustus Gossage Robinson, Vicar of Wantage	resigned
1921-1945	Arthur Thomas Loyd, MP., Lockinge House	died
1921-1934	Edward Brookes Ormond, Wantage, solicitor	resigned - moved away
1923-1949	Reginald Arthur Loyd, son of A.K.Loyd	resigned
1923-1930	Sir Mortimer Singer KBE, JP., Steventon	died
1924-1934	John Nicholas Arbery, Brooklands, Wantage	died
1926-1941	Thomas More Eyston, East Hendred	killed in action 1941
1926-1937	Edward John Belcher, Wantage	died

1930-1949	Charles John Baker, JP., Letcombe Regis	died
1931-1933	Dr Amelius Cyril Birt	resigned
1932-1957	Rt. Rev. Bishop Roscow G. Shedden, DD., Vicar of Wantage	resigned
1932-1953	Kaye Aspinall R. Ramsden Sugden In-town governor to 1940; out-town from 1940	resigned - moved away
1933-1947	Henry Robins, Wantage	resigned due to ill health
1934-1957	Percy Staner Clark, JP	resigned due to ill health
1934-1951	Howard Farnham Arbery, Wantage, son of J.N. Arbery	died
1937-1965	Cyril John Alfred Kent, Woodlands, Newbury Street, Wantage	died
1940-1966	Henry George Thurston, JP., Thermidor, Wantage	resigned
1942-1972	Major Michael Lavallin Wroughton, Woolley Park	
1944-1983	Albert Cartwright Castle, Charlton; became an in-town Governor 1958	died
1945-1995	Lieut. Christopher Lewis Loyd, Lockinge, son of A.T. Loyd	
1947-1973	John Lewis Sale, JP., Priors Hold, Wantage	
1949-1966	Henry John Wasbrough	resigned
1949-1956	Sir Roger James Ferguson Chance, Letcombe Regis	resigned - moved away
1951-1973	George Frederick Penney, Dunnehome, Lark Hill, Wantage	
1953-1960	Rev. Arthur Charles Ashton Chetwynd-Talbot, Vicar of Wantage	resigned - moved away
1957-1978	C.W.F. Rudgard, East Hendred	
1957-1999	J. Wilson Sharp, Sparsholt, later of Shellingford	
1958-1960	Hon. Justice E.C. Ormond, Hanney	resigned
1961-1974	Lord Norrie	
1961-1984	Rev. Johan H. Schaufelberger, Vicar of Wantage	resigned
1966-1993	John Alfred Kent, Wantage	
1966-1969	W. G. Buckland	resigned
1966-1990	Arthur Smith, Elms Farm, Grove	
1969-1973	J.P. Baldwin, JP	
? - 1980	D.W. Hawkins	
<1981-1983	Mervyn R.T. Scott	
1979-2010	Mrs Anne Winifred Shone, Letcombe Bassett. First female Governor	
1983-1994	Sidney Woodroffe	
<1983-1986	Canon Douglas Alfred Pearce, Vicar of West Hanney	died
<1983-1996	Lord Herschell, Ardington	
<1983-1996	Maj. Gen. R.H. Whitworth, Letcombe Regis	
1982-2007	Mrs Mary Mackinnon, East Hendred	
1983-1992	Rev. Robert Wright, Vicar of Wantage	
1983-	David Castle	
1986-1995	Mrs A. Tyser, West Hanney	
1991-2008	Richard Smith	
1993-2009	Geoffrey Bailey	
1995-2000	Matthew Green	

1995-1998	Mrs Linda Badger
1996-1997	Mrs Fiona Malcol
1996-	Thomas Loyd
1996-2003	Edward Froud
1996-	Anthony Prior
1998-1999	William Wasbrough
1999-2002	Rev John Salter, Vicar of Wantage
1999-	Robert Sharp
1999-2009	Paul Hexter
2001-	Ian Hermon
2003-	Terence Clark
2003-2009	Michael Bellinger
2007-2009	Rev. Anthony Hogg, Vicar of Hanney, Denchworth and East Challow
2008-	Mrs Moya Lee
2009-	John Naish
2009-	Peter Cecil
2010-	William Jestico
2011-	Dr. Ann Boon
2011-	William Roycroft

Appendix 2

Teachers at the schools

GRAMMAR SCHOOL or FREE SCHOOL		ENGLISH SCHOOL or PETTISCHOOL	GIRLS SCHOOL
1598	John Wirdnam		
1599-1600	Mr Charlton		
1600-1604	Mr Harford		
1604-1618	Hugh Floyd		
1604-1630		Thomas Otes or Oates (d. 1630)	
1618-1622	Mr Hill		
1622-1633	Mr Keepe		
1631		John Cooke	
1632-1634		Mr Eastmode (Robert Estmonde?)	
1633-1639	Mr Surman		
1634-1637		Henry Greene	
1637-after 1644		Edward Silvester (d. 1660)	
1640-1643	Mr Lyttle		
1644- ?	Mr Willcocke		

———————————————— (gap in records here) ————————————————

<1659- ?	Mr John Heron		
1660- ?	Mr Francis Slade the younger (on accession of Charles II, possibly did not take office)		
<1665-1670	Mr John Heron		
1670	(Mr John Hunsdon) (not appointed by governors but by John Heron)		
1670-1688	Mr Samuel Jennings (or Jennens)		
1689-1693	Mr John Byrch or Birch		
1693-1707	William Sloper (or Sloaper)		
? -1699		Mr Daniel Freer	
1699-1715?		Thomas Fewtrell	
1707-1749	Mr Phillipp Barton		
1711			person chosen by M. Barenburgh
1726		Schoolhouse to be let to tenants	
1733-1734		Joseph Humphreys (d. Dec. 1734)	

1738-1753		Mr Pratt
1749-1756	Rev Mr Jacob Freer	
1755-1756		Joseph Green
1756-1763	Revd. Mr Belcher	
1756-1775		Thomas Austin
1763-1764	Rev Mr George Goldwyer	
1765-1768	(vacant)	
1765-1770			Mrs Mary Brown
1768-1770	Rev Mr Hodgson	
1771	Rev Mr Bickley	
1771-1773			Mrs Green
1772-1775	Rev Mr Bailey	
1774-1780			Miss Povey
1775-1831	Rev Mr Daniel Robins	
1775-1812		Mr Ashur Packer
1780-1816			Mrs Mary Packer
1813-1842		Mr William Butler
1816-1823			Miss Packer
1823-1834			Mrs Packer
1832-1849	(no master)	
1835-1849			Mrs Yeatman (or Yateman)
1843-1851		Mr William Warner

At this point the Grammar School was rebuilt and the other schools were replaced with a new National School

1851-1856	Rev Edmund John Smith
1857-1868	Rev Cornelius Hargrave Crooke
1869-1884	Mr Henry Cook
1884-1893	Rev William Pace Rigg
1893	Edmund John Piggott

In 1893, a new scheme was set up by the Charity Commissioners and the Governors of the Wantage Town Lands handed over responsibility of the school to newly elected School Governors.

Appendix 3

Rules of the Grammar School
as given at a meeting in May 1851

1st   That the Governors as Visitors shall have general control over all matters connected with the management of the School

2nd   That the system to be carried on in the School shall comprehend sound religious education, together with the Classics, English Grammar, Mathematics, Reading, Writing and Arithmetic, and useful learning, and that the hours of attendance and other necessary arrangements shall from time to time be settled by a majority of the Governors present at a Meeting.

3rd   That the Governors shall elect and appoint from time to time a Master who shall have graduated in arts at one of the English Universities, but in case no person so qualified shall offer himself, or in case any person so qualified shall offer himself and not be approved of, then the Governors shall elect and appoint the best qualified person who in their judgement may offer.

4th   That the Master shall be provided with a sufficient house and premises without charge for rent, but he shall pay the Parochial Rates, Parliamentary and other Taxes, and shall keep all the Premises in tenantable repair, the Governors doing all substantial repairs and finding Timber and Materials for that purpose. That his Salary shall be £50 per annum.

5th   That the Governors shall have the following power over the scholars (viz)

1st   By sending all Boys who claim to be instructed in Latin Grammar being residents in the Parish free of all expences except that of Books.

2ndly By sending a number of Boys not exceeding 12 who may appear to the Governors as fit objects for a free Education to be admitted to instruction in all the subjects taught in the School free of all expences except that of Books.

3rdly   By sending 12 Boys being residents in the Parish at a payment of £5 per annum free of all other expences except that of Books. Every Boy sent by the Governors shall be presented to them previously to his election and no boy shall be sent to the School under the age of 8 nor be continued beyond the age of 16.

6th   That the Master shall be at liberty to educate private Pupils, provided such education does not interfere with the general management of the School.

7th   That the holidays shall be five weeks at Christmas and five weeks at Midsummer, the afternoons of Wednesday and Saturday, together with Good Friday, Easter Eve, and Wantage Michaelmas Fair Day, and that the Master be bound to report to the Governors all cases of negligence in attendance not well accounted for, and that he have no power to dispense with attendance except in circumstances to be stated by the Governors.

8th   That in case it shall at any time appear to the Governors that any such Master so appoined as aforesaid shall have been negligent in the discharge of his duties or shall be unfit or incompetent to discharge them properly and sufficiently, either from immoral conduct, incapacity, age, or any other infiirmity or cause whatsoever, it shall be lawful for them at a Special Meeting to be convened for that purpose (at which Meeting two thirds at least of the whole body shall be present) to enquire into the circumstances of the case and at their discretion either to suspend such Master or remove him from his appointment or act therein as they may deem expedient.

(No 9th point given)

10th That these Rules may be altered from time to time, at any Special Meeting called for the purpose, (at which Meeting two thirds of the whole body of Governors at the least shall be present) and in the event of the votes being equal upon any question put from the chair, the Chairman for the time being shall have the casting vote, the Chairman voting only once.

Rules of the Grammar School as given at a meeting on 9th December 1868

I   The Governors shall have general control over all matters connected with the management of the School

II   The system to be carried on in the School shall comprehend sound Religious Education, together with the Classics, French, English Grammar, Mathematics, the Elements of Physical Science, Reading, Writing and Arithmetic, and the hours of attendance and other necessary arrangements shall from time to time be settled by a majority of the Governors present at a meeting.

III   The Governors shall elect and appoint a Master who shall have graduated in Arts at one of the English Universities, but in case no one person so qualified shall offer himself, or in case any person so qualified shall offer himself and not be approved of, then the Governors shall elect and appoint the person who in their judgement is best qualified.

IV   The master shall be provided with a house and premises without charge for rent, but he shall pay the parochial rates, parliamentary and other Taxes, and shall keep all the premises in tenantable repair, the Governors doing all substantial repairs and finding the Materials for that purpose. The Master shall not underlet or part with the possession of any part of the premises without the permission of the Governors. The payments to be made to the Master by the Governors shall be, (1) a fixed salary of £80 per annum, (2)

£2 10s per annum for every junior Governors' Scholar, (3) £10 for every Governors' Scholar who shall pass the Oxford or Cambridge Middle Class Examination with a first class Certificate, £5 for every such Scholar who shall pass the examination with a second class Certificate, and £2 10s for every such Scholar who shall pass the examination with a third class Certificate.

V   The Master shall hold his appointment at the pleasure of the Governors but shall be entitled to six months notice before dismissal for any cause other than that of immorality, and the Master shall give six months notice of his intention to resign.

VI   (1) All boys being resident in the parish of Wantage may be instructed in Latin Grammar free of expense for Books and Stationery.

(2) The Governors may elect 12 boys, not under the age of eight years, as junior Scholars, who shall be instructed in all subjects taught in the school upon payment of £5 pa, and the Book and Stationery fees.

(3) The Governors may also elect by competitive examination from amongst the junior Scholars, twelve senior Scholars who up to the age of 16 years shall receive instruction in all subjects taught in the School free of expense, except the Book and Stationery fees. No senior Scholar shall be entitled to remain in the School after attaining 16 years of age without the express permission of the Governors.

(4) All Governors' Scholars shall pay 10s pa for books and stationery.

(5) All Educational and Book Fees must be paid half-yearly in advance to the Treasurer who shall at the end of the current half-year pay the whole amount to the Master, and no boy shall be received as a scholar at the beginning of any half-year, without producing to the Master, a Certificate from the Treasurer that such Fees are paid.

(6) The Master shall be at liberty to educate private Pupils, provided such education does not in the opinion of the Governors interfere with the general management of the School.

(7) Examinations of the whole School shall be held half-yearly, conducted by Examiners to be appointed by the Governors, after which any vacancies among the Governors' Scholars, shall be filled up.

VII The Holidays shall be five weeks at Christmas and six weeks in the Summer, together with good Friday, Easter Even, Ascension Day, Monday & Tuesday in Easter week, Monday & Tuesday in Whitsun week, and the afternoons of Wednesday and Saturday. The Master shall report to the Governors all cases of negligence in attendance not well accounted for, and he shall have no power to dispense with attendance except in circumstances to be approved of by the Governors. He shall also give notice to the Treasurer of the Governors at least one month previously of the day on which he proposes that the Christmas and Summer Holidays shall commence.

VIII These Rules may be altered from time to time, at a special meeting to be called for that purpose, at which two thirds of the whole body of Governors shall be present.

Alteration to the Rules of the Grammar School as given at a meeting on 29th February 1892

Alteration to rules of Grammar School:

Rule VI, subsections 2, 3, 4 & 5

The Governors shall have power to send to the School any number of Boys not exceeding 24 who have attained the age of 10 years and are able to pass an Examination by or under the direction of the Head Master equal to the 4th Standard of the Education Code 1890-1 and who may appear to the Governors to be fit objects for a free Education. Such Boys to be entitled to Instruction in all the subjects taught at the School, free of Expense. But priority of Admission to the School shall be given to residents in the parish of Wantage.

All sets of rules appeared in the Governors' Minutes BRO: D/QW6

Appendix 4

Property belonging to the Wantage Town Lands

IN WANTAGE

The almshouses, the inns, the workhouse and the chantry house were dealt with in sufficient detail in Chapters 7 & 8, but the history of other property is summarised here.

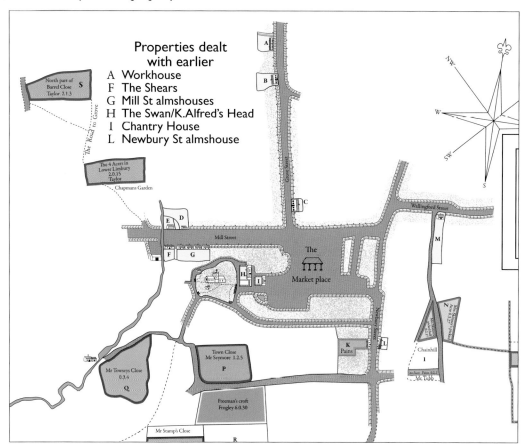

A map made in 1753, showing the property belonging to the Town Lands in and around Wantage town

Grove Street

(Originally known as Loveshill and later as Abingdon Street)

PROPERTY B: Not sure exactly where this property was, but possibly where nos 47 & 47A Grove Street are now. Also not sure when it was acquired by the Town Lands, although possibly some time in the mid 17th century when the accounts were missing. It may have been a property referred to in 1661 as "the South part of a messuage in Loveshill called 'Govers' or 'Wheelers', ..." which did not belong to the Governors at that date. It was a Town Lands' property by 1680, when the accounts are once more in existance. Land, possibly in Grove, went with the property. Simon ARNOLD held the lease at a yearly rent of £1 3s 4d, although sometimes the rent was paid by John SYMONS (or SIMONS).

Possibly site B, now numbers 47 & 47A Grove Street

Site C, number 4 Grove Street, sold 1922

The following history for B seems the most probable.

1703   SYMONS of Lockinge was granted the lease - he was told to build a new chimney.

Some time between 1730 and 1740, Francis BERRY took over the lease, with his widow or his trustees paying the annual rent for the next 20-25 years, after he died. It is most likely that the Berrys did not live there but sub-let the property.

1753   On the map on page 176 Joseph DURNHAM was shown as living there, most probably renting it from Berry's trustees. He died in1755, being classed as 'old' in the burial register.

1763   The lease of this house and garden passed to Thomas WHITEHORN, still at an annual rent of £1- 3s- 4d. The property stayed in the WHITEHORN family for at least the next 70 years.

1837   A report of the Charity Commissioners recorded that the house had lately been pulled down and there was only a workshop left there. It was still let to a Thomas WHITEHORN, and the rent was still £1 3s 4d a year.

By 1853 Thomas CLEMENT was the tenant.

1871   The Governors sold the property to Mr George DIXON for £120, when it was described as a "garden and shop" (the shop was probably the workshop referred to in 1837).

PROPERTY C: NOW NUMBER 4 GROVE STREET

It is possible that this site was one of the original properties of the Governors in 1597, as there is no evidence for its later purchase. In the early days it consisted of a cottage in Grove Street; with a close of meadow near Priors Mill (probably the land at the bottom of Locks Lane) and an acre of arable land in the Town Close Ham (where King Alfred's School now stands) being part of the tenancy.

1641   The first person who was definitely the tenant there was William WILLIAMS. Later, among others, it was rented by John FROGLEY, a clothworker, and Samuel STEVENS, a tobacconist.

By 1834 Thomas CHURCH, a labourer, was living there and paying 2s per week rent.

After Thomas CHURCH died in 1866, the MARKWELL family were tenants.

1882   The dilapidated house in Grove Street, in the occupation of Mrs MARKWELL was to be pulled down and rebuilt - it was now a shop and house.

1922   4 Grove Street was sold by auction for £390

Mill Street

PROPERTY E (BY THE BROOK) - LATER 36 MILL STREET

The land next to the brook, on the opposite side of Mill Street to the Shears, most probably belonged to the Wantage Town Lands in 1597. It is not possible to be sure who leased it, however, until John STEVENS paid a rent of £1 for some "Mill Street tenements" in 1750. At the time, John STEVENS was also renting the Governors' property in Wallingford Street.

1753   Widow STEVENS was one of the tenants, with 2 families - the ARROWSMITHS and the SILVERSIDES living here or in Property D

1778   Samuel PLUM took over the property - described as three tenements which had originally been two cottages, plus orchard and garden.

The property passed down through the PLUM (or PLUMBE) family, for over a hundred years.

The property which became 36 Mill Street, as it looked in 2012. See aslso the old photo on page 120, looking up Mill Street with this house on the left

1837   Two more small houses had been built on the land at the back.

1896   Two of the cottages had been made into one house - the nephew of the last PLUMBE, Joseph ALDWORTH, was living there. There were several outhouses at the back - a closet, a wash house, sheds to store wood and coal, a greenhouse, a former stable; plus a garden at the back. The third cottage, now a house and shop, was let separately to James HORLICK. Three thatched cottages had been built next to this with the BEAVIS, GREEN and WORNHAM families living in them. The orchard had now become a drying ground for these cottages.

The number of little houses on this land varied each time it was mentioned. In the 1881 census, there was a group of houses behind the main part of Mill Street, called Gawlers Court, which had five families living there, two of them with the same names as the people living in the three thatched cottages in 1896 (BEAVIS and WORNHAM), so Gawlers Court could have been the little group

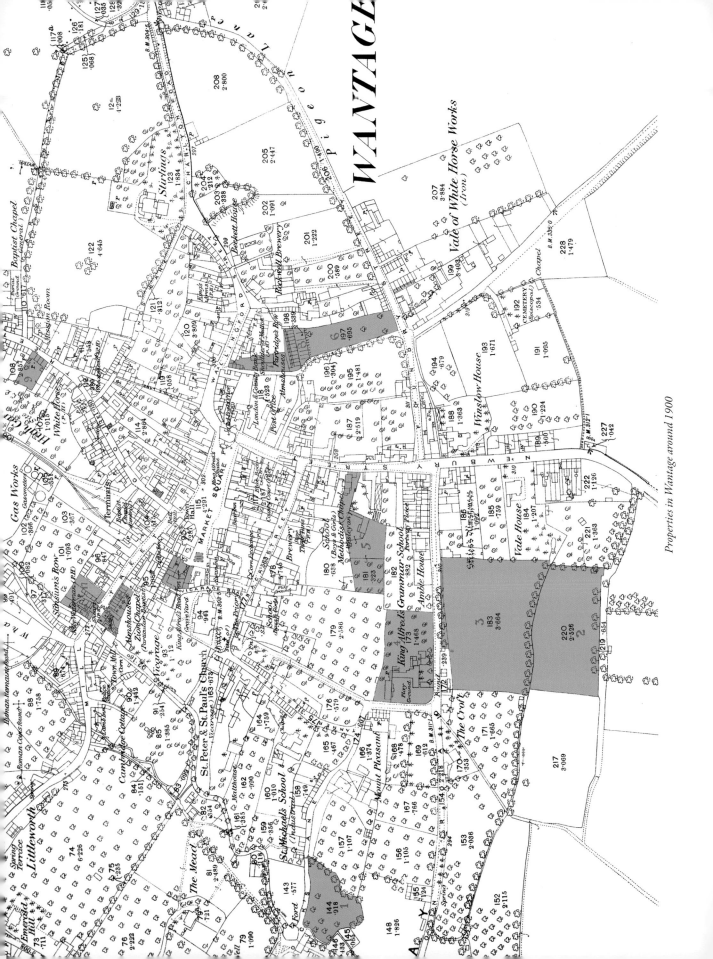

Properties in Wantage around 1900

of closely packed cottages behind the Mill Street Governors' house and shop.

1934   The buildings were very dilapidatcd and over crowded - Wantage Urban District Council ordered that they should be demolished. There was a house and shop (number 36 Mill Street), three dilapidated cottages (numbers 30, 32 and 34) and the site of two cottages, which must have already been pulled down.

1936   Shop let to Mrs KIDD - she was there until her death in 1949

1949   Shop in very bad condition - not economic to improve it - it was put up for sale at £500, and was sold to Ft/Lt GEORGE, with numbers 30, 32 and 34 as well, so these houses had not been pulled down .

Property D - later 24 Mill Street

This Mill Street property, next door to the property, E, above, was also most likely to have belonged to the Wantage Town Lands in 1597, but tracing the tenants for the next hundred and thirty years is not possible.

1730   Tenant was Richard COX, paying a rent of £3-10-0. For the next 50 years, the COX family remained tenants of the two cottages with outhouses and gardens

1786   John COX was made bankrupt and had to give up the tenancy.

GOFF family, who were clothiers, took over

1817   Richard GOFF made bankrupt.

The HAZELL family, then John PLUMBE and later Henry John FARMER became the tenants. There was a workshop at the back, which had earlier been a timber yard.

1881   Mr FARMER was a toy dealer, so one of the cottages was now being used as a shop.

1935   The two cottages had become three houses some time previous to this - shop was number 24, also numbers 26 and 28 were on the site. All three houses were classed as unfit for human habitation by Wantage Urban District Council and ordered to be demolished.

Mrs Cummins' shop, 24 Mill Street, before it was pulled down to make room for Limborough Road.
The building to the left is 36 Mill Street.

1939   Small plot of the land at the back of property D was sold to WUDC, in order that the town swimming pool could be extended - Governors' plot was next door to the pool.

1955   Mrs CUMMINS, who rented the shop, wished to retire - the building was described at the time as being very old in parts and likely to collapse.

1957   Wantage UDC were planning a car park behind Mill Street - wanted the site of these premises.

1960   Property sold to WUDC for £400. The plot became Limborough Road, leading into the car park. (The road can be seen on the photo of 36 Mill Street, shown on page 179)

Newbury Street

PROPERTY K - BECAME 22 NEWBURY STREET and is now shops and part of the Civic Hall car park

1617   Robert PAYNE of Abingdon (born Wantage) gave this house, garden, orchard and a half acre close of pasture land; with 7.5 acres arable in the common fields of Wantage and Grove.

1617-37   Richard WESTBROOK held the lease

Then there is a long gap where it is impossible to find who rented Newbury Street.

1818   Joseph BLISSETT, breechesmaker, took the lease of the property in Newbury Street - it was now 3 dwellings with a yard and outbuildings

1819   From this date, for over 50 years, the orchard was let separately from the cottages and outbuildings

1872   Homestead, garden, and orchard all let to Mr John WHEELER, builders, as yearly tenants

1884   Property now described as house, garden, orchard and premises in Newbury Street

1914   Small house, 2 cottages, yard, orchard - let to Miss JOTCHAM

1917   The Governors inspected the cottages - found them beyond repair - said they should be pulled down at the end of the war.

1925   Sister Superior of St Mary's School complained at state of old thatched cottages in Newbury Street - in dangerous condition.

1927   Trustees of Community of St Marys leased orchard and garden ground.

Mr Henry WARNER leased other part - Governors laid on water, built a wash house, and carried out some repairs.

1935   St Mary's bought St Anne's Orchard and other land in Newbury Street for £350 after negotiating price down from initial £700

1936   Edgar HUMPHRIES rented small house, yard and premises - 22 Newbury Street

1948   22 Newbury Street sold to Mr Edgar HUMPHRIES at auction for £1,000 (net £920)

(See photo of present property on the site on page 4)

Wallingford Street

PROPERTY M - NOW THE POST OFFICE AND ROWE'S SUPERMARKET.

This property most probably belonged to the Town Lands at the time of the Act of Parliament, but it is not

The site of the "cottage and garden" in Wallingford Street sold to fund the rebuilding of the Shears Inn.
It eventually became the first town cinema, ... then a bicycle shop, here in 1972 ... and now Rowes Newsagents & Post Office

possible to work out who rented it in the early days. It was originally a house and garden, with out-buildings and an orchard behind.

1641   Richard HARDING rented the property
          Various HARDINGs had the lease from 1641 until 1724

1724   John HYDE became the tenant and in 1726 the Governors decided that the house was to be rebuilt - they supplied timber towards this and in 1731 paid men for the work of taking down the old house.

1732   John STEVENS the younger was granted the lease of the ground and dwelling house, called [Strod], in the occupation of John HYDE with the Backside and Orchard belonging to it and of the two acres of arable land (the land was in the fields outside Wantage). The Stevens family were tenants until 1768.

1768   William HAZELL (or HAZLE) took over the lease and agreed to build a brick wall to the garden the whole length of the garden against Harding's Lane (the lane running up the right hand side). Members of the Hazell family had the lease until 1856

1857   John LAWRENCE, sadler, took over; followed in 1900 by George RICHINGS

1912   The Wallingford Street property, now 2 cottages and a garden, was sold to George RICHINGS for £225. This money was used towards the rebuilding of The Shears

LAND IN WANTAGE

As explained in Chapter 6, the Governors owned farm land, both arable and meadow, from before late Elizabethan days and more was added to this by gift and by purchase. In those early days, as can be seen from the map on page 184, much of the Wantage land belonging to the Trust existed as many small strips in the open fields, which would have been the arable land. Nearer the town, were small closes and patches of meadow or orchard. Barwell Close (or Barrel Close as it is shown on the top left of the map - later part of Grove) was a large meadow, with only part of it belonging to the Town Lands. Similarly, the meadow near this called Lower Limborough (or Limbury on the map) was only partly owned by the Governors. After Wantage fields were enclosed at the beginning of the nineteenth century, the land allotted to the Wantage Town Lands was consolidated into fewer, larger, areas of land, as shown in the map on page 185.

These areas of land were gradually given away or sold, as detailed below:

1851   Town Close had the Grammar School built on it

1873   The land on Chain Hill was sold for £300

1894   Pound Close was given to the school - it had been used as the school playing field for many years, being rented by the head master.

1920   The land at Charlton was sold for £65
          The orchard in Locks Lane was sold for £150
          The arable land in Manor Road was sold for £700

1928   The meadow in Willow Lane was sold to King Alfred's School for £300

1951-1976 Eagles Close was sold off in several parcels of land (see Chapter 8)

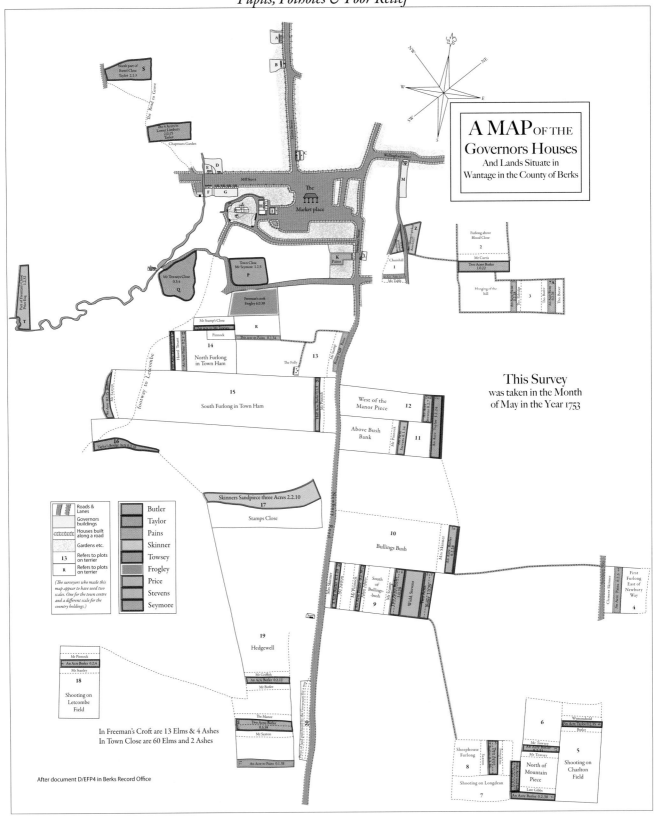

Governors' land in Wantage after enclosure

PROPERTY OUTSIDE WANTAGE

Three properties outside Wantage had houses on them, at Grove, Steventon and East Hanney. The Town Lands' properties at East Challow and Stanford-in-the-Vale were land only.

GROVE

The Governors owned land at Grove at the time of the Act of Parliament which set up the Trust. The Grove lands were in more than thirty strips in the common fields until the parish was enclosed in 1804, although tenants mostly rented several strips each, at any one time. There was a cottage from an early date on a plot of ground by the brook, called Spicers Close but later known as Brook Meadow. See page 188 for the house in 2012.

At enclosure, the land holdings were concentrated into six plots. The largest of these was in Swinhill (or Sunhill) Field, which became known as Grove Hams Farm. A house and dairy were built on this farm in 1865, and in

A **MAP** OF the
Governors Lands
Situate in Grove in the
Parish of Wantage in the County
of Berks 1753

N

After document D/EF P5 in Berks Record Office

Scotlands

Mr Butler

Mr Tubb

An acre 0.1.8 Alder

Mr Butler

An acre 0.2.17 Alder

Mr Dyve

Mr Butler

Mr Dyve

Mr Grove

An acre 0.2.17 Alder

Mr Dyve

An acre 0.2.31 Alder

East of College Coppice

Norton Field

Southdapland

To Hanney

2 Acres 1.0.7 Alder

John Simmonds

Spicers Close
3.2.8 Heding

Thorsons Close
3.0.15 Alder

THE GREEN

Orchard
0.1.18 Alder

Mr Butler

Mr Grove

North Field

Hanging furlong
north west of
Wick Green

Wm Shepherd

two three yeerslces
0.1.6 Hobs 1.1.16

Mr Towsing

Three acres
3.3.4 Hobs

John Cowdrey

Mr Butler

2B one acre Hobs 3.3.12

Mr Lamborn

West of the Leys

Mr Lamborn

Two acres 0.3.2 Hobs

Mr Butler

The Leys

On Gilmans Lane

Town Close
1.0.31 Taylor

Gilmans Lane

Swinhill Field

Wick Green
10.0.28 Hobs

Durman Burs
1 acre 0.3.2

Marsh Close
1 acre 0.2.12 Durman

Alder
Governors

0.2.17

or Butler

THE STREET

To Grove

Barrow Lane

Hobs
Alder
Heding
Taylor
Durman

Mr Church

John Cowdrey
The Manor

John Smart
Shooting on
10 acre furlong

Ten acre furlong

Mr Grove

The Manor

Mr Godfrey

John Godfrey

Duck Furlong

The Manor

Two acres 1.2.23

John Cowdrey

John Hobs

John Hobs

The 9 halfs
4.1.39 Hobs

John Hobs

Nine half
Furlong

Black
Breach

White Breach Furlong

The Manor

White
Breach

Brook furlong

Fran. Simmons

Two acres
1.0.20 Hobs

Mrs Weston

Two acres
10.1.1 Hobs

Late Pinners

an acre Durman
0.2.16

an acre Durman

poor half furlong

John Simmonds

Manhill Field

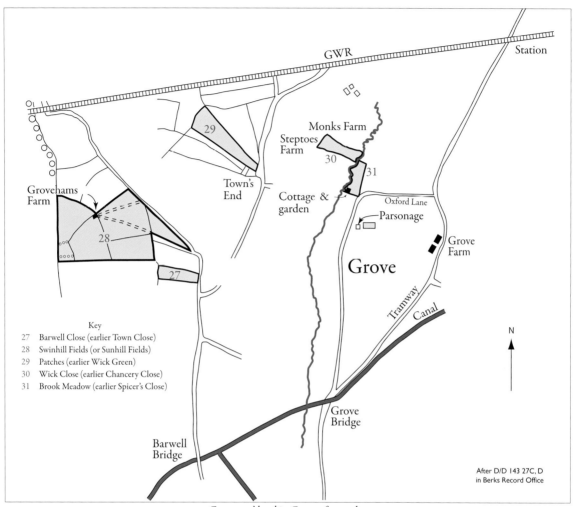

Governors' land in Grove after enclosure

1893 a new fifty foot long cattle shed there replaced an old thatched building which had fallen in and was beyond repair. Almost all the Grove property was sold in 1920, various members of the COTTRELL family paying over £4,300 for Grove Hams Farm, Wick Close, Brook Meadow and Patch Meadow. William STEVENS bought the meadow in Barwell Lane for £333. The vicar, the Reverend HOWARD, paid £25 for the little meadow behind his vicarage. In 1921 the last small plot in Grove, part of Wick Close, was bought by Mr GODFREY for £50.

STEVENTON

Property in Steventon was part of the Town Lands at the time of the Act of Parliament in Elizabeth I's reign, when Ellis DIGWEED was paying a rent of ten shillings a year for it. After that the HOPKINS family were the tenants for nearly 140 years. Initially there was a farmhouse, barn and other buildings by the Green, with strips of land in the outlying fields. When Richard TYRELL renewed his lease in 1834, the property was described as, "A homestead and buildings, cottage and garden and a close, with eleven field lands" (the field lands being in 12 strips as two were only half acres). After the parliamentary enclosure of the fields in 1883, the Governors were

187

The cottage at Brook Meadow, Grove, in 2012

The site of the Governor's house on the Causeway at Steventon

awarded two plots, one arable and the other meadow, but both a long way from the farm. In 1886, there was a fire at the homestead, which burnt down the buildings. Although they were insured, so could have been rebuilt, it was decided that because the fields were well separated from where the farm had been, it made financial sense to let the empty land as a meadow, rather then put up new buildings. All the property in Steventon was sold in 1920: the arable field to Mr BETTERIDGE for £200 and the two plots of meadow (the distant field and the small close where the farm had been) to Mr CARTER for £175. A modern bungalow was built later on the site of the farmhouse (see photograph opposite). Maps of the Steventon land before and after enclosure are shown on page 98.

EAST HANNEY

The East Hanney land belonged to the Town Lands before 1597. At that time Robert BROOKE(S) paid rent of 20s per annum. There were two plots of land and a house, barn, and other premises. For a hundred years, the property was leased to various members of the BROOKE(S) family, although they perhaps did not farm it themselves as one of them, Edmund BROOKES, was 'of Oxford'. In 1689, the lease passed from another Edmund BROOKE 'of the Citty of Oxon' to Richard BELCHER of East Hanney, who was a cordwainer (a shoemaker). BELCHER repaired the house and outhouses in 1691 and built new stables in 1710. He only lived in part of the house.

From 1720 to 1862, first the COLLINS family and then the GODFREYS were the tenants, by which time the house had become two thatched cottages, along with a barn and five stables. The cottages

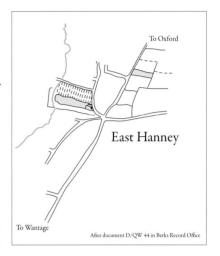

To Oxford

East Hanney

To Wantage

After document D/QW 44 in Berks Record Office

did not seem to be in good repair and suggestions for rebuilding cropped up on more than one occasion. The cottages were not rebuilt although repairs were carried out several times.

In 1891, the cottages were burnt down in a fire and it was decided to rebuild a house and sheds with the insurance money.

The meadow was behind the house, between the house and the stream, while the arable was alongside the road to Oxford. All the property in Hanney were sold in 1920 to Frank HERMAN for £585

(See photo of the rebuilt house on page 93)

EAST CHALLOW

Some of the East Challow land was already part of the Wantage Town Lands in 1597, but as was explained in Chapter 1, more land in East Challow was bought shortly after this, using money given by several benefactors. The small close of about 2 acres, called Town Close, was part of this transaction. Later, in 1713, Thomas WILLIS left yet more land in Challow to be used for the benefit of the Town Lands. As with other land belonging to the Governors in the early days, the land was mostly in the form of strips in the fields, as shown in the map on page 95. Some of this land had been enclosed in 1659, by agreement with the Challow inhabitants, but most of it was enclosed much later in 1801 by an Act of Parliament. A map of the Challow land after enclosure is shown on page 96.

An area of arable in South Field, alongside the road to Letcombe Regis off Portway, was sold to Mr CROCKER for £650 in 1901. Shortly after this, in 1907, the Wantage Rural District Council asked if the council could construct a small reservoir in the meadow know as Town Close, behind the village school. This would be used to supply some of the village houses with water at the times of year when the water in the parish well was low. Permission was given and the RDC dug a well in Town Close. The council agreed to maintain a pump to bring up water from the well and store it in an underground reservoir next to the well, paying a rent to the Governors for this. When a piped water supply was laid on in the village in 1937, the reservoir was no longer needed and the Rural District Council decided not to renew the lease when it ran out in 1942. Town Close was sold to Mrs ALDER, who owned the farm next to the close, for £150 in 1946. The remaining three areas of meadowland in East Challow had been sold in 1920: Copse Ground to Richard BARNARD for £717, one of the meadows in White Mead to Mrs MIDWINTER for £166, and the other meadow in White Mead to Mr NALDER, who owned the engineering works in Challow, for £181.

STANFORD-IN-THE-VALE

The meadow land in Stanford was bought by the Governors in 1715 from Farmer MAYOW. The land was in a part of the parish known as Gentlemans Mead and measured seven acres. The meadow was enclosed in 1783, when the Governors, for some reason, were awarded less land than they had originally; their plot being approximately three and a half acres. Perhaps they had been given land in a better part of the meadow. Where before, their land would have been part of the whole meadow without any hedges or fences surrounding it, they now had to put up a boundary and they made a mound round their land and planted a new hawthorn hedge on this mound. Gates and gate posts had to be provided too. The meadow brought in a rent of between £5 and £6 during the C18th but it was increased to £9 for most of the C19th, falling to £8 at the time of farming difficulties in the 1890s. As with most of the Governors' land, it was decided to sell Gentlemans Mead in 1920 and Mr DAWSON bought it for £178.

(Map of the Stanford land is shown on page 5)

SOURCES

The main sources of information for this book were the following:

Berkshire Record Office (BRO):

Governors' Minutes	1656-1715	D/QW4
	1716-1829	D/QW5
	1830-1893	D/QW6
Governors' Accounts	1598-1644	D/QW7
	1680-1733	D/QW8
	1733-1789	D/QW9
	1790-1851	D/QW10
Governors' Waste Books	1768-1789	D/QW11/1
	1834-1865	D/QW11/2
	1865-1883	D/QW11/3

In Governors' hands at time of writing:

Governors' Minutes	1893-1971
Governors' Accounts	1852-1944

Various plans, documents, letters etc

Other sources of information are given below for each chapter.

CHAPTER 1 - IN THE BEGINNING ....

p2   Transcription of Act - *Charity Commissioners' Report* (HMSO 1908)

Petition re William Wordnam - *1908 Report*

Dates of Henry VI & VII - R. Hamilton, *Now I remember* (Pan 1964)

Many towns turned chantries into lay organisations - L. Garnish, *Wantage 1550-1650 Schooling* (1987)

p3   Early chantry and probably Bouchier family involved - *Wantage Schooling*

Definition of 'water bouget' - http://www.heralds.org/saitou/parker/jpglossw.htm

p4-8 Later donations - *Report 1908* & W.C. Jotcham, 'The Charities of Wantage' in A. Gibbons & E.C. Davey, *Wantage Past and Present* (1901)

p5-7 Willis/Payne and other charities become part of general fund - *Wantage Past & Present*

p9   Life of Walter Kirby - http://www.sacredheart.school.nz

CHAPTER 2 - THE RUNNING OF THE TRUST

p12 Names of original Governors - transcription of Act - *Charity Commissioners' Report* (HMSO 1908)

Where first Govs lived - L. Jotcham, 'List of Governors of the Wantage Town Lands' in *Wantage Past & Present*

Will of Thomas Aldworth - PCC wills from The National Archives Ref: PROB 11/93

Collins family of Betterton - E.Lockinge parish registers (transcript produced by Oxon Fam. Hist. Sy.)

p13 Legality of in-town & out-town Governors - *Report 1908*

p48 Laying of foundation stone of new Grammar School - *Jacksons Oxford Journal* 1850 Aug 3

p51 Moules dry earth closet - L. Picard, *Victorian London: The Life of a City 1840-1870* (Phoenix 2005)

p52 Nos. of boys in 1865 - *Report 1908*

p55 School buildings in 1868 - *Report 1908*

p58 Highfield built for retiring Mr Cook - *Short History of Wantage School*

Mrs Cook designed window in church - *Short History of Wantage School*

Cricket field used for grazing - *Report 1908*

Formation of Wantage Water Company in 1877 - Report of Wantage Urban Sanitary Authority 1877 - in The National Archives MH12/328

p59 Baby Pace-Rigg born - Wantage parish baptism register - D/P143/1/20

Assistant staff salaries: Comment from report at school of 1892 - *Report 1908*

p60 Annual sports day at King Alfred's School - *Reading Mercury* 1893 April 22nd

CHAPTER 5 - HELPING THE POOR OF WANTAGE

P62 Comparison of relief from WTL and from poor rates - Vestry Minutes 1730-1748 BRO DP143/8/2

Percentage of Berkshire population on poor relief 1800-03 - http://eh.net/encyclopedia/article/boyer.poor.laws.england

p63 Old Age Pensions 1908 - http://en.wikipedia.org/wiki/Old-Age_Pensions_Act_1908

p64 Definition of thatching 'sprays' *Bailey's Dictionarium Britannicum* (1730)

p65 William Nias died 1782 - Wantage parish registers of burials (transcript by Oxon Family History Society)

p66 William Wells, shoemaker, keeping bawdy house - BRO D/P143/18/5/2

p68 Numbers of clothiers in 1790s in Wantage - *British Universal Directory* (c1791)

p69 First mention of fire engine in ... 1704 - K. Philip, *Victorian Wantage* p105

Fire hooks in church - Wantage baptisms register 1653-1704 (transcript Oxon Family History Society)

Buying of third fire engine and leather buckets etc - Churchwardens' Accounts 1758-1844 BRO D/P143/ME329 5/2

p70 Family histories - Wantage parish registers (transcript by Oxon Family History Society)

Helping the Poor in Sickness

p72 First inoculation - http://en.wikipedia.org/wiki/Lady_Mary_Wortley_Montagu

Inoculation of Parson Woodward's children - D. Gibson, (ed) *A Parson in the Vale of White Horse: Letters from East Hendred 1753-1761* (1982)

p73 The itch - H.M. Murray, (ed with others) *Quains Dictionary of Medicine* 3rd Edition (Longmans 1910)

p76 Radcliffe Infirmary; date of opening and rules - www.oxfordradcliffe.nhs.uk/aboutus/ri%20history.aspx

Royal Berkshire Hospital - http://en.wikipedia.org/wiki/Royal_Berkshire_Hospital

p77 Cotton as cheap woollen cloth - N. Cox & K. Dannehl, *Dictionary of Traded Goods & Commodities 1550-1820* (University of Wolverhampton 2007) - URL: http://www.british-history.ac.uk/report.aspx?compid=58731

Legislation re burying in woollen - J. Richardson, *The Local Historian's Encyclopedia* (Historical Publications 1986)

Food Given to the Poor

p78   Man going to church to get food - from vicar's diary - BRO: D/P143/28 (1853)

Clothing Given to the Poor

p79   Foulweather cloth made in Wantage - *British Universal Directory* (c1791)

79-80 Foul weather great coat for bellman - BRO Wantage Vestry Minutes 1730-48 D/P143/8/2

p82   Cloth given out in 1836 - Charity Commissioners' Report of 1837 in *C. C.s' Report* (HMSO 1908)

       6 great coats given to deserving married out-door labourers - *Report 1908*

Helping Poor Children

p83   William Patient a cooper - Wantage parish registers

p85   Legal settlement with apprenticeship - J. Waller, *The Real Oliver Twist* (Icon Books 2005)

       Finding father of an illegitimate child - BRO Vestry Minutes 1730-1748 D/P143/8/2

       Story of Jane Toby and William Harding - Wantage parish registers

p86   Jane Toby moved to Daventry - Wantage Overseers Removal Orders BRO   D/P143/13/3

CHAPTER 6 - PROPERTY BELONGING TO THE WANTAGE TOWN LANDS

p87   House in Mill Street with lease for lives - BRO D/QW23

p88   Growing beans - M.A. Havinden, 'Agricultural Progress in Open-field Oxfordshire' in
       http://www.bahs.org.uk/09n2a1.pdf

       Jethro Tull seed drill - hhtp://www.saburchill.com/history/chapters/IR/004f.html

p90   Origin of Queens College quit rent not known - *Report 1908*

p92   Agricultural depression in late C19th - C. Miller, (ed) *Rain & Ruin: the Diary of an Oxfordshire Farmer, John Simpson Calvertt 1875-1900* (Sutton 1983)

       Decrease in rentals - W.C. Jotcham, 'The Charities of Wantage' in A. Gibbons & E.C. Davey, *Wantage Past & Present* (1901) p156

p93   Land Tax - www.history.ac.uk/gh/landtax.htm

Land belonging to the Town Lands

p97   Number of parliamentary enclosures 1760-1850 - K. Tiller, *English Local History: An Introduction*

       Results of enclosure - A. Young, *General Report on Enclosures* (London 1808, reprinted NY 1971)

p100   Definition of 'mound' - *Bailey's Dictionarium Britannicum* (1730)

p102   Position of Barwell Close - Grove part of Wantage inclosure map 1803 BRO: D/P143/26B plot 158

       Definition of 'faggot' and 'cord of wood' - *Dictionarium Britannicum*

p103   Fuel in Vale - W.F. Mavor, *General View of the Agriculture of Berkshire* (Board of Agriculture 1809)

       Elms growing mostly in hedgerows - *General View of the Agriculture of Berkshire*

p104   Increase in price of trees at beginning of C19th - *General View of the Agriculture of Berkshire*

CHAPTER 7 - HOUSES BELONGING TO WANTAGE TOWN LANDS

p108   Wantage Improvement Act banning thatch - K. Philip, *Victorian Wantage* p16

       Thatched roofs on fire in Garston Lane - *Reading Mercury* 1872 Apr 13 p108 Thatched roofs on fire in Mill Street - *Reading Mercury* 1893 Jan 21

Water Supplies

p111 Wantage sewerage improvement - Sanitary Report for Wantage Rural Sanitary District - The National Archives (TNA) MH12/327 1874

Grove water - Papers of Rev Tomlinson, Vicar of Denchworth; Reynolds Building Trade Circular Feb 12 1877; & Report of Royal Sanitary Commission 1868/69

Formation of Wantage Water Company - TNA MH12/328 Jan 1878

Water supply to Grove etc - TNA MH12/328 Sep 18 1878

The Swan ... which turned into King Alfred's Head

p114 Church tax for Swan - Churchwardens Accounts 1564-1656 (transcript at Vale & Downland Museum)

Contents of Swan rooms - Will and Inventory of Richard Webb - Swindon & Wilts RO P23/143

p116 Assemblies held at Alfred's Head Inn - *Jacksons Oxford Journal* 1801 Feb 21st & March 28th

p117 Cottages bought in Cat Street - BRO D/QW30

The Shears Public House

p119 The Savorys of The Shears - Wantage parish registers & the following wills:

       1716 Wm Savory, blacksmith of Wantage - Swindon & Wilts RO   P5/15Reg/352A

       1800 John Savory, blacksmith of Wantage - S & WRO   P5/1800/14

       1828 William Savory, blacksmith of Wantage - S & WRO   P23/938

The Old Workhouse

p122 Setting up of workhouse in Grove Street - BRO: Wantage Vestry Minutes 1730-1748 D/P143/8/2

Agreement for care of poor in workhouse in 1750 - BRO D/P143/18/4

Possible hemp manufactory - *Jacksons Oxford Journal* 1802 July 24th

Nicholas Clement's house in Grove Street - BRO: D/QW16

Map showing Workhouse on Manor Road - Wantage Enclosure map BRO: D/P143/26B

p123 Description of old workhouse buildings in 1837 - *Charity Commissioners' Report* (1908)

p124 Description of the 4 cottages - *North Berks Herald* 12th September 1952

CHAPTER 8 - THE GOVERNORS' ALMSHOUSES IN WANTAGE

p125 William Fetiplace's donation to almshouse of 1526 - *Report 1908*

Stephen Fordeham's will - L. Garnish, 'Documents of Tudor Wantage' - Vale & Downland Museum leaflet - Local History series www.wantage.com/museum/Local_History/

Early almshouse burial references - Wantage parish registers (transcript Oxon Family History Society)

p127 Number of rooms at almshouse - *Report 1908*

Streatley Wharf - J. Collins, *The Rev. John Aldworth & his Parish of E. Lockinge 1684-1729* (Black Swan Press Wantage 1989)

Photographic Credits

The author would like to thank the following people and organisations for the use of their photographs. Please contact them individually for permission to re-use.

Author: 94 *bottom*, 101, 188 *bottom*

C.E. Brown: *Frontispiece*, pp. *1, 2, 3, 4, 7, 8, 15, 22, 25, 26, 28, 30, 36, 40, 47, 48, 50, 54, 56, 93, 110, 113, 115, 116, 117, 118, 119, 120 bottom right, 123, 126, 130, 133, 135, 136, 137, 148, 151, 153, 178 right, 179, 182 right, 188 top*

Margaret Hall: *178 left*

Terry Ryland: pp 28, 110

Wikimedia Commons:

       Musphot: p *51*

       Public domain: pp. *66, 67, 94 top, 147*

Vale & Downland Museum: *69*

Centre for Disease Control & Prevention PHIL 7762: p *71*

Oxfordshire Health archives: p *76*

Gordon Collier collection: p *120 top*

David Castle: pp. *120 bottom left, 141, 142, 181, 182 left*

Stiles Trustees: p *155*

Index of People

Index